How to Live
on Almost Nothing
and Have Plenty

Drawings by RACHEL BROWN

HOW TO LIVE ON ALMOST NOTHING AND HAVE PLENTY

A PRACTICAL INTRODUCTION TO SMALL-SCALE SUFFICIENT LIVING

BY JANET CHADWICK

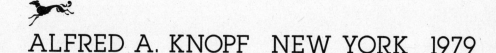

ALFRED A. KNOPF   NEW YORK   1979

THIS IS A BORZOI BOOK

PUBLISHED BY ALFRED A. KNOPF, INC.

Copyright © 1979 by Janet Chadwick

All rights reserved under International and Pan-American Copyright Conventions.

Published in the United States by Alfred A. Knopf, Inc., New York,

and simultaneously in Canada by Random House of Canada Limited, Toronto.

Distributed by Random House, Inc., New York.

Library of Congress Cataloging in Publication Data

Chadwick, Janet, 1933–

How to live on almost nothing and have plenty.

Includes index.

1. Agriculture—Handbooks, manuals, etc. 2. Country
life—Handbooks, manuals, etc. 3. Agriculture—Vermont.

4. Country life—Vermont. I. Title. II. Title:

Small-scale sufficient living.

S501.2.C42 1979   630   79-2246

ISBN 0-394-42811-0

ISBN 0-394-73753-9 pbk.

Manufactured in the United States of America

First Edition

To Ray . . . who taught me
the real meaning of the words
"to give of yourself"

CONTENTS

PREFACE AND ACKNOWLEDGMENTS

Possibly a conscious or subconscious feeling stirring within you has urged you to pick up this book; then you suddenly realize that you don't know how to milk a goat or raise chickens. WAIT! Don't panic. Don't put the book down and leave. Your shoes are in the same place ours were several years ago. As gardeners, we certainly couldn't be called God's gift to the world, and our only experience with animals till then had been our mongrel puppy and our "male" cat, who later presented us with five kittens.

We wanted a more self-reliant life-style so much, however, that I picked up and read every book I could on the subject. While parts of this book may sound like excerpts from a TV situation comedy, this is only because, if there was a mistake to be made, we made it. However, our mistakes have not only given us something to laugh about as time went on, they've taught us things that we never found described in the many how-to books that we read. There have been some frustrating moments, but even the worst of these could not change our love for this rich, rewarding experience.

I've written this book for you the beginner. I've included a library of reading and several years of experience, mistakes and all, between its covers in the hope that it will be the only major source of information you will need to help you to begin your new life. Throughout the book I suggest other reading material that you might find interesting and helpful. I've tried to make my instructions as easy to understand as possible.

I'd like to thank my husband, Ray, and our daughters, Mary and Kim, whose enthusiasm for learning and experimenting with our new life-style has equaled my own. Without their help and encouragement this book could not have been written.

I'd also like to thank my mother and father, Florence and Harold Bachand, for demonstrating to me all of my life that there is a difference between being a *house-*

keeper and being a *homemaker* and that hard work brings its own rewards.

A very special thanks to Jane Garrett, my editor, who refused to accept anything from me but the best I had to give, to Rachel Brown who did the artistic illustrations, and to Anne Eberle, who contributed the index. Thanks also to Claire Smith, who typed the final manuscript after I had an accident.

I'd like to thank all of our friends and relatives who shared our learning experiences with us, especially my daughter and son-in-law, Karen and Philip Marcelino; our sons, Gary and David, who gave all they had to give when they were home; and a very special little boy named Brian. It's too late to thank my grandparents other than my grandmother Emma Bachand, who is still with us, for teaching me to love the land and appreciate fine craftsmanship, but I'll be forever grateful to them for the wonderful memories of my childhood that fueled my excitement for our "homesteading" experience.

Monkton, Vermont   —JANET CHADWICK
May 1979

How to Live
on Almost Nothing
and Have Plenty

1

CHANGING LIFE-STYLES

My husband, my children, and I have developed here at Sunnybrook what, for us, has become a completely food-sufficient, and partially energy-sufficient, life-style. We have become less dependent on world resources and more dependent upon our own. We raise all of our own foodstuffs—vegetables and fruits, milk, eggs, meat, grains, and herbs—with the exception of flour, coffee, and spices. We make our own bread, butter, cheese of all kinds, yogurt, ice cream, wines and liqueurs, and many gifts, including soaps and candles. We do go to the grocery store for paper supplies, cleaning products, and some just plain junk. But the important thing is that if we couldn't buy these things, it would in no way change our way of living. We also heat entirely with wood and have our own supply.

The fact that we raise a great deal of meat seems kind of sacrilegious in a world where there is such a scarcity of high-quality protein, but there is a balance to everything, and we are applying it to our own situation. We have about twenty-six acres of tillable land, and if we raised all grains and seeds, I'm sure that we could feed half the town we live in. But we do not have the equipment to till, plant, and harvest all this acreage. Letting it lie unused would not solve anyone's problems, either. It makes far more sense for us to raise grazing animals that forage this acreage for us and then turn this forage into protein. Because we know what we feed our animals, we don't have to worry about the quality of the protein we are eating. Selling surplus meat, eggs, dairy products, and vegetables and raising some of our grains keeps our grain costs to a minimum.

I was forty years old and my husband forty-two when we decided to change our life-style. We had already worked hard all of our lives, and many people wondered what would make us get involved in something that was going to be a great deal of work and take even more of our time. Why did we do it? Well, there wasn't any one answer. Instead, it was a culmination of all the things we had felt most strongly about in our lives, starting with our conviction that we should live each day of our lives so as not to hurt anyone else and in such a way that we help to make this world a better place to live in for everyone.

We've always been concerned about poverty and the uneven distribution of the most important substance in our survival, namely food. Some people have so much that they can't use all of it, and others have so little that they've never eaten enough to feel full, not even once in their lives. But trying to tackle this dilemma by solving the problems of people thousands of miles away is like trying to start out in a new company as its president. In either case, you don't stand much of a chance for success. We need to start solving the problem right here at a grass-roots level. Right here at home. What we don't drain off world supplies will be available for the people who need it. There are some of these people right here in this country, right here in your community. We all should feel a need to do something about that.

I had been brought up in a family of hardworking people with pride in themselves and their heritage. They set high values for themselves to live by. Their doors were always open to others, and they lived a life-style that was filled with dignity. Money was not always in abundance, yet one would never have guessed this. Their homes were gracious and warm, and they set the best tables I have ever eaten at. There was always room for extra people. They had something special: They had faith, they loved each other, they weren't afraid to work, and they were creative. From their homes came beautiful needlework such as you seldom see today.

My maternal grandmother was our Santa Claus. Even though she had many grandchildren and little money, each Christmas brought boxes of homemade gifts for everyone. During the war years she turned the flower-printed grain bags into beautiful aprons, blouses, nightgowns, and tablecloths with matching napkins. All with beautiful embroidery, tatting, and crocheted edgings. She would start each year in January and work until the following Christmas. My mom is just as clever, and a talented artist besides.

I'd like to tell you a story about my great-grandmother. She lived in Montreal with my great-grandfather, who was a doctor. They were very wealthy, and my great-grandmother had servants for everything. She did nothing herself but needlework. During the last years of my great-grandfather's life he became very ill, and the illness used up all the money, so that when he died, he left her penniless, with a large family to bring up. Never having worked before in her life, she didn't know what to do and at first she tried to take in needlework to support her family. That not being enough, in her late thirties she finally had to sell her home for money to live on. Well, she bought a small run-down house and started fixing it up. She papered, painted, and cleaned it until it looked so much better that she was able to sell it at a large profit. So she continued doing this for all of the remaining years it took her to raise her family.

In the summer of 1978, my grandmother Bachand, who was ninety-seven at the time, came to visit. I showed her my hundreds of jars of canned goods, and when we came to the section with all my tomato products, Gram turned to me and said, "You know, Janet, now that I live all alone, I don't need very many jars of tomatoes this year, so I only put up fifty-three pints. Of course, I did put up a few other fruits and vegetables." I wanted to shout, "Hallelujah, lady!" This wonderful woman still keeps house alone on the farm. Though her son lives nearby and runs the farm, she still puts in a huge garden every year and goes out to the barn to check on things once or twice a day. What's happened to that kind of courage over the last couple of generations?

In the last few generations we Americans seem to have fallen apart. We have stopped trusting one another. You can live in a neighborhood for years and still not know the people who live next door. Young people seem confused and frustrated. Values we had always been so proud of seem slowly to be dissipating. We have watched young people with no leadership lash out at the world and, in their confusion and frustration, try to escape with drugs and alcohol. Others have been trying to think things through and just seem to become hopelessly muddled and discouraged. There has been no one there to help them, and they don't seem to know how to help themselves.

In the midst of this, I have had six children to raise. I began to feel regrets that they were going to be deprived of all the joys and beauty of their French-American heritage, a culture that I had grown up in but, like so many beautiful cultures, one whose customs are being set aside in favor of the fast pace of our modern society. My children were going to be pulled in directions that seemed disastrous, and faster than we could teach them about all the things that we thought were special and that would make them special individuals. We wanted to give them reasons for having the strength to hold out for what was right and just in this world. We were worried, too, that with unemployment growing by leaps and bounds they would not be able to take care of themselves, even with the best of educations. So many young people graduate from college every day and yet can't get decent jobs. How do they provide for themselves in the meantime? Many have never learned any basic everyday living skills. Finally, to top everything off, food and energy costs have been rising at such a fast pace that no matter how hard I tried, the diet I was feeding my family was becoming more and more inadequate. Everything seemed to be a food substitute or to be loaded with food additives.

We Reached a Decision

We felt that we had to do something to improve our life-style, and we did. Years earlier, when our oldest son was twelve, we were told that if he would live long enough, he might be able to overcome his kidney disease by having a transplant. So we decided to build a small summer home on some land we owned about twenty miles south of Burlington, Vermont, where we lived. Hopefully, when the time came for him to have surgery, we would be able to sell or mortgage it to pay the cost. It was a small house, built in sections in our backyard in the city and trucked on a flatbed trailer to our site, where it was assembled. It turned out to be a pretty sturdy little home, and when in later years, after three years of dialysis and a transplant, our son died, the little home was still there, and there was nothing to hold us in the city anymore. My husband worked at the medical center in Burlington, but since it was within commuting distance, we began to plan our move. We accomplished this in June 1974, and by December 1974 we had built a small barn to house our livestock. We enlarged the house, put a cellar and root cellar under it, and we were ready to go.

In the twenty years that we had been married, I had always done a great deal of canning and preserving, and from the time we first bought our land, we had had a large garden every year. I had always cooked everything from scratch, so we had a pretty good start in the field of self-sufficiency.

I spent the first six months of our move reading how-to books, and all our animals except the pigs arrived on December 23, the Saturday before Christmas. We started with two milk cows, two milk goats, two pigs, and several rabbits, chickens, ducks, and geese—and the disapproval of our friends. They thought we were foolish to try something like this at our age. We heard remarks such as, "I'm going to do a lot of living in my life." But, like many other things, we still felt that quality was more important than quantity, and we thought we'd like the quality of our life much better.

I want you to know that when I say I learned how to milk a cow with the cow in one hand, and the how-to book in the other, I am not joking.

We put up a greenhouse, and in spite of setbacks that first year, we grew all our own plants, plus enough to sell to pay for all our seeds and garden supplies. We raised enough meat to last a year and preserved and root-cellared enough fruit and vegetables to get by till the next summer's garden without buying any.

We've learned to make everything go full cycle. We've learned to put back better than what we take from our soil and the woods, so that our abundance will increase, not decrease. By using the excess garden produce such as corn, soybeans, nuts and seeds, and extra milk and whey, we have been able to reduce our grain needs to very little, and sales of extra eggs and milk pay for most of that. All of our animal manure goes back into the gardens to fertilize the soil and replenish the nutrients that we have used, so that we continually build our land into more productive soil. This year I have canned and frozen better than one thousand jars and packages of fruits, vegetables, pickles and preserves, fruit juices and sauces. We fill a huge root cellar and two very large freezers besides. There will be preserves and relishes, wines and liqueurs, and herbs and cheeses for Christmas presents. Enough to share with others less fortunate than we, enough to barter for work that we cannot do ourselves, and bushels of extra potatoes to go with the extra milk that we raise our winter pigs on.

I feel good about what we are doing, and I'm proud of my hardworking husband and children. When I tell people that I'm a career woman, they look at me in surprise. They consider me "just a homemaker." But I have made homemaking a challenging career, and I'm willing to bet that I am faced with more challenges in a day than the average career woman is in a month. I know that not everyone could turn to this life-style as totally as we did. It wouldn't be desirable either because, as in all things, there must be a balance. But all of us can change our ways of thinking, buying, cooking, and the way we make use of the earth's resources, so that we can reverse this trend toward world poverty and starvation. We are all responsible for the lack of humanitarian values that make it possible for one man to sit and eat steak while he watches his neighbor starve. These are things that everyone can do something about.

We're Not Different

When people meet our family after they have already heard about us and what we are doing, they seem surprised to see that we look, talk, and dress just like everyone else. We aren't any different than the rest of you. Our home is medium size, furnished with a mixture of old and new; we take our faith seriously; and our children attend the local union high school just like all the rest of the children. My husband has a regular job in the city, twenty miles away, and commutes daily. You can live as austere a life-style as you want, but it isn't at all necessary to become a hermit. Other than that we feel more tuned in to the good things in life, our workday has taken on a new look, and we live much better for less, our lives have not changed all that much in most ways. Our friends are the same, our social life follows much the same pattern, we still dance and go to parties, and when we give parties in return, we enjoy them more because we don't feel the cost so much. We don't travel a lot, but then, we never did before, nor do we feel inclined to in the future. I'm sure, though, that if we wanted to take a vacation now and then, we would be able to have someone in the surrounding community take over the chores on our small homestead for a few days at a time.

We are not "nonconformists," nor are we antagonistic to the existing social system. But we care about what happens to our family, friends, and all the people of the world. We feel that we *are* our brother's keeper, though we *are not* his judge. We don't want to tear down our social system, but we do want to make it better. I personally would like to take all the best parts of my grandparents' lifetime and combine them with the best parts of ours. I'd like to see a stop to the fashion of throwing out the good in the old ways of doing things just because a new idea has come along. We are, in effect, throwing the baby out with the bath water.

Change should mean improvement, adding to what is already good. This way is less costly and less wasteful. It helps to sustain a people's pride in their workmanship, and somehow that faith in themselves gives them trust in the other people around them. We owe it to our children and their children not to lose sight of where we have been and where we are going in the future. We owe it to them to develop ways of getting to that future without destroying all that is good that we have already learned. There should be enough for everyone in this world, and there would be if we all cared enough to do our share. I guess that what I'm trying to say, what this all adds up to, is that we are doing our best to take care of our needs, and we are doing it with pride and self-respect. At the same time, we are teaching our children to do the same thing. We hope that they will teach their children, and because of this, we will have helped to instill in a few young men and women of the future a knowledge that they have the ability to survive along with a feeling of responsibility toward the other peoples of this world. We hope that they will develop a creed that will encourage them never to take any more than they need, to share what they have in abundance, and to put back in proportion or better what they use of this world's natural resources. I'm not afraid for my children any longer.

Other Benefits

Our life-style has accomplished so much besides developing habits of self-sufficiency. We've watched these changes take place daily in our home. Our children have learned responsibility, the value of hard work, and compassion from working with small animals. I'm sure that that compassion will spread itself to every living thing around them as they grow. They've learned to garden and to milk cows and goats. My youngest daughter does most of the evening chores in the barn before my husband gets home, and she can handle a milking machine that weighs almost as much as she does. In fact, we bought our secondhand equipment because of her. She wanted to milk so badly, and her little hands just weren't big enough to milk the cow. The children can cook, can, and freeze foods. My fifteen-year-old daughter did all the cooking and made all our bread and butter this summer in order to free me so that I could have the time to write this book. She learned to make such beautiful bread that she developed a small business for herself, selling to the teachers at her school.

We've had the long summer days of working together to talk about what values in life are really important, time to talk about the children's grandparents and great-grandparents and the kind of courageous ingenuity they had all possessed, the same kind of ingenuity that was now being demonstrated right in our own home. It gave them an opportunity to relate to all that was best about the past and to find a place for it in their future.

My sons and daughters have learned arts and crafts, using the natural and beautiful products available to us at no cost from the fields and woods. Christmas is a wonderful time of the year for us. We start getting ready for it at canning time, and we try to make it mean what it's really supposed to—a time of sharing and love. Not a contest to see who can spend the most money and get the biggest present. The children have learned to give. Give without expecting anything in return except the satisfaction that comes from sharing. These kids have learned how to get high on life. I couldn't give my children my happy memories of growing up in a closely knit family, so we as a family had to create our own. But with today's high prices, homesteading was the only way we could accomplish this. Our family celebrations here are wonderful, and they have given our brothers, sisters, aunts, uncles, and cousins the incentive to have them too.

Our health has improved a great deal since we moved from the city, in spite of what appears to be much hard work and long hours. But I think that my husband and I are much like the children in that this life is so rewarding that we, too, seem to get high on it. We do feel that the absence of a great number of food additives and large amounts of sugar from our diet has contributed to our better health. There is more and more evidence to prove that we are bringing up a generation of children with physical and emotional problems that are directly related to excessive sugar and food additives. Some scientists believe that if this trend is not reversed soon, these children will suffer irreversible brain damage before they are twelve years old.

We have not made as many strides in energy conservation as we would like to have done by now, but that will come soon. In the meantime, we heat entirely with wood and in the winter do some of our cooking on our wood stove. We own an electric clothes dryer, but we don't use it unless we are having very bad weather for several days. We hope eventually to harness some of the energy that is in the raging brook by our house and to couple stored energy with solar and wood heat to provide most of our needs.

Food and energy costs are rising more rapidly than any other factors in our economy today, yet these are the two areas of inflation that are most controllable on a personal level. You can keep your family's rate of inflation down to a percentage of the national level by becoming more self-sufficient.

You, Too!

I'm sure that if you talk to some people about what we are doing, they will tell you that any fool can be a farmer. Well, let me tell you something. You can't be a fool and make this life-style work. "Anyone" can do it, but it takes planning, a desire to learn, and patience—and you can't be afraid to get your hands dirty. Many was the time in those early days of learning that I found myself thinking, "Good heavens! What have I got myself into!"

There are those who have tried and failed, and they failed because they didn't want to take the time to do things right. The soil is complex, and you can't just dig a hole, plant a seed, and then wait for it to produce a tomato for you. At least you won't be able to do it for long before the nutrients in that particular hole are used up and it stops producing your tomatoes. If you don't believe me, just read a few good articles about what has happened to some of this country's best farmland because the farmers took more from the land than they were willing to return.

Start with a Practical Attitude

The suggestions that I'm going to set forth in this book are just that—suggestions on how to get started on a life-style that will be rich and rewarding. There are many ways of doing things, and eventually everyone develops new ideas and ways that are best for himself. It doesn't matter how old or how young you are or how much you don't know about gardening and raising small animals. Take it slow, and use a lot of common sense. The best advice I can offer you is, Don't attempt too many new things at one time. Rome wasn't built in a day, and neither is a more self-sufficient life-style. Unless you have thirty or more acres of land, a good-size nest egg, plenty of practical skills, and full time to devote to farming, there is no point in trying to become completely self-sufficient. It would be impossible, furthermore, if you have only one or two acres of land to dream of raising a herd of whiteface cattle, but you can certainly plan to raise all your own fruits and vegetables; honey; chickens for eggs and meat; a few ducks, geese, rabbits, and pigs for meat; and one or two little milk goats to provide you with milk for making butter, cheese, yogurt, ice cream, and at least a couple of kids a year for meat. If you have never eaten chevon, I can tell you it's delicious.

With whatever time and space you have available, plan to do just as much as you can to fill your needs. There's something here for everyone.

Learn to Laugh at Yourself

Setting your goals too high doesn't leave any room for failure, and some failures you are going to have. Learn to laugh at yourself. Being able to laugh at your mistakes is one of the biggest assets you'll ever have for this or any other life-style. Many things may go wrong from day to day, most of them very minor, and for the newcomer to this way of life it can be very discouraging and frustrating at times, especially if you can't find something funny about the situations you will get yourself into.

I think my most discouraging episode occurred late in March 1975, the first year of our new life-style. My son David usually milked our Jersey cow, Ginger, but David had the flu, and I was elected to milk. The day was bitterly cold and windy, with a late-season storm brewing. Now, Ginger was a lovely lady, but she was shy and nervous, and she didn't make friends easily. She wasn't used to being milked by me; until then, I had usually been the one who just patted her on the head and said comforting things to her while she was being milked. I pulled up the milking stool and sat down, but I didn't get very far before she really let go with her hind leg, and I found myself sailing right into the gutter. There I lay, holding the milk pail on high—I hadn't spilled a drop—and covered with manure from head to foot, I gingerly picked myself up off the floor and set back at my task, determined that I was going to accomplish it, which I did, although by the time I had finished, I was soaked through and cold. But I decided I would complete all the barn chores and feed all the animals before I went back to the house because I knew that if I gave myself the shampoo and shower I badly needed, it would be a while before I warmed up enough to come back to the barn. So I cleaned the gutter, fed the animals, filled my pockets with eggs, and, loaded down with the milk pail on one arm and the feeding buckets on the other, left the barn. I had a difficult time latching the door, so I sort of hit it with my hip—well, you can imagine what it was like to scramble six eggs in your pocket all at once.

The wind seemed to blow right through my wet clothes, and by the time I got to the house, with my arms loaded, raw eggs running down my leg and into my boot, and very large tears streaming down my cheeks, I was quite a sight, and I felt about as sorry for myself as any human being could. Gone were my daydreams of the gentle Jersey cow, contentedly chewing her cud and pouring gallons of rich, creamy milk into my pail. Subconsciously I must have pictured myself in denim bib overalls with a little red-checkered skirt, gaily tripping down from the barn with the egg basket swinging from one hand and the milk pail from the other. I'm certain that I never pictured myself manure-soaked, tear-stained, and cold, with raw egg running down into my boot. I had *finally* come to terms with reality. But a good hot shower, clean clothes, and a hot cup of coffee had me laughing about the whole incident in less than an hour.

Taking Time

If you haven't learned basic skills in carpentry, mechanics, wiring, and plumbing, don't give up; they are easily learned. On the other hand, don't try to tackle all these projects plus vegetable gardening and small-animal husbandry all at once. Start with a simple plan (see pages 12–13). Make it your goal the first year to put in a very good vegetable garden along with a few small fruits such as strawberries, rhubarb, and melons.

Three breeding doe rabbits with one buck will provide you with an average of ninety-two 1½- to 2½-pound fryers per year. Ten little bantam hens and one rooster will provide you with enough eggs for a year plus next year's flock, and though these little chickens aren't too meaty, at the end of their laying year they can be used for stewed chicken. About twenty-five or more frying chickens can be raised quickly and inexpensively during the first summer, too.

I would not consider it too ambitious to include two pigs in your first year's plan, though you might want to wait until the second year. They do not take up much space, can be fed mostly from your garden surplus, and they will provide you with plenty of top-quality pork, ham, bacon, sausage, and lard. If you have more lard than you can reasonably use, you can make a good supply of homemade soap. Add to all this all the organic fertilizer you will get for your garden for the following year, and I think that you will be off to a good start the first year.

Make sure that your plan leaves you enough free time to learn the basic skills that you will need and provides you with time to build the animal shelters that will become necessary as your plan grows. Chickens and rabbits will manage nicely through that first winter in simple pens if you take care to protect them from the cold winds and rain or snow. I'll give you instructions in later chapters.

PLANNING THE FIRST YEAR

In order to design a plan for your first year of homesteading, you must establish how much time the members of your homestead are going to be able to invest in this experience. You will have to take into consideration the availability of pens and buildings to house your animals, and the costs involved in getting each project established and running smoothly. The expense will include building projects, basic tools, stock, feed, seed, and slaughtering of your animals, if you do not intend to do it yourself.

It might help to have some idea of how much time it takes for various homesteading projects.

RABBITS (three does and one buck): Five to eight minutes twice a day to feed and water them, and half an hour per week to keep the pens clean.

POULTRY (ten hens, twenty-five meat birds, and a few ducks and geese): Five to eight minutes twice a day to feed and water them, another couple of minutes to gather the eggs, and half an hour per week to clean each pen. If ducks and geese are allowed to range free, they take very little time.

PIGS (two): Five to eight minutes twice a day to feed and water them. Pigpens with cement floors will have to be cleaned at least twice a week. Outside pens or ones with dirt floors do not need to be cleaned as often. The amount of time required to clean pigpens will vary with the length of time between cleanings. Figure on a minimum of forty-five minutes per week for cement pens, and thirty minutes per week for dirt-floor pens.

GOATS (two does): Five to eight minutes twice a day to feed and water them, about ten minutes to milk, and goat pens should be cleaned daily if the goats are confined in warm weather. It takes twenty minutes twice a day to clean milking equipment and cool the milk.

VEAL CALVES (two): The same as goats less milking and milk-handling time. The pens of veal calves *must* be cleaned daily; however, it seldom takes more than a few minutes.

BEES (one hive): Bees require only a few hours per *year*, but it costs about two hundred dollars to get started, so be sure to keep that in mind.

Growing your own fruits and vegetables will require about an hour two or three days a week in the early stages, and then up to an hour each day as the plants grow larger and require more care. This will depend a great deal on how many plants you decide to grow, and the size of your garden, but for the average-size homestead garden of about 80 feet by 100 feet, I plan on at least that much time.

Vegetable gardening will require at least ten to twelve hours per week (possibly more if you plan to raise some of your own stock feed) during the early gardening season to till, prepare the soil, and plant. You will need at least that amount of time for fall cleanup. Weeding, cultivating, watering, and fertilizing can be kept to a minimum during the growing season by following the instructions that I give in Chapter 2 on mulching. This same amount of time can be put to good use in the winter months. It will provide time for reading informational booklets. A bibliography of the reading material that I found most helpful will be found at the end of this book.

So, to boil it all down: Determine how much time you will need for each project you are interested in, and how the work will be divided (who will do what). Investigate what small pens or buildings there are available to be used for housing animals, or the costs and time required to build needed housing. Decide on the size garden you would like to put in, and the costs of all stock, feed, seed, and equipment you will need for the various projects. On the basis of these determinations you should be able to choose the projects that would be reasonable for you to include in your first year.

If you go slowly, you won't strain yourself financially, either, so that by the time you get to your second year, you will already have realized a large savings on your grocery bill and will be better able to afford to build whatever housing you need. We'll discuss what kinds of housing each animal requires in the chapters on individual animals.

Basic Tools to Start With

Besides a well-thought-out plan and a sense of humor, that first year you should have a few basic tools. You'll need basic carpentry, plumbing, and wiring tools. A good circular saw, electric drill, and chain saw are practical investments. You'll also need good gardening tools: rakes, hoes, spades, and forks, and a tiller are all important purchases. Buy secondhand tools if you are sure they are in good condition. A few butchering tools are going to be necessary. You'll need a hand meat saw, a cleaver, a butchering knife, a boning knife, and a good-quality knife sharpener. This seems like a lot, but actually the investment is small compared with what the return will be.

If it's at all possible, you should have a truck. When you find out how important one is to your homestead, you might even want to trade in your car for one if you can't afford to run more than one vehicle. Many things are available at little or no cost if you can transport them yourself, such as sawdust, mulch, organic material for your garden, and slabwood to build and heat with. Slabwood is the outer layer of wood trimmed from logs when trees are being milled for building materials.

By the time you get to your second year, your ideas of what you want to accomplish may have changed. Hopefully, your plan will grow from year to year. There may be some projects that you will want to discontinue because they have not proven to be rewarding enough for you. There will certainly be new projects that you will want to try.

New Types of Equipment? New Techniques?

When deciding whether or not to use a newly developed piece of equipment or a new technique, ask yourself the following questions: Is this new product or theory in conflict with my effort to conserve natural resources? Will it serve to make my life better or easier without being a threat to someone else's welfare (either because of its manufacturing process or because its use might pollute the air or waters)? Does it make my life-style more productive? Are the costs involved reasonable when balanced against what this product or theory will do for me? (Remember that some things will be very good for one person but not a reasonable investment of money, time, or effort for your particular situation.)

After answering all these questions in a sensible way, you will have to decide if you want to try the new equipment or ideas. There is certainly no harm in making your life easier and more productive—if there will be no far-reaching consequences. Good luck!

2

STARTING YOUR OWN SEEDLINGS

Because this book takes in all aspects of small-scale self-sufficient living, I feel it's important to include instructions for starting your own vegetable and flower plants indoors at home. There are great savings to be realized from starting your own plants from seed as opposed to buying seedlings from a nursery. Furthermore, it's a wonderful way to spend the late-winter and early-spring months. Recently, as I was transplanting my first seedlings of the season, the phone rang. It was my son Gary to tell me that his wife, Gail, had just delivered a beautiful baby boy, my first grandchild. When I returned to my tiny seedlings, I couldn't help but feel somewhat awed by all the new life around me. I can't understand how anyone who works with growing things can ever feel that life is passing him by.

There's something about the tiny bright green seedlings that shoot up at the beginning of each gardening season that make you feel that you, too, have a new chance on life. It's the beginning of a new day for you, a new dream, and new hope for your future. The whole universe seems to be waking after a long rest. As the seedlings that you are working with grow into strong, sturdy plants, somehow you feel that you've been given new strengths and the courage to go on and seek a better life.

Greenhouses

My first little greenhouse, built lean-to fashion off the kitchen door of our city home, gave me one of the happiest experiences of my life. It was 8 feet by 12 feet, constructed of wooden strapping frames, and covered with 6-mil plastic. We put a large window in one end for ventilation; heated it from the house, with the kitchen door open a crack at night; and when it got too hot, late in the spring, we put a large fan on the end opposite the window. I can't tell you what a great feeling it was, up here in northern Vermont, to be able to walk out of the kitchen on a sunny day late in February, with freezing temperatures outside, and feel as if I was walking into springtime. Our little solar greenhouse did a lot to help us keep our heating bill down that winter, too. On a sunny day, with the kitchen door open, it heated the entire back of our house.

I won't include building instructions for large greenhouses, but I will tell you the least expensive way to get started, as well as everything you need to know to start all your annual vegetable and flower plants successfully. Regardless of what type of greenhouse you have, the same growing principles apply. If you do have the money and the time to construct one of the larger greenhouses, one of the best booklets I have seen on this subject is "Hobby Greenhouses and Other Gardening Structures." It can be obtained by writing to The Northeast Regional Agricultural Engineering Service (N.R.A.E.S.), Riley-Robb, Cornell University, Ithaca, New York 14853. It costs $2 and it is well worth every penny. It contains complete plans for many different styles of greenhouses.

Our second greenhouse, the one that we built here after we moved from the city, was not as happy or as productive an experience. It was built on the south face of our new little barn, and we had many problems with it. This second greenhouse was the same size as the old one, 8 feet wide and 12 feet long, with two tiers of shelving. It was built of fiberglass panels attached to redwood strapping. It had vents, fans, and heaters, with automatic heat and humidity controls. There was a heavy screened door (to protect my plants from straying chickens) leading into the barn. Panels were constructed to cover the screen at night. This allowed the heat from the greenhouse to help keep our barn warm on sunny days, and by putting the panels on at night, we prevented heat loss from radiation through the clear fiberglass panels of the greenhouse.

Advantages

- There was extra heat for our barn during cold weather.
- A built-in water line in the barn also served the greenhouse.
- Electrical units were connected to the barn's electrical system.

Disadvantages and Possible Solutions

Because the large front wall of the barn collected heat as well as the greenhouse, it became much too hot for the ventilating system I had installed.

SOLUTION: Install a large ventilating system, and hinge sections of the roof so that they can be opened at least 1 foot on warm days.

The fiberglass roof did not protect the plants from the burning rays of the sun in the late spring, and we lost many dozens of plants on the top shelf in just one day.

SOLUTION: Place slats (snow fencing works well) over the roof to filter the rays of the sun, or use a specially made type of fiberglass that is manufactured just for greenhouses.

Because of the animals in the barn, we felt that for safety's sake we had to use electric heat. This proved to be very costly.

SOLUTION: I can't honestly find a solution for this, because I still feel that other types of heaters are dangerous. You never know when a small animal might get loose and go through the door, possibly knocking over a kerosene heater.

Our hayloft was attached to one side of our barn, and in spite of our best efforts, rodents nested in the hay. Rats would burrow into the greenhouse and feast on my seedlings.

SOLUTION: Building your greenhouse on a cement foundation should prevent this problem.

The last disadvantage was one that was important to me, though it might not be to you. Our barn is back of the house by some 100 feet, and I missed the pleasure of being able to fuss a few minutes at a time whenever I wanted to. So finally I abandoned the use of that greenhouse in favor of the units that I am now using inside the house. These units do everything that any good greenhouse should, and until I can afford to build another greenhouse off my kitchen door, they suit me fine. The units I use are not expensive to build, and even if you want a larger one in the future, I would suggest that you start your first year with a small unit. It will help you to decide exactly what you want when you eventually put up your permanent greenhouse.

My plant-starting area consists of two units, each 6 to 8 feet high, 4 feet wide, and 2 feet deep, with 32 square feet of growing space per unit, or a total growing space of 64 square feet. This is growing space equal to what you would have in a freestanding greenhouse 8 feet square. These units can be used for years.

Gathering Materials for the Units

If you have scrap lumber or can encourage a donation of any from a friend or relative, that's all you need for these basic units, but if you have to buy wood, slabwood is fine, and that's what I used to build my two units. You'll need a roll of 4-mil plastic that is 10 feet wide and 50 feet long, plus four 4-foot fluorescent shop lights. Buy these when they go on sale, which is usually in the late-fall months in my area. Other than that, all you need are some nails and heavy-duty hooks to support your grow-lights, and of course a little confidence in yourself.

You will be able to maintain warmth and humidity in these small units, but they will be slightly more difficult to control than greenhouses that have heat and humidity controls. This problem is very minor, though, and you have the added advantage of being able to use household heat and electricity for lights.

You should have your first unit ready to use by January, because it takes just a little longer for some plants than others and you have to allow a couple of weeks more for plants that will not be exposed to a great deal of sunlight to develop to the transplant stages. One unit should be built inside the house. You do not have to have light from a window because you are going to be supplying your own light. You can put it on any available wall space as long as it is at least 6 feet from a heater and the room has a window that can be opened for ventilation. The second unit, which will be built outdoors, need not be built until early April. Now, I'm talking about northern climates. For warmer climates, you simply adjust the start of your project to your own local growing season. The inside unit should be built five months prior to outdoor planting time, and the outside unit, which will be used to harden off your plants (see page 27), should be built two months prior to outdoor planting time.

To construct each unit, cut four uprights, each 6 to 8 feet tall. Their height will depend on the height of your room; you can make the outside units as tall as you want to. Cut ten cross supports, each 2 feet long. The boards *do not have to be of uniform width and thickness,* but they do have to be sturdy enough to support plenty of weight. I used slabwood of differing thicknesses, and it didn't make any difference. Finally, you will need to cut 4-foot lengths of shelving. It is very important that the wood used for shelving is of uniform thickness on each shelf. That does not mean that you can't use some 1½-inch lumber and some 1-inch lumber if you have it. Just construct some shelves of the 1-inch and some shelves of the 1½-inch. The boards do not have to be of uniform width either, so long as when they are put together, they form a shelf 2 feet deep.

The last four boards that you will have to cut will be for cross supports at the top and bottom of your frame to tie it all in together and make it sturdy. You can't cut and measure these ahead of time unless you know the exact thickness of your uprights. (If you're using 2-by-4's, for instance, you wouldn't have any problem, but it's more difficult when using odd-size lumber.) When you have your side sections built, cut four pieces of lumber that are each 4 feet long *plus* the combined thicknesses of your two uprights; these will be your cross braces.

Putting the Units Together

Lay two uprights flat on the floor exactly 2 feet apart to the *outside edge,* as in the sketch. Starting at the bottom, nail a cross support across the bottom, one at the top, and the other three equally spaced in between. Construct two sections like this. With someone to help you, turn these sections up on their sides, spacing them with the *inside edge* of the uprights exactly 4 feet apart. Attach these two sections at top and bottom, as in the sketch, using two of the four cross braces that are 4 feet wide, *plus* the thickness of your two uprights. Attach these cross braces to the outside of the section. Turn the unit over and put the other side together in the same way. Your frame now looks something like a huge box kite.

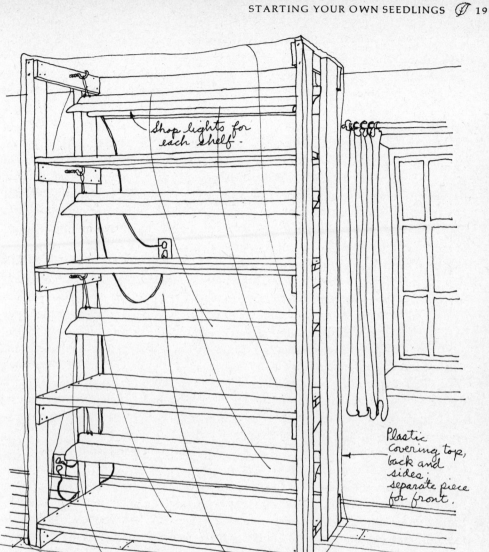

shop lights for each shelf.

Plastic covering top, back and sides: separate piece for front.

PLANT STARTING UNIT

Raise the frame to a standing position and nail your shelving on, as in the sketch shown here. Staple all the plastic securely to the top, back, and sides. Cut another face piece of plastic to fit the front, with just a little to spare on each side. Staple this to the *top* only. This face sheet will help you to control the heat and humidity in your greenhouse. It will also protect your tender young plants from dan-

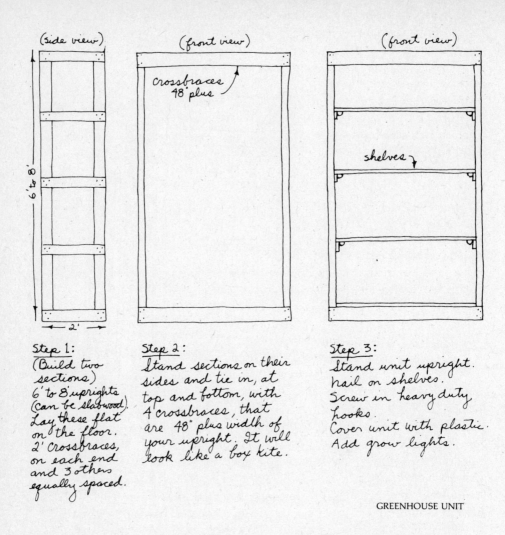

(side view)   (front view)   (front view)

crossbraces
48" plus

8' to 6'

shelves

2'

Step 1:
(Build two
sections)
6' to 8' uprights
(can be slabwood).
Lay these flat
on the floor.
2' crossbraces,
on each end
and 3 others
equally spaced.

Step 2:
Stand sections on their
sides and tie in, at
top and bottom, with
4 crossbraces, that
are 48" plus width of
your upright. It will
look like a box kite.

Step 3:
Stand unit upright.
Nail on shelves.
Screw in heavy duty
hooks.
Cover unit with plastic.
Add grow lights.

GREENHOUSE UNIT

gerous fumes that can be produced by gas or open wood fires. Screw the heavy-duty hooks to the inside center of each cross brace to support your four fluorescent lights, and you're ready to start planting.

Starting Your Seedlings

Almost any used plastic containers or tin cans will do to germinate your seedlings in. Just make sure that they are very clean and have holes punched in the bottoms for drainage. Plastic-coated milk cartons cut on the length make good containers, as do Styrofoam egg cartons. To use these latter, separate the top from the bottom. Place your starting medium in each little cup of the bottom half, plant a seed or two in each one, then set the filled bottom of the carton inside the empty top of the carton for extra support.

The cheapest, and I think the best, starting medium that I have used so far (and I've used them all) is sawdust. You can also buy vermiculite in building-supply stores. It goes by various insulation trade names. If you buy it in a garden supply store, you will have to pay about five times more for it. I like sawdust for many reasons. First of all, most of the time it's free. It's clean, it holds moisture, but it drains well too. Root systems of plants started in sawdust seem to be exceptionally sturdy. Vermiculite has the advantage of being sterile, but I honestly feel that it runs second to sawdust in every other way. In spite of the fact that sawdust is not sterile, I know that my rate of germination is excellent.

Again, it's up to you. You can buy sterile preparations in garden supply stores, though they are very expensive, or you could try to sterilize some soil of your own at home. The way to do this is to mix equal parts of garden soil, peat moss, and either sand, vermiculite, or perlite. Then sterilize this mixture in a shallow pan by placing it in a preheated oven at 200 degrees F for 1 hour. The problem with this is that it gives off a terrible odor and just about drives everyone out of the house.

Choosing Seeds

Some types of plants do better in one area of the country than in another, and the best way to determine which seeds or plants do well in your area is either to go to your nearest garden supply store and ask or to sit down with catalogs from various seed supply companies and read about each different variety. I personally think that this latter is much more fun. I usually send for as many catalogs as I can get free just before the Christmas holidays. The catalogs usually arrive right after the holidays, and they give me a few long winter evenings of pleasure just looking at them. Your local extension service is also a good source of information.

Many books on gardening advise you not to plant more than you need for your family. I'm going to tell you to do just the opposite. Seeds are inexpensive. Since you are probably a novice, some plants will be lost to experience along the way; others you will be able to sell to people you know and thereby, hopefully, pay for the cost of planting your own garden. We've done this almost every year. If you are left with extra plants at gardening time, put them in your garden. There is always a market for extra fresh produce, tomatoes especially. Many times you can trade extra vegetables for things you need or for extra help with some project. This past year we traded extra meat and vegetables with our son-in-law for the labor it took him to enlarge our small barn. Good carpenters are very expensive, but paying for the work this way was easy for us. Any extras make good feed for many of your small animals.

Plants to Start Inside

Broccoli, brussels sprouts, cabbage, cauliflower, celery, eggplant, head lettuce, onions from seed, peanuts, green peppers, hot peppers, sweet potatoes, tomatoes, cucumbers, melons, and summer and winter squash can all be started ahead of time and set out as plants. In our short northern growing season there is no other way to grow them.

Onions from seed should be started five months ahead of planting time in order to get good-size plants to set out in early spring. As the seedlings grow to about 4 inches in height, cut them back to 1 inch to promote growth of the bulb. You can cut them back as often as necessary. It doesn't pay to transplant onions to other containers in the house; they would require too much space. It doesn't matter if they grow thick in the containers they were started in.

Eggplant and celery should be started four months before the date of the last hard frost in your area.

Two and a half to three months before the date of the last frost is the time to start tomato and pepper plants. I like good-size, sturdy plants to set out, so I start my plants a little earlier than most gardeners recommend, and I have never been sorry. Early cabbage, cauliflower, and head lettuce can also be started now.

Two months before the date of the last frost you can start off the rest of your plants except those of the cucurbit family (pumpkins, cucumbers, squash, etc.).

Be sure to start plenty of marigolds at this time, too, for pest control in your garden (we will discuss this later on, in Chapter 2). Marigolds started from seed in the garden won't bloom in time to be effective against the first onslaught of bugs in early summer. This is also the time to get annual flower plants started.

If you'd like to try a few hills of sweet potatoes, six to eight weeks before the date of setting out is the time to get these started. If you're lucky enough to find some sweet potatoes that have not been treated, by all means buy them. If, though, like most of us, you have to settle for potatoes treated with preservatives, be sure to rinse them well in lukewarm water, then stand them in a glass of water, root end down. After a while little shoots will sprout. When these shoots are about 6 inches long, remove the shoots from the potato and put them in a glass of water to form roots. When they have developed a good root system, plant them in individual pots.

Wait until one month before the date of the last frost in your area to start cucumbers, melons, and summer and winter squash. The best way to start these is to take several sheets of paper towels, wet them well, and lay them flat on a shelf or table. Sprinkle your seeds on these, and roll them up. Put them in plastic bags, and place them where it's warm. In a few days they will have germinated, and you can plant them either in individual pots or in pieces of sod. Since they do not transplant well, make sure that the containers you use can be transplanted directly into the ground or start them in sod. To start plants in sod cut little squares of sod about 3 inches square and about 3 to 4 inches deep. Turn them upside down and plant your seed in the soil. When the seeds have germinated and it's time to plant them in the garden, plant them with the grass side down, and your new little plants will be nourished as the grass decomposes.

I'd like to add just one note here. If you are not using the little greenhouse unit described in this chapter but are using a regular greenhouse instead, you should subtract two weeks from all the starting dates I have given here for the various types of plants, except for the cucurbit group. Plants exposed to direct sunlight grow faster and need less time.

Don't be afraid to experiment with seeds that are usually started right in the garden. If you have time and can afford extra containers, you can try anything you think you would like to have an early crop of, such as sweet corn, beets, chard, and so on. Root crops do not transplant well; these must be started in peat pots, fertile cubes, or peat pellets.

How to Start

Start your seeds in moistened containers of sawdust or the starting medium of your choice. Wet your containers well, then let them drain until they are free of excess moisture. Very tiny seeds need only to be sprinkled on the top of the soil and pressed down with a piece of flat board. Larger seeds should have a light sprinkling of soil, or whatever you are using, over the top; then firm them down with the palm of your hand or a piece of board. Slip these containers into plastic bags or cover with several layers of newspaper. Seal the bags, then place the containers in your greenhouse until the seeds have germinated.

If the room maintains a fairly warm temperature, you will not need to turn on your lights until the seeds have germinated. If the room cools to below 65 degrees F most of the time, you should plan on using your lights to maintain a temperature of at least 65 degrees F. Seeds germinate best between 65 and 70 degrees F. Temperatures below this will slow germination and could cause some of your seeds to rot. If your room is really cool, you may find it necessary to tape down the sides of the face sheet of plastic (see page 19) to the front of the unit to help the lights to maintain an even temperature in the greenhouse unit.

One morning, after about a week to ten days, you'll get up to discover that some of your seeds have germinated. You'll be so thrilled that you'll probably feel ridiculously foolish—it's like giving birth to something. Now is the time to take off the little plastic bags.

It is important to maintain constant humidity, and the easiest way to do this is to place your flats of germinated seedlings in shallow trays or pans that have about 1 inch of crushed stone in the bottom. Adding water to these trays affords all the humidity that your young plants will need. I tried to buy some crushed stone from a local gravel company, but I needed so little that they gave it to me. After your plants have germinated, you should try to maintain about 75 to 85 percent humidity. An inexpensive thermometer that registers temperature and humidity can be purchased from all garden supply stores and most hardware and farm supply stores.

Pour water into your trays of crushed stone until it just barely reaches the top of the stones. You don't want to get it too high, or your flats of seedlings will get waterlogged. Keep your lights on fourteen to sixteen hours a day. At this point, if you can afford to replace one fluorescent bulb in each unit with a grow-light, your plants will do much better. The fluorescent bulb provides warmth, and the grow-light provides the ultraviolet rays of the sun, giving your plants the best growing conditions possible.

Watering and Fertilizing

Maintain the water level in your trays, and as your flats of seedlings dry out, moisten them with a weak solution of fertilizer. The best rule to follow is this: Mix a solution of Miracle-Gro or Rapid-Gro that is only one-third strength, using room-temperature water. Let your flats of seedlings get quite dry, then water them thoroughly, but don't drown them. Don't water them again until they have become quite dry.

If you are using an open fireplace or a gas or oil heater in the same room where your greenhouse stands, be sure to keep the face piece of plastic in place. The fumes could kill your plants. If you notice that moisture is running down the inside of the plastic, it means that the humidity is too high. Correct this by opening the face piece. Short exposures to toxic fumes are not too disastrous.

When warmer weather arrives, in early March, and you get a mild sunny day, open a window and allow some fresh air in. Just be careful not to expose the seedlings to any really cold air or drafts.

Transplanting

After your seedlings have developed to the four-leaf, or what is called the two-true-leaves stage (see sketch), they must be transplanted into other flats to give them room to grow. Now you will need a good soil mixture. I use one part good garden soil that is free of weeds, one part sand, and one part vermiculite or sawdust. Mix this well and it makes a good friable potting soil. It is not necessary to sterilize this. Transplant your seedlings carefully, using full-strength fertilizing solution to prevent root shock.

When transplanting, give each little plant at least 1 square inch of growing space. Poke a hole in your potting mixture with your finger or the blunt end of a pencil. Water flats of seedlings thoroughly first; then carefully lift your seedling and snip off the first two leaves, the ones that are not true plant leaves, then tuck the root end very carefully into the hole and gently firm the soil around the plant. As the flats dry out, water as you did your seedling trays.

Tomato plants can be transplanted as many times as they outgrow their containers. Always take off all but the top cluster of leaves and I promise you the most beautiful tomato plants you have ever seen. Other plants may be transplanted again, too, but I don't recommend that they be transplanted as often as tomato plants.

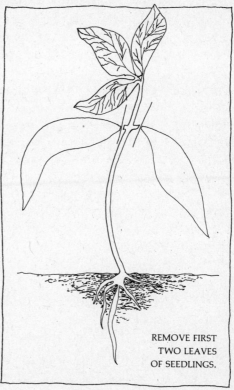

REMOVE FIRST
TWO LEAVES
OF SEEDLINGS.

Greenhouse Problems

When working with plants, you should be sure to wash your hands carefully before you start. This is especially true if you are a smoker. The nicotine that adheres to your fingertips is toxic to tomato plants and will kill them.

Once in a while you may notice that some of your flats have mold on them. This is not harmful; if it bothers you, just scrape it off. Another thing that can happen is what is known as damping-off. Your plants seem to be growing well, and then all of a sudden they just fall over. When I first started out to grow my own plants, I read that if you always used sterile soil, this would not happen. I found that information to be misleading, however. It is possible that the incidence of damping-off is less with sterile soil than with other growing mediums, but it happens just the same. The best solution I have been able to come up with is to buy seeds that have been treated with Captan or else buy some Captan myself in a garden supply store and treat my own seeds. Sometimes it is sold by another name, so if you can't find it, tell the sales clerk what you want it for and he or she will be able to tell you what to buy.

Aphids, mealybugs, spider mites, and scales are the most common pests in the greenhouse. They feed by sucking juices from the plants, which causes irregular growth, stunted plants, or curled leaves. Aphids are about 1/16 inch long. There are green, pink, white, red, and black aphids. They have soft little pear-shaped bodies and are usually found in clusters along the stem or underside of the leaves. Mealybugs are tiny dusty-white, waxy-looking bugs that form clusters on plant stems and the underside of the leaves, especially on the veins of the leaves. Scales are oval-shaped brown bugs about the same size as aphids; they eat the stems and leaves of plants. Spider mites look like little red spiders and are barely visible to the naked eye. Large infestations of this bug result in a frail, silky webbing over the plant.

Keeping your greenhouse and the containers you use clean will help to prevent insect problems. Never throw weeds or extra seedlings on the floor and leave them there; this is a good way to start a problem. If bug problems do develop, you can control them by washing each plant with warm sudsy water, if it's just a plant or two, or wiping it with a swab dipped in alcohol. If you have a large infestation, though, you will have to use a spray. Malathion is a good all-around spray that is not too harmful, and Pyrethrum is a good spray for aphids. Spray again in ten days to prevent a repeat of the problem.

Lighting

In the beginning try to keep your lights just about 1 or 2 inches above the seedlings; as the plants grow, keep raising your lights. As the plants grow larger, increase the distance between plants and lights to approximately 6 inches. If your plants seem to be growing leggy, it's usually because they are too far from their source of light and warmth. If they're not too bad, try lowering the lights first, but if the problem has progressed too far transplant them into deeper containers before you lower your lights. This will set the plants back a little, but they will develop stronger roots and become sturdier.

Hardening Off Your Plants

About eight weeks before the date of the last frost in your area, build your outside greenhouse unit (see pages 18–20, 27 for instructions). Try to have it on the south side of your house, where it will get sun all day, and as near to a door as possible. If it is conveniently located, it won't be such a nuisance to go out and cover your unit if a cold snap arrives.

Now start moving your hardier plants outside. Choose a warm day. Cabbages, cauliflower, broccoli, brussels sprouts, celery, lettuce, and onions should be moved out at this time. This will give you more space in your indoor greenhouse for the warm-weather plants, such as tomatoes, peppers, eggplants, and sweet potatoes, which are beginning to outgrow their space by now. In a month's time the hardier plants will have slowly become adjusted to outside temperatures and will be ready

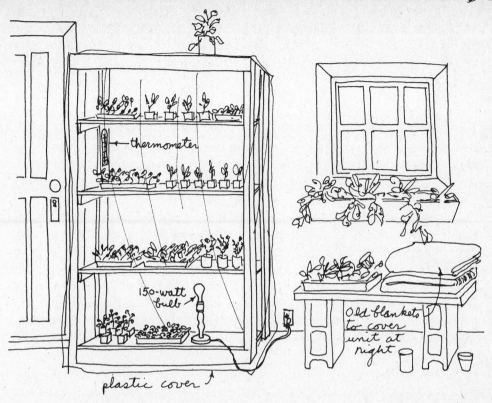

OUTSIDE GREENHOUSE

to be moved into the garden just about the time that some of your cole crops will be going into the garden, and your hardening-off unit will have room to accommodate the next batch of warm-weather plants.

Daytime temperatures will be moderate enough to harden off your plants without damaging them, but at night the plants will need a little extra protection. In the early evening place a short table lamp on the bottom shelf of your little greenhouse and put a 150-watt bulb in it. Don't use a shade, but be careful to keep the plants on the bottom shelf far enough away from the heat of the bulb, at least 8 inches. Just before the sun goes down, cover your unit with a couple of old blankets and turn on the lamp. This will keep in the warmth of the day's sun and maintain an above-freezing temperature during the night.

Be sure to hang a thermometer inside the unit, and when the temperature gets above 75 degrees F, raise the front piece of plastic. As the days get longer and warmer and the nights less cold, increasingly expose your plants to the outside air. You should protect your young plants from the burning rays of the sun by placing a piece of cardboard or something on top of the greenhouse during the warmest part of the day. Plants that are just becoming acclimated to the outside air need protection from the wind too. Windburn can be just as damaging as sunburn.

3

GROWING
VEGETABLES

People are returning to vegetable gardening today in larger numbers than at any time since World War II, when the so-called Victory garden was a national project. When you stop to think about it, it isn't too hard to understand. When you shop at the grocery store and see the prices that rise daily, the produce of poor quality, the packages that contain more substitutes and additives than real honest-to-goodness food, it isn't too hard to understand what's driving most people back to growing their own fruits and vegetables.

For my family there are other factors just as important. Planting a tiny seed such as a tomato seed and watching it grow into a strong plant that will produce up to ½ bushel of tomatoes plus hundreds more seeds never fails to fill us with awe at the miracle of reproduction.

Then there is the excitement of waiting for each new taste and texture to come along every spring. Starting early in the season I walk through the garden daily, searching for each new special treat. The first to put in an appearance is fresh chives, which I snip to top my baked potato. Following soon is horseradish, so tangy that it makes your nose smart. Right on its heels appear the first multiplier onions of the season (the taste of spring itself), along with rhubarb, new shoots of fresh mint, perennial herbs, and parsley that has wintered over. While I eagerly watch for the first new shoots of fresh asparagus, I'm busy putting in early peas, lettuce, onions, swiss chard, spinach, and radishes. I love to snap the first stalks of asparagus and eat them raw or stir-fried tender-crisp. Asparagus needs very little seasoning to enhance its subtle sweet taste. Then, in just three weeks, the first radishes put in an appearance. Pulling up a radish with its hot, snappy taste and eating it right there in the garden can bring tears to your eyes. Soon the lettuce, sweet basil, and cherry tomatoes that I started early in the greenhouse are producing abundantly. I can never wait for my first large crop of sweet basil; I make pesto, pungent with fresh garlic and grated Parmesan cheese. (Most recipes call for oil, but we always have so much homemade butter available that I make ours with that instead.) This bright green, tasty, buttery sauce is served over noodles or spaghetti. I love it so much that I grow a small amount of fresh basil year-round for an occasional treat that reminds me so much of summer. And there isn't any way I can begin to describe to you the taste of your first big red sweet juicy strawberry, eaten while you are standing ankle-deep in your own strawberry patch.

Before long, warm-weather crops are in, and the new peas are ready. When I was a little girl, I couldn't wait for the taste of the first fresh garden peas in late spring. To me, there was no greater taste treat on earth than those tiny new peas. Even the sight of their glossy green pods and the sound of them popping open would make my mouth water. I can remember my grandmother scolding me, saying, "Janet, the peas are just about ready, now you stay out of them so the rest of the family can have some." Of course, I was always grateful to Gram for that scolding, because if she hadn't given it to me, I wouldn't have known that the peas were ready. She'd no sooner get the words out of her mouth than I would hightail it out to the garden for my first fistful of the bright little green jewels.

By early summer there is such an abundance of tastes and textures to savor that it's hard to choose. This is when it's time to can, freeze, dry, or preserve the extras at the peak of their vitality and taste. Midsummer brings fresh sweet corn. Ahhhh, sweet corn, there is nothing to equal it. I am firmly convinced that anyone who does not love corn on the cob must surely have something wrong with his or her taste buds. I've been known to sneak out to the garden early in the morning and snitch the first few ears of the season to eat for breakfast. My favorite way to cook corn is to husk it fresh from the garden, place it in a pot, and cover it with cold water. Bring the water to a boil and shut off the stove, leaving the corn in the water for three to five minutes. Cooked this way and lightly seasoned with salt and butter, its sweet juiciness just pops right out at you.

One season of growing your own fruits and vegetables will be enough to convince you that even if you aren't saving any money (which of course you are), nothing can compete with the fresh flavors and textures of homegrown fruits and vegetables.

Gardening needs to be approached with a generous sprinkling of good old-fashioned common sense; otherwise, you'll resemble the overwrought mother who constantly has one finger on her son's pulse and a thermometer in his mouth. Gardening should be fun, not a hassle. The basics of good gardening never change. They involve some method of turning and breaking down the soil, developing a productive soil environment, planting, nourishing the plant life, keeping the garden weed- and pest-free, harvesting, and cleaning up in the fall. However, though the fundamentals remain the same, the methods of good gardening have become better, easier, and more exciting with every passing year. Enough food can be harvested from a garden 80 feet by 100 feet to feed a family of four for a season of fresh vegetables and fruits, with enough left over for winter keeping. New methods of gardening even include terrace, rooftop, and container gardening for people without space, and community garden projects are springing up all over the United States. In this chapter I am going to address myself to the small-scale homestead, but these practices are basic and can be used in any type of gardening.

Basic Equipment

Like all other projects on the homestead, gardening takes forethought. You must plan where you are going to locate the garden, what you are going to plant in the garden, and what equipment you will need for your gardening project. The amount and type of equipment you will need is going to vary with the size of your garden. For small gardens, under 50 feet square, you could get by with simple gardening tools such as shovels, spades, hoes, rakes, weeders, a wheelbarrow or cart, and watering equipment. Push-types of cultivators work well in small gardens, and they allow you to plant your rows closer together, thereby increasing the yield of the garden. Larger gardens require more expensive equipment: a good rotary tiller or, for large truck gardens, possibly a small tractor.

Ray and I use a Troy-Bilt tiller with the tines in the rear for both our small kitchen garden and our much larger (9,000 square feet) garden, which is farther from the house. Other companies, such as Sears and Montgomery Ward, are now carrying this type of tiller. While it is more expensive than tillers with the tines in the front, it has many advantages and is well worth the money. It is easier to handle, making it possible for older and handicapped people to enjoy gardening. It does a thorough job of breaking up even virgin soil and leaving a smooth seedbed.

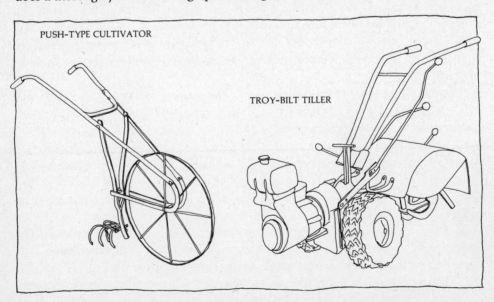

PUSH-TYPE CULTIVATOR

TROY-BILT TILLER

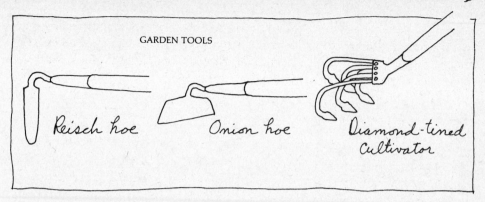

GARDEN TOOLS

Reisch hoe   Onion hoe   Diamond-tined Cultivator

And because it pulls the weed roots right up to the surface, the weeds are eliminated much faster and weeding is kept to a minimum. When fall comes, it chops the remainder of the stalks and vines into mulch, which is tilled right back into the garden to decompose and add organic humus and nutrients to the soil without all the extra work of pulling everything up, composting it yourself, and putting it back into the garden.

This type of tiller allows you to walk along the rows beside it instead of behind it, so that you do not pack down the fine tilth of your soil. This feature alone has many advantages. Loose, aerated soil gives your roots room to grow; it captures even the smallest of rainfalls, letting the water get down to the root system where it will do the most good; and the weed seeds are pulled up, not packed back down into the topsoil, where they will set roots and grow again. Tractors do pack down soil, making it very firm, and in clay-type soils this makes it all but impossible for some crops, especially root crops, to grow. A tractor needs more room to turn around, and if you are short on garden space to begin with, this serves to cut down on your space even further. Over all, I recommend a rear-end tiller rather than a garden tractor. You'll find that it doesn't require any more time to use this type of tiller, and special attachments can be purchased for every type of gardening task.

There are three other little garden tools that help make gardening easier, and they aren't costly: The Reisch hoe is a narrow elongated blade; it's small and very handy for getting to weeds between plants that are growing close together, such as onions that are planted in wide rows. The onion hoe is a small-bladed, lightweight hoe that can be used for every gardening chore except hilling, which requires a hoe with a wider blade. Last is a diamond-tined cultivator. This is especially handy for getting between the rows in small gardens or for loosening up crusty topsoil in years when rain is scarce.

Stick to lightweight garden tools. The heavier type of tool might look as if it's sturdier and longer lasting, but when it comes to enjoying your experiences as a gardener, you'll find the lighter-weight tools far less tiring to use.

Take good care of your garden tools. Tillers are expensive to replace, and even small tools cost enough nowadays. To make small-tool cleanup easier, take a 5-gallon pail of coarse sand and pour in some old oil (oil saved from an oil change in the car or tiller will do just fine). After gardening chores are over each day, push your hoes, rakes, and so forth up and down in the sand a couple of times before you put them away. This cleans and oils them at the same time. It prevents rust, and the tools will last much longer.

Read your tiller manual well and keep up the maintenance program that the manufacturer recommends. I can tell you from experience that reading the manual that comes with new equipment can save hours of frustration. Ten years ago, after about three years of gardening, Ray and I decided that we wanted a much larger garden. We felt that in order to handle a larger garden, we should have a good tiller. We ordered a heavy-duty 8-hp front-end tiller, and it arrived only partly assembled. It didn't look as if it would be too complicated to put the handle and tines on, so, greenhorns that we were, we finished assembling the tiller without reading the assembly instructions—and we put the tines on backward. We tilled all summer with them on the wrong way. It was terrible! Operating that tiller was like taking a bull by the tail. We were hauled and mauled until every bone in our bodies ached. We never discovered our mistake until we lent the tiller to a neighbor to do fall cleanup and he noticed that it had been assembled wrong. I have to be honest, though, and tell you that even with the tines on right, these heavy-duty front-end tillers are no picnic to use.

Where to Locate Your Garden

There are many things to be taken into consideration when you decide where to plant your garden: convenience to the house, availability of water supply (I will discuss alternatives on pages 59–60), drainage, exposure to the sun, composition of the soil (sandy versus clayey), condition of the terrain (too rocky, too swampy, too much brush or shrub to be cleared, too hilly, ledge formations only 6 to 8 inches beneath the topsoil). However, for some of you, in the end, there will be no choice; there will be one spot and one spot only where you must locate your garden.

Don't despair; any type of terrain or soil can be made to grow a garden. Granted, if you have soil that won't grow weeds, it certainly isn't going to grow vegetables either, but that soil can be improved over a period of time to become just as rich and productive as the best. It will just take more time, work, and patience. Steep slopes can be terraced, and areas where there is a ledge can be used by building raised beds. Railroad ties, slabwood, or 1-inch lumber that is 12 inches wide can be used to build frames that are a foot deep and as long and as wide as you want them. When these frames are filled with a good topsoil mix, you can grow anything in them. Because raised beds dry out and warm up faster than soil

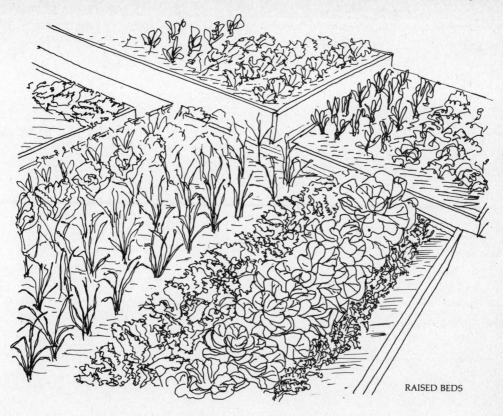

RAISED BEDS

In an area 20' x 40' you have room for eight raised beds with ample paths between — similar to the garden shown above.

in the ground, you can get a head start on your garden in the spring. Even shaded areas can be used when you use a little ingenuity. Putting a wall of some type of reflecting material such as tin, tinfoil, or aluminum on the north side of your garden can give you the benefit of sun that you would ordinarily not get to shine on your garden at all.

Most vegetables do best in a deep, sandy loam that has good drainage and is well aerated. This type of soil is the first to dry out in the spring and the fastest to warm up. Land that is gently sloped to the south or southeast is the best: Vegetables must have sun to grow, and though some crops, such as the cool-weather crops (e.g., cabbage, leaf crops, and onions) will grow in partial shade, even these must have sun for half of the day.

TINFOIL REFLECTING WALL

Land that is low and that stays wet must have some kind of drainage system set up before it can be used. Deep trenches containing tiles or drainage pipes and crushed stone placed every 20 to 30 feet in the garden (depending on how wet it is) can be helpful. Be sure to pitch these to the lowest area of your land in order to get maximum benefit. These trenches, or swales, need not take a lot of time and effort to dig if you have a tiller that has a furrow attachment. Set the furrower to go as deep as it can and furrow out your trench. Then put in a couple of inches of crushed stone, lay down some 2- to 4-inch PVC drainage pipe, and cover the pipe with crushed stone to the ground level. Gardens planted on steep slopes should be tilled and planted across the slope and mulch used between the rows to prevent moisture loss and soil erosion.

Preparing Your Soil

Heavy clay soils can be made more like humus by adding organic matter. Rotted organic matter is called humus, and heavy clay soils need more of this to loosen up the particles of clay that mat together to create the heavy compactness of the soil. Roots have a very difficult time growing in this type of soil. Corn is about the only crop that seems to do well in clay soils, so you might want to concentrate your soil-conditioning efforts on the parts of the garden where you will be growing other crops. Tilling in green corn stalks at the end of the growing season is a good soil builder in itself.

Light sandy soils also need extra humus. However, in this case, it is to hold in moisture and nutrients; otherwise everything just drains right out of them. This type of soil must be made spongy.

Preparing your soil for gardening should start with soil testing. Most agricultural extension services will test your soil for you for a small fee. Today there are some inexpensive soil-testing kits on the market that you can buy to test it yourself. They are available at any garden supply store. The less expensive test kits tell you only the pH (acidity or alkalinity) of the soil. The more expensive kits and the more thorough extension service tests give more information plus recommendations for improving your soil.

Once you know your soil needs, the steps to soil improvement are pretty basic and uncomplicated. You must break up the sod if it is a new garden area. This can be done with a shovel, spade, tiller, or tractor and plow. This step is best undertaken in the late fall. It allows time for the soil to get broken down by winter frosts. Even in warmer climates it is wise to till at the end of each gardening season. Soil becomes more friable and easier to handle when worked this way. If you must start in the spring, work the soil as soon as it's dry enough for you to get into the garden, after the frost is out of the ground. A good rule of thumb to follow is that the soil is ready when a fistful of it squeezed in your hand crumbles and falls apart when your fist is opened. If it sticks together in a moist mass, then it is not ready, and trying to work the soil at this point will only cause it to mat together in hard claylike chunks.

When you've determined that the soil is ready to work, till it thoroughly. If it's a new garden area, remove any large rocks and stones as you go along. Wait a day or two and go over it again, tilling in the opposite direction. Continue to till new garden areas this way every few days until you have worked out most of the larger rocks and stones and the soil is worked down to a reasonably crumbly tilth. It need not be smooth and lump-free.

Fall is the perfect time to add organic matter to the soil, for it will have all winter to decompose. But if you must wait until spring, you can still take some steps toward soil improvement. Well-rotted manure, shredded leaves, old hay, mowed grass, homemade compost, soybean and cottonseed meal, seaweed, disease-free crop residue, shredded newspaper, and food garbage that has been put through the blender with a little water (this is a good quick way to get nutrients into the soil) are all good organic matter that will add humus and nutrients to your garden.

Recently I accompanied my husband to the city, where he made a business call at a complex that housed doctors' offices. While I waited in the car, I watched workmen rake up the old rotted leaves from around the buildings and load them into a truck to be carted away. I got out of the car and asked where they took the leaves and was told that they were paid to take them to the nearest dump. I asked whether anyone would be allowed to come along with plastic bags and fill them with these leaves, and the men said that this would be fine as long as whoever took them made sure to do a good clean job. For those of you who have a hard time coming up with enough good organic matter to improve your soil, this could be a good cheap way to get the very best. Just be careful not to take leaves from areas that have pine trees. Pine needles will increase the acidity of your soil, and the only plants that grow well in acid soil are blueberries, flowers of the rhododendron family, and potatoes and peppers. If this is the only type of mulch that you have available, it can be used, but you must compensate for its acidity by adding lime to the garden. The pine needles should be tilled into the soil in the fall or as early in the spring as you can work the ground so that they will have time to break down. Be sure to test the soil to determine how much lime should be added at planting time.

Homemade Compost

Compost is as good a fertilizer as manure; in fact it can be even better if the manure is full of weed seeds. You can make neat compost storage units that are wood sided or made of cement blocks or wire cages, or even use plastic bags or barrels. Put garbage, leaves, hay, weeds, shredded newspaper, and so on in a pile about 3 to 4 feet in diameter. Pile it in layers of coarse material, then a handful of bone meal (use about 1 pound of bone meal per bushel of material), another layer of coarse material, and so on. Moisten the pile thoroughly but don't saturate it. Try to keep the center of the pile loose, so that air can reach it. In order for the compost to break down properly, all of its components—air, bone meal, coarse material, and moisture—must be in contact with one another. The reason that bone meal is used is that you must have a natural high-nitrogen activator if you want to make fast compost. If you follow these instructions, the pile should heat up in a week to ten days.

Now it's time to turn the pile. Mixing everything well, try to get the materials that were on the outside of the pile into the center this time. Wet the pile again. The heating and breaking-down process will slow or come to a stop in about three to four weeks, and your compost will be ready to be put into the garden. If you have a lot of food garbage in the compost pile, do not turn it, or the food will attract mice and rats. Keep it loose and wet it occasionally. Spread slake lime over the pile to control odors. It will take longer to break down this way, but it will prevent problems with rodents.

Another method, and a way to make a small amount of manure go farther, would be to layer coarse composting material between layers of manure. The natural nitrogen in the manure will give you the same results as the bone meal, making your small amount of manure much more valuable. Compost made this way will not give you the rich black compost of a manure pile that has been allowed to sit for a year or more, but even with its coarser texture, it will still be excellent compost for your garden. Tilling it into the soil will complete the process of breaking it down.

A compost pile should not smell bad. If it does, it is not working properly. The most common cause of inadequate decomposition is that the pile has not been turned often enough.

Preparing Your Seedbed

Prepare your soil as described on pages 35–36, *then* till in the organic matter if you did not do so the previous fall, wait two weeks, and till again. This may seem a lot of extra work, but if you are going to provide a fine tilth for the seedbed, it is important to work the soil and remove the rocks first, as described on page 35. Attempting to till in compost at the same time that you work up virgin soil will only make your job more difficult, and the added stress on the engine of your tiller could be damaging. Usually by the time you are ready to plant, the organic material will have started to break down and its nutrients will be available to your plants. When adding organic matter in the spring, stay away from hard-to-break-down materials such as fresh sawdust and wood chips. These require much longer periods of time to break down into usable compost, and while they are decomposing, they tend to use up much of the nitrogen in the soil. Save these for adding in the fall, and then try to add a good amount of hen manure along with them. This manure is very high in nitrogen and will replace the nitrogen that the wood product uses as it breaks down. Lacking hen manure, you can use bone meal sprinkled over the wood material. Remember that plants need well-aerated soil, and only by building up a friable seedbed of humus can you be sure of a healthy, productive garden.

Lime and Fertilizer

Lime has many important functions in the soil. It neutralizes acidity by reducing the amount of hydrogen in the soil. It adds calcium and magnesium. Magnesium is especially important for potatoes and many other crops. In soils that are sandy or soils that have not had the benefit of manure compost, magnesium is especially needed. Dolomite limestone corrects this deficiency. Lime reduces the toxic elements of whatever aluminum, manganese, and iron you have in your soil. These toxic elements are most common in acid soil, and liming neutralizes this toxicity. Aluminum and iron tend to chemically bind phosphorus that is added to the soil, in effect making it unavailable to plant life. You could actually be adding phosphorus to your garden to no avail if the pH level is not right. Finally, when you add lime, it makes nitrogen available to plant life by helping the soil organisms to decompose organic matter.

For best plant growth of most vegetables and fruits, the pH level of your soil should be between 6.3 and 7.0 (which is neutral). For blueberries, peppers, and potatoes the pH should range from 4.5 for blueberries to 5.5–6.0 for potatoes and peppers. All of them do better in slightly acid soils. If your soil test indicates that you need to adjust the pH of your soil, lime should be added before you till for the last time. Unless specific recommendations have been made, use 1 generous quart of lime or wood ashes for every 100 square feet of garden space. (Wood ashes can be used in place of lime. This will present a savings to those of you who heat with wood in the winter.) Broadcast this evenly over the garden and till it into the top 2 to 3 inches of your soil. Lime enters the soil at the rate of about 1 inch per year, so if you don't till it in, it won't get down to the plant roots where it's needed. If you repeat this procedure every three years, it should keep your soil pretty neutral. Yearly testing is the best way to determine need.

With proper liming and a good supply of well-rotted manure, you may not need any additional fertilizers for your garden. For those of you who are not practicing organic gardening, you might want to add an all-around general fertilizer such as 5-10-10 or 5-10-10-2. These figures refer to the percentages of important minerals needed for plant growth: nitrogen, which is needed for dark green foliage; phosphate (phosphorus), which is important to the development of root crops; and potash (potassium), which is needed by the entire plant for healthy growth and helps keep it disease-free. The final figure, 2, if present, refers to the percentage of magnesium that has been added. If you have used lime on your garden, the chances that you will need magnesium are not very great. Dolomite limestone is one-third magnesium. I don't know why, but plants grown in shaded areas do not require as much nitrogen as the same plants grown in full sun.

When it comes to chemical fertilizers, some beginning gardeners make the mistake of thinking that if some is good, more is better. This is not true. Adding too much fertilizer, especially nitrogen, can cause your plants to grow heavy foliage but not bear many fruits. This is especially true of the legume crops. These crops fix nitrogen in the soil; adding more would have the effect of a double dose. And root crops that are fed too much nitrogen will grow large tops and almost no roots, so go easy. Broadcast fertilizer the same way that you would lime, using 1 generous quart of fertilizer per 100 square feet of garden area. The fertilizer should be mixed into the top 2 to 3 inches of soil. If you are using a tiller, set the cultivating tines so that they cultivate only to a depth of 2 to 3 inches. This should be done one day before planting, otherwise the chemicals might burn your plants; but if you fertilize too far ahead of planting, the fertilizers will have had a chance to leach out of the soil before you get to plant. Here again, organic fertilizers prove to be superior because they break down slowly over a long period of time.

When using only organic manure compost as a fertilizer, it's a good idea to add some rock phosphate to the soil. This is the one nutrient that manures are lacking in. However, if you are using a variety of organic materials, the chances are that rock phosphate will not be necessary. If you only have chicken manure, use it sparingly or mix it with sawdust to reduce the high nitrogen content, otherwise it will burn your plants.

It's important to realize that when using chemical fertilizers in your garden, you might be adding nutrients that your soil requires but you aren't doing anything to improve the condition of the soil. That is, if you have heavy clay soil or a very light sandy soil, you will still have to make your soil more like humus. When you stop to think about it, as long as you have to do this anyway, and good organic material adds plenty of nutrients to the soil, it's really a waste of money to use chemical fertilizers. There is one exception to this rule, as I see it. When starting off with very poor soil, soil that can't even grow a decent weed, you can be pretty sure that these soils do not contain many nutrients of any kind, and any soil improvement project is going to take at least two years in this type of soil. As a matter of practical psychology, I recommend working as much organic material into the soil that first year as you can and at the same time adding a little chemical fertilizer. You are going to want some harvest from that first year of hard work, and you should have some, so the addition of chemicals that first year while your organic material is breaking down will help to ensure against total crop failure. Even for the most dedicated, reasonable success the first year is important to your morale.

While it takes more than one year to improve poor soil, if you follow the above guidelines, you should be ready to plant your first garden and be able to expect reasonable results. It's important to continue each of these steps year after year to attain and maintain healthy, productive soil. Rain and winds are constantly eroding the topsoil, and unless you take care to replace it, even the best of soils will become unproductive.

All of our gardens here at Sunnybrook have been developed from pastureland, that is, heavy clay soils that were stony and in poor condition. We've worked them year after year, and now we have what we consider reasonably good humus soil. With the exception of the first year, we have not added any chemicals except for a superphosphate (we use 10-15-15) that we always use for potatoes. Rock phosphate can be used instead, but I have not been able to find a good source of supply in this area.

If organic matter is at a premium around your homestead, you could use what is called green manure to improve your soil. Annual rye, buckwheat, clover, and many other crops make excellent organic matter for your garden. Many of these cover crops are planted early in the fall and tilled in just before winter to decompose by spring. Others are allowed to grow and mat down during the winter and then in the spring they're plowed in. All legume crops make especially good cover crops while providing a food crop as well. Just till the vines in after harvest in the fall. Legume crops add a great deal of nitrogen to the soil. State extension services have information on what types of cover crops make the best green manures in your area.

Planting cover crops has another advantage. After one or two years of using them, the weed population of your garden will be pretty well choked out. Last year we decided to use buckwheat in an area of our garden that was especially weed-infested. We planted it between the rows late in August and tilled it in early in October, just after it blossomed. This year we couldn't believe the difference in that area of our garden. It's more expensive than some of the other cover crops, but we intend to do another section of our garden this year.

What to Plant

Pictures in seed catalogs tend to be a little deceptive at times, but the catalogs offer a wide variety of every type of seed and plant available. What I like best about them is that they give you information about the newest varieties of seeds and plants being developed each year. Many of the newer hybrids are developed for small gardens, such as the bush type of melons, cucumbers, and squash, so that by reducing the space requirements of your plants, you can increase the yield of your garden. Read the seed catalogs and arm yourself with information before you go shopping for your seeds.

Each year it seems that some crops do better than others. There are many variables in the weather that usually account for this: Perhaps it has been too dry, too wet, too hot, too cool, or there has been too late a spring or too early a fall. Sometimes a particular bug infestation is responsible, but in ten years, without exception, we have always had one or more successes that we could boast about.

If you are using seeds saved over from the previous year, be sure to check them for germination. Take a piece of paper towel and dampen it, scatter approximately ten seeds over the paper, and roll it up. Wrap this in plastic and set it in a warm place for a few days (the top of a self-defrosting refrigerator is a good place). If only half of the seeds germinate, you'll know that if you want to plant these seeds, you'll have to plant twice as many. It's a good idea to mix them with new seeds.

Whenever you are using your own seeds, always save the seeds from the most perfect plants you have. Seeds saved from hybrid plants will grow and produce the following year, but because hybrids are developed by cross-pollinating two different types of plants, you can't expect to have exactly the same type of plant as you grew with the original seeds.

Plan Your Garden

As a homesteading family you needn't worry about planting too much garden as long as you have the time to take care of it, because all of the extras can be used for animal feed or sold to pay for grain or some other project you are planning. That doesn't mean that you don't need a plan for your garden, though. For instance, you might waste much time and effort if you were to plant tall crops, such as corn, so as to block out the sun from tomatoes and eggplants, which must have lots of sun to ripen and grow. Sweet corn and popcorn cannot be planted in the same garden, or they will cross-pollinate. We've had good luck planting sweet corn and several rows of field corn for our animals in the same garden, though. In addition, pumpkins and winter squashes should not be planted together for the same reason. Though pumpkins and squashes grow well and taste fine, they do not store well. If you are going to can or freeze them at harvest time, you can disregard this warning.

Start your plan by deciding which crops go in early and try to use the part of the garden that dries out first for these. Tall crops such as corn, pole beans, and sunflowers should be planted in the northwest corner, or along the northwest edge of the garden. Perennial crops such as rhubarb, strawberries, raspberries, asparagus, herbs, horseradish, Jerusalem artichokes, and multiplier onions should be planted wherever they can remain indefinitely. If you're lucky enough to have room for more than one garden, as we do, you could keep all your perennial fruits, vegetables, and herbs together in a separate garden area.

I advise against planting perennial plants the first year unless you have exceptionally good soil, because these plants are expensive, and it would be a shame to waste money and hard work on plants that won't stand much of a chance of survival. You would be better off to wait one year and work up your soil into a better condition. Even one year of intensive soil conditioning would give these plants a better chance for success. In the meantime, you might want to plant a legume crop such as peas or bush beans in the area that will be used for perennials. After harvesting the vegetables, till the vines in while they are still green. This simple project alone would be a good soil conditioner, as legume crops add a great deal of humus material and nutrients to the soil.

I will not get into herbs in this chapter; they deserve a book by themselves. The best book I've read to date is *A Cook's Guide to Growing Herbs, Greens, and Aromatics* by Millie Owen (published by Alfred A. Knopf, 1978).

DWARF ORCHARD

Sour Cherry

McIntosh Apple

Delicious Apple

Reliance Peach

Bartlett Pear

Dutchess Pear

Manchurian Apricot

N
W E
S

80 Grape Vines

Blueberries

Red Raspberries

Black Raspberries

Asparagus

Asparagus

Asparagus

Garlic

Shallots

Multiplier Onions

Horseradish

Strawberries

Salad Lettuce

HERBS

Rhubarb

P Mint

P Fennel

P Winter Savory

P Oregano

B Caraway

A Summer Savory

A Dill

P Thyme

P Lavender

P Rosemary

P Tarragon

P Camomile

A Coriander

A Basil

P Chives

P Lemon Balm

P Sage

A Marjoram

B Parsley

A Chervil

A Anise

Tomato and Cuke Plants

SALAD AND PERENNIAL GARDEN

GARDEN PLAN

VEGETABLE GARDEN

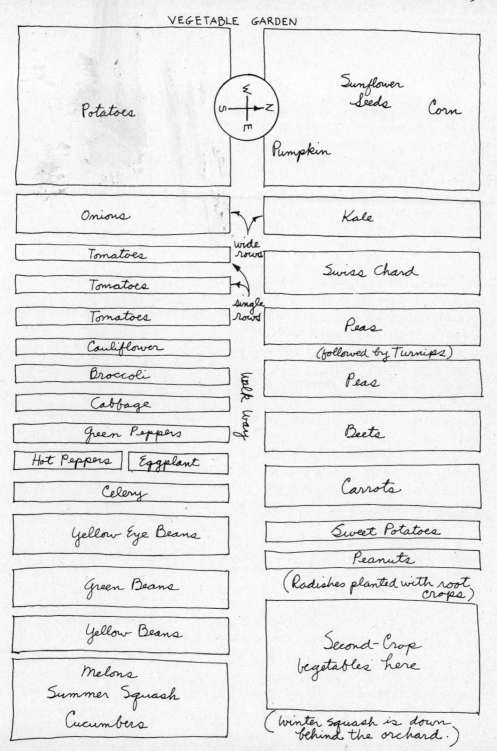

GARDEN PLAN

When to Plant

In the area of the garden that dries out most quickly, plant early crops. These hardy crops include beets, carrots, dill, early peas, kale, kohlrabi, lettuce, mustard, onion seeds, onion sets, radishes, and spinach. These vegetables need cool weather to grow well. There are two main ways you can plant these: You can use early-maturing varieties and pull the spent stalks and vines or till them in when harvest is done and then plant another crop. Or you can companion-plant by combining a short-season crop, such as radishes, with a crop that takes longer to mature, such as carrots. This will give extra garden space and greater production.

Succession Planting and Companion Planting

Though I've tried planting carrots with peas, as some gardeners have suggested, I have not had good results. I feel that the reason for this is that peas fix nitrogen in the soil, and carrots do not do well with extra nitrogen. They grow large tops and no root. This is exactly what happened to mine. Good combinations that you might try are radishes with onion sets or seed or parsnips with cabbage seed. As you pick the radishes, you automatically thin the other vegetables. Onion sets, lettuce, or celery interplanted with cabbage and spinach, lettuce, or swiss chard interplanted with corn are other good combinations. By the time you've harvested the early vegetables, the later ones are just beginning to require more room.

Many people plant pole beans a couple of weeks after corn or sunflowers by putting a couple of bean seeds into each hill of corn. As the corn and beans grow, the corn provides a pole for the beans to climb on. We do not like pole beans (we prefer bush types), so I have never tried this, but I have seen it done very successfully.

Plan to harvest as long a season of fresh vegetables as you can. This means getting the early vegetables into the ground as early in the spring as you can work in the garden. Then plant again in two months for a fall crop. Many vegetables adapt to two plantings in a season: green and yellow beans, broccoli, cauliflower, chinese cabbage, carrots, endive, kale, kohlrabi, radishes, spinach, turnips, collards, and lettuce. Second-crop root vegetables are the best ones for winter keeping, and winter potatoes should be started in late spring, around the end of May.

As the ground warms up and nighttime temperatures stay above freezing, it's time to put in more of your garden. Some plants tolerate a fair amount of frost and can be put in before the date of the last frost in your area. They are called semi-hardy, and they include early cabbage, head lettuce, onion sets, and cauliflower. Brussels sprouts and turnips could go in at this time, too, but these two crops do

PLANT PROTECTORS

best if planted late to mature in the fall because frost actually improves their flavor. But if heavy frosts are predicted, you should cover the plants at night with plastic jugs, tin cans, or newspaper; just be sure to uncover them in the morning. Broccoli can stand some light frost if the plants have been hardened off carefully, so I put a few in early, but I save the others till the danger of frost is past to be on the safe side. We have too large a garden to be able to cover everything at night, and I usually lose about half of the early broccoli plants, but at least I have a few plants producing early in the summer, and I love broccoli enough to be willing to sacrifice a few plants. Broccoli started from seed in the late spring right in the garden will mature later in the summer. These plants are much freer from worms and their taste is better than that of plants set out in either spring or midsummer.

We like to start early potatoes under a hay mulch as soon as the frost is out of the ground. Seeds for tender crops that need warm weather, such as bush beans, corn, and so on can be planted ten days before the date of the last frost in your area. Once the danger of a frost is over and nighttime temperatures average about 50 degrees F, it's time to put in your plants of tomatoes, peppers, sweet potatoes, eggplants, summer and winter squashes, pumpkins, melons, and cucumbers that you have started in peat pots.

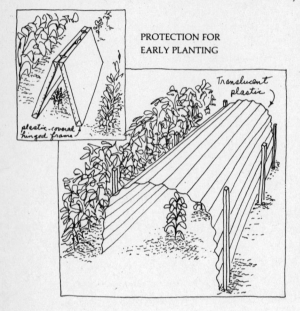

PROTECTION FOR
EARLY PLANTING

Translucent plastic

plastic-covered hinged frame

You can get a head start on Mother Nature and put some of your plants out early by building a miniature greenhouse to place over each plant or a larger one to cover several plants, or by covering each plant with a clear plastic container that can be removed on warm sunny days (see sketch on page 45).

Methods of Planting

Wide-row planting is increasing in popularity, and it's not hard to understand why when you know the advantages: greater yields (up to five to eight times as much in the same area) and less work (you can weed or pick the equivalent of a 15-foot row by working in just a 3-foot-square area, the reaching distance of your arm). Because crops that are grown in wide rows have thicker vegetation, the soil is kept shaded. This retards weed growth and loss of moisture from the soil on hot sunny days. Of course, you can still plant in single rows if you want to, but we have never enjoyed gardening as much as we do since we've adopted wide-row-planting techniques.

To plant in wide rows you must first prepare a smooth seedbed. It's not necessary that the entire garden be level and smooth, just the area that you are going to plant. Stake out your row at each end and stretch a string the length of the row along the two outside edges. Rake this area smooth and level it off as much as possible. If you are hand seeding, broadcast the seeds between the strings and cover them with soil from between the rows. Seed should be covered to a depth that is approximately four times their diameter. Very fine seeds need only to be

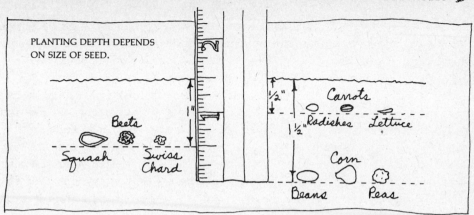

PLANTING DEPTH DEPENDS ON SIZE OF SEED.

Beets

Squash

Swiss Chard

½"

1½"

Carrots

Radishes   Lettuce

Corn

Beans   Peas

scattered over the top of the loose soil and firmed down with a broad hoe or walked on. Seeds must come into firm contact with the soil to germinate well.

We like to plant our larger seeds, such as peas and beans, by means of an even easier way. We scatter the seeds over the prepared area, we set our tiller tines so that they will till very shallow, and we till the seeds in. Then we walk the rows to firm up the soil. When we plant this way, we use a few more seeds than we ordinarily do because some of the seeds go a little deeper than others. The advantage of this, besides being less work, is that the seeds nearer the surface germinate and

grow quickly, and as you harvest the vegetables, it makes room for the seeds that went in a little deeper. As you pull vines that have been harvested, the less mature vines grow in their place, and this prolongs the harvest season for each crop by several weeks without having to plant over again. We have planted swiss chard and beets this way too. Last year we harvested 5 bushels of beets from a row that was only 25 feet long by 18 inches wide. When seeds planted this way first start to grow, some areas of the row may look sparse. Don't panic; before you know it, the row will fill in, and you might well have to thin it.

All root vegetables except potatoes can be planted in wide rows. Other vegetables that do well are kale, lettuce, onion seed and sets, peas, spinach, and swiss chard. If you like small heads of

TILLER-PLANTED ROWS

Plants of varying maturity

cabbage, you could try planting these three to four across in a wide row. They will not grow as large this way, but for a small family, the smaller heads might be just right. Celery that does not need to be blanched will also do well planted in wide rows. Larger plants, such as broccoli, cauliflower, eggplant, brussels sprouts, green peppers, and tomatoes, should be planted in single rows because they need room to expand.

In the past, we managed to lose half of our corn each year to the birds—they'd dig it out of the soft ground as fast as we'd plant it—until two years ago when we came up with an easy, inexpensive way to stop them. First of all, I soak the corn seed overnight in room-temperature water to give it a head start on germination. The next day we cut strips of newspaper 2½ to 3 inches wide. Making shallow trenches 2 to 3 inches deep with our hoe, we space our corn in double rows with 8 inches between them and 24 inches between each double row. After we drop our corn seed in the row, we cover it with the strips of newspaper, and then fill in the shallow trenches with dirt from the outside rows. When the birds try to dig it up, they hit the newspaper, and this stops them. Planted this way, the corn germinates quickly and is above the ground in about seven to ten days. By the time it has grown large enough to be above the ground, it has also set down good enough roots and the birds can't pull up the young seedlings, either. Now we have full rows of corn without having to replant it two or three times, and the double rows give us twenty-four rows of corn in the same space it previously took to grow twelve.

Corn needs to be hilled for support as it grows taller. Pull the dirt from between the rows and up around the base of the stalks. Do this at least once when the corn is about 1 foot tall. Corn must be planted in blocks (of rows of four) for good cross-pollination. If you are planting more than one variety to mature at different stages of the summer, then you should still plant them in blocks.

Onions from seed are planted the same way as all fine seed. Onions from sets can be planted in either single or wide rows. The simplest way to plant is to work the soil until it is loose and crumbly. Take each onion set and push it down into the soil, 1½ inches apart, root end down, until the top is beneath the top level of the soil. We do not firm the soil over our sets, and the green tops are above ground in about one week. As soon as there are any large enough to eat as scallions, we start thinning the plants, picking every other onion. This leaves room for the onion bulbs to develop on those that are left. As you pull the scallions, run your finger around the tops of the onions you leave and remove the dirt from the top two thirds of the bulb. Onion bulbs grow mostly above the ground, and if the soil is not removed, they will remain very small. As the onions planted from seed grow to scallion size, follow the same procedure.

To grow potatoes under mulch, start by broadcasting some rock phosphate or superphosphate over an area of ground the size that you want your potato patch, using 1 quart of fertilizer for each 100 square feet to be planted. Wet the fertilizer down well, and let it set for two days. If you use rock phosphate, you should wait a week or more. Meanwhile, on the day you fertilize, cut the seed potatoes into pieces that have at least two good eyes in each piece. Put the potatoes in a spot that is protected from the sun and rain, in order to dry the cut edges, for two days. This protects the potato seed from rot after it has been planted. Scatter the seed over the fertilized area of ground and cover it with at least 6 inches of old hay. That's all there is to it. No weeding, no tilling, and when it comes time to harvest the potatoes, just pull back the hay and pick them up. Last year we planted about 8 pounds of Kennebec seed potatoes in an area 50 feet square and harvested close to 200 pounds of nice large potatoes. Furthermore, during the summer, we took some of the tiny ones to cook with peas. Ten pounds of seed will produce anywhere from 200 to 300 pounds of potatoes, depending on weather conditions and the type of soil they are grown on or in.

We decided to go one step further and leave all the potatoes that were still tiny by fall right there in the potato patch. We covered the patch with an additional 2 feet of old hay mulch for the winter. Ray and I couldn't wait for spring to arrive to see what would happen. It took longer for the frost to go out of that area of the garden because of the heavy mulch, but much to our delight, once it had gone, we discovered that the potatoes and the mulch had worked down into the topsoil during the winter, the tiny potatoes had already germinated, and a new batch of potatoes was growing. I added a light sprinkling of superphosphate to the top of the mulch, which by this time had reduced itself to about 6 inches deep. The entire patch of potatoes grew beautifully, and we dug 117 pounds of potatoes this fall from this experiment.

Potato seed is very expensive, but there are ways to get around this problem if you just can't afford to buy it. As the potatoes you are using develop eyes in the early spring of the year, save the eyes when you peel the potatoes to cook them. Just dig the eye out and plant the eye instead of the potato. Some gardeners will tell you that these small pieces produce weak vines and do not produce well, but while they might be slightly lower in production than good seed, they are also lower in cost (they are free), and they still grow good strong vines that produce a crop of good-size potatoes. You can plant more seed to compensate for lower individual plant yield. I've used this method several times myself, and I feel confident in advising you to do this. But never use potatoes for seed that are sold for commercial consumption. These potatoes often carry many diseases and have been treated with a preservative. Naturally, good-quality, disease-free seed potatoes are your best bet for a good crop.

Potatoes planted in the ground must be planted deeply, because tubers form up the stem of the plant and not at the root ends. This can be done in two ways. Either dig a trench 6 inches deep with a furrower or a hoe, or dig individual holes. If you plant trench-style, lay the potato pieces 12 to 14 inches apart in the trench with a handful of 10-15-15, or whatever superphosphate you choose to use, between each piece. Fill in the trench and firm the soil. If you dig holes, space them the same distance apart, place a small handful of fertilizer in the bottom of the hole, cover this well with another handful of dirt (especially important if you are using a fertilizer with nitrogen in it, or it will burn the seed), and put in your potato seed. Fill in the hole with soil and firm it. As the potato vines grow, they must be hilled to give the tubers additional soil to grow in.

Sweet potatoes are grown from plants, not seed, as I mentioned in Chapter 2. They need a long growing season and can't be planted until after the ground warms up. They need an average of 145 days to mature. A good way to get a head start with them is to plant the slips early in large-size peat pots in your greenhouse. This gives the root development a head start. Unlike Irish potatoes, sweet potatoes grow on the root ends. They like a sandy, fertile soil, not too high in nitrogen (as with all root crops). Our soil tends to be heavier, so we plant ours by making a trench and putting 2 inches of well-rotted manure on the bottom. We cover with loose soil until we have built a ridge 6 to 8 inches high above the ground level. Then we plant our sweet potato plants in this ridge, spaced 18 inches apart. Sweet potatoes do not tolerate wet soil, and planting them in ridges helps to keep heavy soils drier.

Growing Asparagus

Those of you who love this hardy perennial should give special consideration to starting an asparagus bed the first year of gardening, as it requires three years to get a good crop. Since the fern that develops when this plant goes to seed grows quite high, be sure to place it in an area of the garden where it will not block out the sun for later-maturing plants.

Asparagus should be planted in well-fertilized ground as early in the spring as the ground can be worked in the northern climates (it should be planted in the fall in the South). Work as much good organic matter into the soil as you can and give it time to decompose well before planting asparagus. When you're ready to plant, dig or furrow trenches 8 to 10 inches deep, with the rows at least 4 feet apart. Make mounds of soil mixed with compost every 12 inches along the trenches. We use nursery-grown disease-free crowns that are one to two years old. Drape them over the mounds of soil. Fill the trench in and firm the soil down well.

Asparagus beds need three years to mature, and each spring they should be side-dressed with a good fertilizer. Do not cultivate too deeply because asparagus has a very shallow root system. The first year after planting, do not pick any of the young shoots but let them grow to ferns and berries. This is important, for it is this process that will give you next year's growth. The second year you can pick for about two weeks. Pick only the shoots that are as big around as your thumb, again letting the rest go to seed. By the third year you should have a well-established bed that will continue to produce for years. At this point you may pick all the shoots that are as big around as your thumb. Leave pencil-slim shoots to develop more plants. The ferns should not be cut down until winter or early spring. We usually burn ours in the early spring. A very effective way to keep your asparagus bed weed-free is to put a heavy layer of rock salt on it in the early spring before new growth has started.

Setting Out Transplants

Plants should not be put into the garden during the heat of the day. The best time to set out your plants is early evening or on a very cloudy day. Tender young plants set out early in the day on sunny days are often burned by the hot sun. If this is the only time of the day that you have to set out your plants, take care to protect them from the hot sun by putting some kind of paper cap over them. *Do not use plastic or tin cans; this only intensifies the heat of the sun.* In hot, dry spells, make sure that new transplants are watered daily until they have become well established.

Cole crops (cabbage, broccoli, brussels sprouts, cauliflower, etc.) are all planted the same way. These are shallow-rooted vegetables, which means that the roots grow very close to the surface of the soil. To plant, dig a good-size hole, large enough to accommodate the root of the plant and whatever soil you can keep from the pot surrounding it. Put a cupful of liquid fertilizing solution, such as liquid sea-weed or Miracle-Gro, in the hole to get the young plants off to a good start and prevent root shock. Then wrap a paper collar that is about 2½ to 3 inches wide around the stem of the plant. Put the plant in the ground with half of the collar above the ground level. This protects your new plants from cutworms. Fill the hole with soil and firm it up around the plant. The paper collar will rot off as the plant grows, and cutworms do not usually bother a plant once it has become well established. Cole-crop plants should be planted 16 to 18 inches apart, with cabbage being the exception if you like a smaller head.

Eggplants are planted the same way, but need about 30 to 36 inches between plants and at least 24 inches between rows. Peppers are planted just like eggplants, but can be planted as close as 14 to 16 inches apart. Old-time gardeners like to place matches in the bottom of the hole. The sulfur in the matches seems to reduce the pH in the soil, and peppers like a slightly acid soil. Peppers do not do well in soil that is low in magnesium. If your peppers are not doing well, this might be one of the causes. While dolomite limestone does contain one-third magnesium, it's not a good idea to lime the garden area where you are planting peppers because they prefer a slightly acid soil. The best solution to this problem is to mix some Epsom salts (magnesium sulfate) with water. Use 1 tablespoon of salts to 6 ounces of water, and spray this right on the plant leaves. This is especially effective if it's done at blossom time. Plants treated like this usually have rich dark-green leaves and produce an abundance of peppers.

Celery that you want to blanch should be planted in trenches that are 6 to 8 inches deep. Set the plant in the bottom of the trench and firm the soil around it. As the celery grows, add more soil, enough to keep the stalks covered. Another

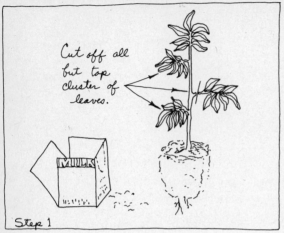

TOMATO PLANTING

effective way to blanch celery is to drive four wooden shingles, box fashion, around the celery plant. Pull dirt up around your "box." This will exclude sunlight and keep your celery from turning green. Many people do not bother to blanch their celery, and it stays green. The outer stalks of this type of celery tend to be a little tougher.

If you followed the advice I gave in the chapter on starting your own plants and transplanted your tomatoes frequently as they grew, you should have tall plants with good sturdy stalks and strong root systems. When it comes time to plant your tomatoes outside, they should be planted almost the same way. Take off all the lower leaves. Make a shallow trench, lay the stem of the plant horizontally in this trench, cupping the top cluster of leaves carefully upright above the ground level with your hand. Add a cupful of liquid seaweed or Miracle-Gro solution, and cover the stem with soil. Firm the soil well over the stem and up around the top cluster of leaves. If it's been particularly warm and the surface of the soil has been getting very hot in midday, it's a good idea to place a small amount of light mulch, preferably old hay or straw, just around the cluster of leaves. This will prevent them from coming in contact with the hot soil and getting burned. Tomatoes planted this way develop new roots all along the stem. This strong root system, close to the surface of the ground, will receive maximum heat from the sun. These plants recover from transplant shock quickly, will bear sooner, and will give greater yields than plants that are planted with the root system set deeply into the soil.

It's also very important that you leave plenty of room between plants, because unstaked tomato plants take up more space. Planted too close together, they would not ripen very well because much of the fruit would be hidden from the sun. Determinate tomatoes (tomatoes that grow to only about 2½ feet and stop growing) should be planted at least 3½ feet apart. Indeterminate tomato plants (plants that continue to grow in height unless they are pinched off) should have 3½ to 4½ feet of space between them. If you decide to stake your tomatoes instead, be sure to drive in the stakes at the time you plant your tomatoes; otherwise you might injure the root system.

If the water supply is going to be a problem in your garden, you might want to plant vine crops such as cucumbers, melons, squash, and pumpkins the way we do. During the year I save all the large plastic and tin containers that I come across. When we plant our vine crops, we take a container, punch holes in the lower edges, and sink the container into the ground, leaving only 2 inches of it above the soil level. Then we plant our seeds or started plants around this container. It makes an ideal way to water and fertilize these plants. Water is poured directly into the container and the moisture and nutrients get right to the root system where they are most needed.

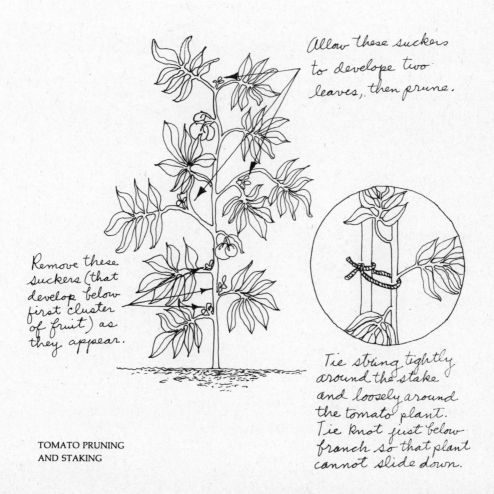

Allow these suckers to develope two leaves, then prune.

Remove these suckers (that develop below first cluster of fruit) as they appear.

Tie string tightly around the stake and loosely around the tomato plant. Tie knot just below branch so that plant cannot slide down.

TOMATO PRUNING
AND STAKING

Thinning and Weeding

As your seedlings germinate and get up above the ground about 1 inch, it's time to thin them. A few years ago Ray and I attended a gardening class conducted by an old hand at gardening. He had many new ideas, and in the course of the program he showed slides on thinning with a rake. It looked so quick and easy that we were really enthusiastic about trying it, but when it came time to do so, we panicked. It looked as if we were pulling all the plants out of the ground, so we did only half of the garden that way and thinned the rest of the vegetables by hand as we had in the past. Within a month's time, it became obvious that the rake method worked beautifully. Plants that were thinned this way looked as good as those we thinned by hand, if not better, and in addition we had pulled up many of the tiny weed seedlings before they had time to spread and choke out our vegetables.

To thin using a rake, you simply pull the rake *across* the row, going in one direction. This does pull up many of the tiny plant seedlings along with the weed seedlings, but when all is said and done, those remaining are spaced just about right for good growth. This method can be used for narrow rows as well. Never cultivate plants deeply after they start to grow. Root systems on many plants spread far into the side rows, and you could damage them severely. We find it best to mulch as much as possible all plants that grow and produce above the ground. Root crops do not present as much of a problem.

Cultivating

Cultivating plants (loosening or breaking up the soil around plants) that are not mulched should start as soon as the tiny seedlings emerge from the ground and you can see where they are planted, or as soon as you transplant your plants. At least once a week, get rid of all the weeds near your plants. You should do this more often in periods of rapid growth. A sharp-edged onion hoe does a good job of slicing off weeds at the surface of the soil. Some of the more succulent weeds, such as milkweed, are easier to pull up. They grow fast and take a great deal of moisture and nutrients from your plants.

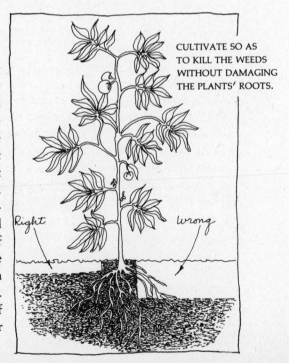

CULTIVATE SO AS TO KILL THE WEEDS WITHOUT DAMAGING THE PLANTS' ROOTS.

Right

Wrong

You might read in some articles on weeding that if you pull weeds and leave them between the rows, they will die, decompose, and furnish some organic matter to the soil, but I have found that if you pull weeds in moist ground, and this is when it's easiest and best to weed, you frequently have quite a bit of soil that adheres to the larger types of weeds; placing this weed material in the rows or on top of mulched gardens seems to furnish another seedbed for them to reroot themselves. Unless you have time to make sure that you get all of the soil off these roots, it's best to pick them up in a basket and put them in a compost heap. The good soil around them, as well as the weeds themselves, will make a good addition, and you can return them to the garden after they have had a chance to break down into good usable humus.

When I started my perennial herb garden, I had a hard time distinguishing between the weeds and the herbs because I wasn't familiar with herb seedlings. I finally looked for a generous sprinkling of seedlings that all looked alike and that were different from any in the other rows of herbs. It wasn't a very scientific way to tell the plants from the weeds, but it worked, and I'm sure you could use the same system with all other fine seedlings, such as carrots and beets. Seed packages often show what the seedling is supposed to look like, but if you look at several seed packages at a time, you'll find that it's pretty hard to tell one kind of seedling from another.

Mulching

Mulching can be used early in the season on cool-weather crops to keep the ground from warming up too fast. This prolongs the harvest season for such crops as spinach, lettuce, cauliflower, and broccoli that tend to bolt quickly in warm weather. Mulch warmth-loving crops, such as tomatoes, eggplants, peppers, and so forth, after the ground has warmed up, usually around mid-June up here in the Northeast. Mulching the garden with old hay, straw, partly decomposed sawdust, or black plastic is a good way to control soil temperatures. It keeps the soil from becoming too hot during the day and from cooling down too much at night. These constant temperatures make for better growing conditions.

Mulch also keeps in the soil's moisture, protecting it from evaporation due to the hot sun beating on the soil's surface. And when gardens planted on steep slopes are mulched, it helps to prevent topsoil loss as well. Finally, a good mulch will prevent weed growth and save hours of work.

If you're going to do a large garden, you will need a considerable amount of mulch for it to be effective. The listing on page 56 tells you how much of the various types you will need. Black plastic for a large garden runs into a lot of money, and you will reduce the savings that you expect to realize by planting the garden in the first place. If you're careful, you can reuse the plastic one or two seasons, but it's still very expensive for large gardens.

TYPES OF MULCHES AND MINIMUM DEPTH REQUIREMENTS

Mineral
Small gravel, 1–2 inches
Crushed rock, 1–2 inches
Vermiculite, 1 inch
Rock wool, 1 inch
Marble chips, 1 inch

Plastic and Foil
Clear polyethylene
Black polyethylene
Aluminized plastic
Aluminum foil

Paper
Newspaper
Magazine pages, 6 sheets
Corrugated paper
Roofing paper
Aluminized paper
Biodegradable commercial mulch
   paper

Organic
Sawdust, 2 inches
Shavings, wood chips, 1 inch
Peat moss, 1–2 inches
Buckwheat hulls, 1 inch
Cocoa hulls, 1–2 inches
Bagasse (sugar cane), 1–2 inches
Pine needles, 3 inches
Lawn cuttings (well dried), 1–2 inches
Shredded bark, 2–3 inches
Shredded newspaper, 2 inches
Clean straw, 6–8 inches
Weed-free hay, 6–8 inches
Excelsior, 3–4 inches
Chopped cornstalks, 3 inches
Leaves, 2–3 inches
Bark nuggets, 3 inches
Brush or stump chippings, 2 inches
Compost, 1–2 inches*
Ground corn cobs, 1–2 inches

We have found that the best solution for a large garden is to save newspaper year-round. When we're ready to mulch, we lay down layers of newspaper, at least six sheets thick. Slightly overlap the sheets, and cover these with old hay, straw, sawdust, or whatever types of mulch you have on hand, using several varieties if necessary. If you can't come up with enough mulch, you can put several light shovelfuls of dirt over the newspaper, just enough to hold it in place. This type of mulching is very effective in maintaining the ground temperatures that you desire, it reduces evaporation of soil moisture, and very few weeds, if any, penetrate through the six sheets of newspaper. You could go on vacation for a week and not have to worry about coming back to a weed-filled, wilted garden.

If you find that you can't or don't want to mulch the entire garden, I would suggest that you at least try to mulch your tomato plants. Wait until the ground has warmed up and then put down your mulch. This way you won't have to stake your tomato plants. The mulch will protect the fruits from the rot that occurs when they come in contact with the ground, and unstaked tomato plants produce a

*Compost is probably the best mulch you can use, and you can make it yourself from leaves, lawn rakings, and other leftover plant materials from your garden.

greater yield. When mulching tomato plants, use a mulch that is free of weed seeds; this will keep small rodents away. They usually nest in mulches that have weed seeds, and after they eat the seeds, they go after the tomatoes.

In the fall, organic types of mulch are tilled into the soil to decompose, and they add some very valuable nutrients to the soil as well as making it more humus. This past year Ray was injured in late October, and we didn't get to till the gardens before winter as we usually do, yet when we went to till them this spring, the newspaper that had been on top of the ground had rotted right into the topsoil, and there wasn't a sign of it left. The chemicals in the ink deteriorate rapidly and evaporate into the air; therefore they do not have a chance to get down into the plant life where they might be harmful.

Our perennial garden is mulched in a special way. The first year we put down one layer, 3 to 6 inches deep, of well-rotted manure, covered by six sheets of newspaper and then a top layer of old mulch hay or straw. Being short of hay or straw some years, we use old, partially decomposed sawdust. This effectively fertilizes our garden, maintains good moisture and temperature balances, and, with minor exceptions, controls the weeds. Our reason for not wanting to cultivate our perennial garden is that plants that are left in the ground year after year develop root systems that travel some distances from the plant itself. Cultivating could damage these root systems. To save ourselves work and losses as well while maintaining healthy soil conditions, we choose to mulch. During the winter this mulch breaks down and sinks into the topsoil, greatly improving it and nourishing the plants. The following spring what might have been originally a total mulch of 8 to 10 inches has partially decomposed and has been reduced to about 2 inches, and we start all over again, adding just what we think we need.

Fertilizing

Plants have the same basic needs as all living things. They require air, water, and nourishment if they are to thrive and be productive. Understanding your own life cycle will help you to understand the needs of your crops better. Human life makes its greatest demands for nourishment during infancy and early growth. If you waited until a child was eighteen years old to give him anything but water, he would have surely died before then. Plant life is not much different. It requires its greatest amount of feeding at the time it is set out as a tender young plant. If you have prepared your soil well and there is an abundant supply of decomposed organic matter in the garden, or at least if you have chemically fertilized your soil before planting, this will furnish an adequate diet for your plants until they are partly grown.

When root crops and leaf vegetables are about one-third grown, they need to be fed again. Cole crops should be fed about three weeks after setting out, and

FERTILIZER
SIDE-DRESSING

fruit-setting plants should be fed at the blossom-set stage. This will give them the extra nutrients they need to get them over this stress period. Fruit-bearing plants, such as tomatoes, eggplants, and so on, will need one additional side-dressing between fruit-setting stage and harvest if they are to produce an abundance of high-quality fruits. *Side-dressing* means to place fertilizer down the sides of the rows or around the plants in a circle that is 6 to 8 inches from the plant so as not to burn it. You may use 1 to 2 inches of well-rotted manure compost or a light side-dressing of 5-10-10. Another type of organic fertilizer that can be used at this time is manure tea. Manure tea is made by taking well-rotted manure and placing it in a bucket or barrel (fill it about one-third full with manure) and then fill the barrel with water. Stir and let this stand for at least twenty-four hours. After it has had time to steep, draw off the "tea" and pour this fertilizer around the plants. Water may be added to the barrel several more times before the solution becomes too weak to be any good.

Root and leaf crops such as lettuce and kale as well as squash and watermelon should not have additional nitrogen. Nitrogen might reduce the yield or quality of the crop. Root crops will do much better if they are side-dressed with a high-phosphate, low-nitrogen fertilizer (0-20-0).

Organic fertilizer is in tune with nature, it is part of all the living things around us, and it supplies all the nutrients a plant needs for healthy growth and productivity. Organic fertilizer in the form of manure compost is made up of plant life that has been fed to animals, digested, excreted, and is now being returned to the soil, thus completing the life cycle of the plant. Organic compost creates a perfect climate for earthworms, which not only aerate the soil but also throw off castings that supply many nutrients to the soil as well. Manures that have not been aged at least six months should not be used as a side-dressing because fresh manures will burn the plants. The exception to this rule is rabbit manure, which will not burn plants when it comes in contact with them; place it in the garden anytime.

Watering

Knowing when to water your plants takes the same kind of understanding that feeding them requires. They must have water to carry nutrients through the plant system to feed the plant and to keep the cell structure from becoming dehydrated. Keep water from a plant long enough and it just goes limp and literally sinks to the ground. Water it thoroughly at this point, and over the next couple of hours you can actually see it revive right before your eyes. Obviously, water is very important to plant life. On the other hand, too much water, especially in clay soils, can stop oxygen from entering the soil, depriving the roots of an important element in their growth.

The problem that most beginning gardeners face is how much and how often they should water. In a well-mulched garden, the summer rains, even if relatively sparse, seem to be enough. This is especially true if the mulch was put down after a good drenching rain. In gardens that are not mulched, the sun quickly evaporates moisture from the topsoil, and a little more effort is needed to determine water needs. (I'd like to point out again here that crops planted in wide rows help to shade the ground and prevent a good deal of this moisture loss.) If plants appear very limp *early* in the day (midday heat sometimes makes even the best of plants look limp), it usually means that they need more moisture. Check the soil to see if the dryness extends more than 1 inch beneath the topsoil. If it does, then you should provide more moisture.

Once you've determined that you need to water the garden, it's important to give the soil enough water, otherwise plant roots will reach up to the surface of the soil for moisture and the burning rays of the sun that penetrate the surface of the soil can damage them. I think it's a mistake to take a garden hose and hold it to spray the garden. Most people do not have the patience it takes to stand there long enough to get a sufficient amount of water into the garden. For one thing, when you're standing there directing a hose, it looks like you're putting a lot more water on that soil than you really are. Unless you spray enough water to drench the soil, you are going to do much more harm than good. The soil must be wet several inches down (at least 3 inches). It's far better to invest in an inexpensive spray arm and let the water run in each section until you can tell (by checking) that the moisture has gone well down into the soil.

Never water during the hot sunny hours of the day. The moisture on your plants will intensify the effect of the sun's rays, and they will be burned.

But here we are talking about hosing the garden when the closest some of you will get to a garden hose is the gardening-supply catalogs. Many, like ourselves, will have a garden located so far from the house, barn, or convenient water supply that hooking a hose to an existing water supply is just impossible. If there's a brook or pond nearby and you can afford a gas generator and a sump pump, you could buy some 1-inch black plastic water line and set up a good irrigating system for yourself. But what are you going to do, even if you have the pond or brook, if you can't afford to set up such an irrigation system? You might not even have that pond or brook nearby. Well, don't give up; that's the position we're in with our three-quarter-acre garden up in the northeast corner of our land.

These are the solutions that we have used in dry years. First of all, we mulch as much as we can, hopefully after a good rain. Vine crops, which really require a lot of moisture, are planted around large plastic or tin containers that have holes punched in the bottom and are set into the ground (see page 53). The containers must be wide-mouthed so that they will catch whatever rainfall there is and direct it right to the root system of the plant, where it is most needed. Furthermore, whenever we water and fertilize that area, the water we have to cart up there goes wherever it will do the most good.

The last method we use is to take several clean 55-gallon barrels and load them in the back of the truck. We fill these with water from the house or barn and truck them up to the garden. Using a garden hose without a spray attachment, we syphon the water to the areas that need it most. Remember that it's better to drench just one small area at a time than to try to do the entire garden. All of these efforts take extra work, but they protect the hours we've already invested. Until we are able to afford a better setup, it's a solution we can live with, and we don't lose our garden in hot, very dry summers.

If there are swampy areas near your garden, you might want to look into driving a well point for a shallow well to draw from. In other words, if you want to do something badly enough, it can be accomplished if you use a little imagination.

Pest and Disease Control

Whenever you mention bug and pest control to the dedicated gardener, the look that comes over his or her face gives you visions of the gardener going out to the garden with a shotgun to shoot potato bugs. As ridiculous as this picture seems, it does indicate the determination a good gardener feels about keeping his or her garden free of pests and bugs. There are several types of bugs and diseases that attack plants, and everyone is bound to get some of them at one time or another.

I've had my share of bugs, but I've had very few plant diseases, so I'm not much of an expert on disease control. Most probably any information I would give wouldn't be of much help anyway, because plant diseases and their treatment vary all over the country. The agricultural extension agent in your area is your best source of information on what type of disease your plants have and the best solution to the problem in your area of the country. The USDA extension service puts out an excellent booklet called "Insects and Diseases of Vegetables in the Home Garden" to help you identify insects and diseases in your vegetable garden. It's Agriculture Information Bulletin No. 380.

The best way not to have any problems in the first place is to prevent them. Good healthy plants, growing in well-cared-for soil, will be able to resist most diseases. If you plant in soil that stays wet all the time or fail to rotate your crops each year, and if you are not giving your plants enough nourishment, especially potash, you are looking for trouble.

Never plant the same type of crops in the same area year after year; for example, if you plant watermelon in one corner of your garden this summer, do not plant other plants of Group A in the same area next year. The following is a listing of the various types of crops that fall into groups.

Group A	Group B	Group C	Group D	Group E	Group F
watermelon	cabbage	tomato	carrot	corn*	bean
cucumber	cauliflower	pepper	parsnip		pea
squash	brussels sprout	potato	beet		
muskmelon	broccoli	eggplant	onion		
pumpkin	turnip		garlic		
	rutabaga				
	radish				
	collard				
	mustard				

Southern climates seem to have a greater incidence of disease and bug problems than we here in the North do. Nematodes, tiny worms that attack root crops, are more common there, and control without pesticides is a greater problem. I have found that putting wood ashes in the row with turnip seeds deters these little worms. Salt on cabbages early in the morning when they are still wet with the dew helps to rid them of cabbage worms. Wrapping a paper collar around all plants set out in the garden will stop cutworms (see page 51). Shallow pans of fresh beer will attract slugs. They just fall in and drown, and you scoop them out. Large bugs can be removed by hand picking or by a forceful spray from the water hose. Some gardeners have found that barricading slugs out with a thin line of wood ash placed all around each row works best. The alkali of the ash is lethal to the acidity of their bodies.

If you don't mind being embarrassed, you could try what I did one year. My pepper plants had become infested with some kind of large bug that I didn't even recognize at the time, and after trying to hit them off and breaking several leaves, I decided to go into the house to see what I could find that would be effective in

*It is not as important to rotate corn as it is the other crops.

getting rid of them. Looking through the closet, I discovered an old feather duster. "That looks like a good idea," I thought, "This won't break off any tender leaves." Back in the garden, I was happily brushing bugs off my peppers when I looked up and noticed that traffic on the nearby road was slowing down. The look of dismay on the faces of the drivers told me in an instant that they were wondering what kind of idiot would go out and dust her garden. It worked, though, because the soft feathers could be brushed back and forth, getting to both the top and the underside of the leaves without damaging them. This can be done as often as necessary without damaging the plants.

Marigolds, mums, calendulas, asters, nasturtiums, basil, onions, and garlic are natural bug deterrents when planted throughout the garden. Every part of the marigold plant is supposed to be effective in some way, but we've found from experience that the blossoms are the most useful part of this plant. Horseradish planted at the four corners of the potato patch does a good job of warding off potato bugs. Radishes attract bugs, so plant them with everything. The bugs eat the radishes and leave the other plants alone. Castor beans planted around the garden keep mice and moles away. Be careful, though, that no one eats the dry castor bean itself; it is highly toxic.

There are very few good organic sprays on the market. I have tried rotenone and not found it very effective against bad infestations. Sevin and Malathion are the sprays most often recommended for general use. While I'm not a purist where chemical fertilizers and insecticides are concerned, I believe that they should be used as seldom as possible. We know now that many of these chemicals can be very hazardous to our health. At the same time you need to use some common sense. I don't feel that you should lose your whole garden if organic methods do not work.

The most serious problem that we ever had with bugs came last year. We had a terrible problem with potato beetles on the tomato plants. I went up to check on our new transplants, and there they were, two hundred plants (by conservative estimate—we put up 500 quarts of tomato products from ketchup to chili) totally infested. Those foolish bugs were just going to wipe my plants right out. Now, I wasn't about to lose all my tomato plants to a bunch of potato bugs who'd gotten sidetracked on their way to the potato patch. I went to the nearest farm supply store and bought some Bonide dust. It's a very effective bug and disease control, a combination of carbaryl (Sevin), an insecticide, and Maneb, a fungicide. It's not an organic pesticide, so be careful, if you use it, to read directions for use, as you should when using any chemical fertilizers or pesticides. Even with this dust, if I didn't dust frequently, the bugs returned. Thankfully, my marigolds finally bloomed with big, healthy blossoms, and that was the end of my bug problem.

Coons in the corn patch are an age-old problem confronting gardeners, and it's pretty discouraging to get your tastebuds all set for the first corn of the season only to find that the raccoons got there ahead of you. Heavy pumpkin vines surrounding the corn patch do a pretty effective job of keeping the coons away. Plant the vines heavily around the entire corn patch. If the seeds in any area do not germinate, transplant some pumpkin seedlings to these areas. If the coons find one little area not covered, they will get in. When the vines start to grow, make sure they become well entwined so that they will form a thick fence around the corn patch. Coons hate the prickly vines and will not walk through them. When people say that their pumpkin vines were not effective, it's usually because they were not planted thickly enough.

Harvesting Your Vegetables

Start harvesting crops as soon as there is something big enough to eat. Thinnings from lettuce, radishes, onions, spinach, and swiss chard make great salad fixin's. Tiny new baby carrots are sweet and delicious. Beets can be thinned as soon as they have enough tops for beet greens and right on up to the tiny-beet stage. Never let root crops grow too large, or they will be tough and cordy. Outside stalks on celery and outside leaves on cabbage, head lettuce, swiss chard, kale, and spinach can be eaten as soon as they are big enough for salads. These vegetables will continue to grow from the inside out, and taking off the outside leaves will not hurt them a bit. Start cutting leaf lettuce back for salads as soon as it is 2½ to 3 inches high. Cut back to 1 inch above the ground. If leaf lettuce is allowed to grow too large, it becomes tough and bitter.

Peas are ready as soon as the pods are full and firm. Don't wait until they are too large, or they will lose much of their tenderness and sweet flavor. Bush beans should be harvested when they are young, and as with cucumbers and summer squash, the more you pick, the more the plant will produce. Summer squash is best when it is small-to-medium size. Corn is ready when the silk has turned brown and the ears are full. Watch it carefully, or it will go by quickly and then it will be tough and tasteless.

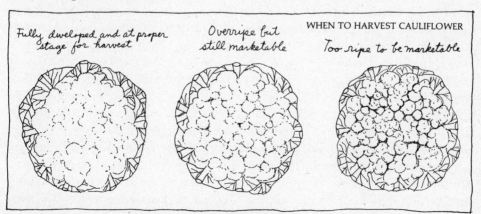

Fully developed and at proper stage for harvest

Overripe but still marketable

WHEN TO HARVEST CAULIFLOWER

Too ripe to be marketable

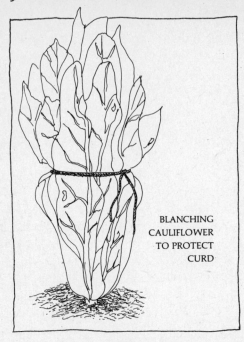

BLANCHING
CAULIFLOWER
TO PROTECT
CURD

Even if you can't use all the vegetables your vine crops produce, keep them picked anyway. As soon as a vegetable grows large enough to go to seed, it has completed its life cycle and the plant will stop producing. Use extras to preserve in your favorite way for winter keeping, give some to others who are less fortunate than you are, sell some, use some for stock feed, and as a last resort, throw it in the compost heap to be returned to your garden next year as rich humus fertilizer.

Potatoes may be picked as soon as there are any large enough to eat (this is usually at the blossom stage), but for winter storage they should be kept in the ground until the tops have turned brown. Winter squash and pumpkins should be picked before a hard frost, but leave them on the vines until the rind is firm enough not to be punctured easily by your thumbnail. If a hard frost is predicted before they have reached this stage, pick them anyway, but they will not keep as well. Kale, parsnips, turnips, rutabaga, and brussels sprouts may be harvested any time they are ready, but these vegetables are best after they have had a light frost. You can even pick these from under the snow in winter.

Preparing Your Vegetables for Winter Storage

There is a great deal to be said about winter storage of vegetables, too much to be included in a book of general information. Owning one good book devoted just to food preservation is a must for every self-sufficient family. My favorite is *Putting Food By* by Ruth Hertzberg, Beatrice Vaughan, and Janet Greene (published by Stephen Greene Press, 1973). It covers everything from root cellars to curing meats, and it's well written in language you can understand.

There are a few things that are important to know at harvesttime if you are going to store vegetables for winter keeping. Beets and carrots to be stored for winter should be left in the ground until late fall, when the weather has become cooler. Dig and store them within twenty-four hours to be sure that they will stay firm and crisp. Cabbages to be stored should be of the solid winter varieties. These keep best. Pull them up by the roots and hang them upside down, until ready to use, in a cool dark place to prolong their storage life. Corn to be used for cornmeal or stock feed and popcorn should be left on the stalk to dry. Beans for baking should be left on the vine until the vines are dead and the pods have started to dry out thoroughly. Drive tall stakes into the ground and pull up the vines. Pile them loosely around the stakes and leave them out in the air and sun until they are completely dried. The stakes will keep heavy winds from knocking over the piles. Rain will not hurt them. Another way to dry beans is to pull them up and hang the vines upside down in a dry airy place to finish drying.

As soon as the onion tops start to fall over, around the end of August or early September, we walk on the rest of the onion plants to break the remainder of the tops down. We leave them in the ground until the tops have all dried, then we dig them up and leave them in a sunny place to finish drying the outside skins and the tops. Onions from sets tend to go to seed faster than onions from seed. If you notice little seedpods developing on the tops of the onions, snip them off, or the onions will stop growing. When the onions have dried enough for the outside skins to slip off easily, they are ready to be stored in a cool, dry place.

Parsnips are best mulched and stored in the ground. Potatoes for winter keeping must be dug after the tops have turned brown. They should be dried in a dark, dry place before storing. Do not wash them. We dry ours for two weeks before storing. If potatoes are left exposed to the sun or light, it will cause them to turn green. This discoloration is caused by the presence of selenium. If any of your potatoes develop a green area on them, cut it off and only use the rest of the potato. Eating the green part will make you sick. Pumpkins and winter squashes should be held at room temperature, 70 to 80 degrees F, for at least two weeks to harden the rind and heal any breaks in the surface of the rind. Then they should be dipped in a solution of 1 tablespoon of Clorox to 1 gallon of water; let them air-dry thoroughly before storing in a moderately warm room. The ideal temperature for these vegetables is 65 degrees F, and if the temperatures go below 50 degrees F, they usually spoil.

Fall Cleanup

Well, you worked the soil into pretty good shape, got the garden in, managed to keep fairly well ahead of the weeds and bugs, and though you got awfully sore and tired by spells, making you wonder if it was all worth it, everything really tasted so good. The freezer, root cellar, and shelves are filled with good things for the winter, and there's even enough extra for the animals. "Now," you say to yourself, "I can sit down and relax." Wait! Not quite yet. Some of the most important steps toward the success of next year's garden should be taken now.

Pull up any diseased plants and burn them. We make a practice of burning our potato plants. We grow such a large crop of potatoes that we don't want to risk any diseases hanging around from one year to another. If you have a tiller, till all the other crop residue into the garden to decompose through the winter. If you haven't got a tiller, pull everything up and compost it for next year's garden. This is a good time to spade or till some organic matter such as manure-composts into your soil or till in that compost pile you've been working all summer.

Just before the first hard freeze, mulch Jerusalem artichokes, parsnips, carrots, and kale left to winter over. These can be dug in the winter by just pulling the mulch back. Wait until you've had a good hard freeze and then mulch everything else that needs winter protection: berries, herbs, and any plants that you want to remain dormant. This will protect them from the frequent thaws and freezes that occur in early winter and late spring. These variations in temperatures do more harm to perennial plants than temperatures that go below freezing and stay there.

Never let a year go by without trying something new. You may end up growing something you don't even like, or if you are experimenting with a new way to grow a vegetable, you might just fail, but the fun of watching and waiting for the new developments of your experiment makes it worth it, and it's also what takes the word *ordinary* out of gardening. In areas that have cold winters, here is a little experiment you can try. Just before you know that there is going to be a hard freeze, put in a few seeds for different plants such as cabbage, cauliflower, broccoli, onions, lettuce, spinach, swiss chard, and even tomatoes. Cover these with a good heavy mulch as soon as the ground freezes hard, and leave the mulch in place until the danger of hard freeze is over in the spring. Some years everything will grow, and other years you might succeed with just one or two types of plants. If you're lucky enough to have success, don't fertilize these plants in the spring until warm weather comes to stay. Fertilizer makes the plants tender and easily killed by fluctuating spring temperatures. This is just a fun experiment, so don't plant a large area. I got the idea when I noticed that tomato and squash plants came up every year in the pigpen. We give the pigs all the extras from the garden and canning each fall, so many seeds are deposited in the soil and trampled in, and they come up strong and hearty each spring. *Now you can Relax!*

There is so much more that I would like to include in this chapter, but I've tried to include all the commonsense knowledge that I have on gardening for you to get started with. There'll always be more to learn, and I urge you to keep reading as you get more involved with your gardening project. New discoveries are being made almost daily about plant life and its relationship to the elements around it. All of this information makes for more successful gardening techniques. There are books that have far more technical information on soil composition and on organic and chemical fertilizer composition and their relationship to soil organisms, but everyone needs a season or two of commonsense gardening before he or she is ready to understand this more complex information. It isn't a matter of how much intelligence you have, it's just that you have to confront a few problems before you even have an idea of what questions you want answered.

4
GROWING
FRUITS

The experiences we had when we started our own little homestead orchard are good examples of why you should not try to bite off more than you can chew the first year. We were in a hurry. We put in huge gardens, put up a barn, built pens, hovered over eggs in an incubator, and started in with enough varieties of animals and poultry to make us resemble Noah's Ark.

Because we were so anxious to do it all at once, we hurriedly tried to put in our first orchard too. We plunged headlong into it without having read enough first and made just about every mistake possible. We planted our dwarf trees too deep. When this happens, it takes as long for them to mature as standard varieties; they also grow much larger. We didn't have time to care for our berry patches, and they were choked out with weeds. And to add insult to injury, Ray went out to scythe down the brush on the bank where we planted our small trees, and my Ray doesn't do things by half measures! Once he got into the swing of things, he managed to mow down half the trees before I could catch up with him. Also, we didn't realize how important cross-pollination is, or that it takes more than one variety of a fruit in order to cross-pollinate most fruit trees. Then we made what I think was the biggest mistake of all: Instead of buying from local nurseries, we sent away to a southern nursery for our trees, and many of them weren't hardy enough for this part of the country. It doesn't take a genius to realize that this first effort was not the kind of success story you write home about.

In the years that followed, we took time to find out what we had done wrong. Some of our mistakes were correctable, and others were not. But we've learned a great deal along the way, and this past year a few of these trees started to bear, though I doubt that they will ever produce abundantly. Last spring we started a new dwarf orchard using all the knowledge we'd garnered over the years, and the difference in our first year's growth alone, as compared with that of our original orchard, has been absolutely amazing.

Annual Fruits

Many delicious fruits are grown as annuals right in the vegetable garden, and because these fruits are started from seed and do not require much time and care, they make ideal choices for that first year of homesteading. Once everything else is running smoothly, you can turn your attention to perennial fruits, berries, and nuts. This list of annual fruits includes pumpkin, all of the melon family, and, in more recent years, plants such as the garden huckleberry, the mango peach, and the husk-tomato, or, as it is often called, the ground-cherry. Except for the husk-tomato, the last group of fruits do not taste good raw, but they make delicious pies, preserves, and jams. Seeds may be obtained from garden supply stores or mail-order nurseries, such as Guerney's, Shumway, and Burgess.

Garden Huckleberry

Actually, this is not a new fruit, but it is a long-overlooked source of fruit for pies, preserves, and jellies. These plants are very prolific. The seed should be started about two months before the date of the last hard frost in your area. These plants need the same culture as tomatoes and do well even in poor soil. When ripe, the berries are about ½ to ¾ inch in diameter and a shiny black color. The fruit isn't good to eat until it is fully ripened. We do not care for it raw, but it's delicious cooked in any way. I mix half huckleberry juice and half apple juice for apple-berry jelly, and many people use this fruit as a substitute for blueberries in pies and preserves. Follow instructions for blueberries in any recipe, but add about one-third more sugar than is called for in the recipe.

Husk-tomato (Ground-cherry)

This cherry-size fruit is grown on low plants. It is started from seed directly in the garden. It is covered with a husk that dries like parchment paper when ripe. An excellent fruit for pies and preserves, it can also be dried in sugar and used in fruitcakes like figs, raisins, and so on. It can be eaten fresh and, if left in the husks and stored in a cool, dry place, it will keep well into the winter.

Mango Peach

This fruit is grown the same way as muskmelon but used only for pies, preserves, and pickling. The fruit is the size, shape, and golden-yellow color of a tree peach. It also has the same food value. The flesh is snow white. The plants are highly productive, but the fruit is not good to eat raw.

Cantaloupe

Plant cantaloupes in rich sandy loam after danger of frost is gone and the soil warms up. If the soil is not a rich sandy loam, it should be conditioned well in advance of planting. Soil improvement techniques are discussed in Chapter 3. Sow four to eight seeds about 2 to 3 inches apart in hills or groups 4 to 6 feet apart each way. (These can be started in peat pots in the greenhouse about one month ahead of planting time.) These plants do better if mulched with black plastic after the ground is good and warm. All forms of melons will ripen faster in the short northern growing seasons if the fruits are raised up by being placed on tin cans or pails turned upside down. Heat from the can as well as the better exposure to the sun help to ripen them faster. Cantaloupes are ripe when they smell very fruity and slip easily from the stem. There are many varieties of melons, such as crenshaw, honeydew, casaba, and several hybrids developed for small gardens. These special hybrids grow on small bush-type plants that do not require much space.

Pumpkin

Pumpkins are another annual fruit popular throughout the United States and a special treat for children on Halloween, when they get to cut fancy faces in them for parties. Plant pumpkins as you would melons and cantaloupes. To grow super-large pumpkins, allow only two or three to develop on the vine; when these are the size of an orange, remove all but the largest one. Cooked pumpkin can be used for pies, puddings, breads, cakes, cookies, preserves, soups, and as a vegetable. Thanksgiving wouldn't be the same in our house without pumpkin pie and whipped cream. Save the pumpkin seeds and roast them for snacks. Some pumpkins, such as the Lady Godiva, are grown for their hull-less seeds. To roast, toss lightly with any good vegetable oil and roast at 225 degrees F, stirring often until done. Add salt if desired, cool, and store in tightly covered containers.

Watermelon

Watermelons used to be grown only in the South, but if started early in the greenhouse, even northerners can now enjoy some success with many varieties. Watermelons are grown like all other melons. To grow extra-large watermelons, allow only one melon to develop on each vine. My sister-in-law grew a fifteen-pound melon here in northern Vermont, and it was beautiful. Chris started the watermelon seeds in peat pots inside, early in May, and did not set the plants out until the ground had warmed up in June. A shovelful of well-rotted manure under the plants gave them an extra boost.

Perennial Small Fruits

I have special memories of berry picking with my grandmother. We would start with the field strawberries in early summer, which were sweeter than any garden strawberry I've ever eaten. No matter how quickly I picked, my grandmother deftly filled her pail ahead of me. I didn't especially like cleaning field strawberries because they were so small, but when Gram served her cake-size biscuit, split in two with berries piled high in the middle and on the top, and everything mounded with a cloud of fresh sweet whipped cream, it was all worth it.

Next came red and black raspberries and finally the huge blue-black longberries. I loved picking these, though heaven only knows why. When we would emerge from the woods, there didn't seem to be one square inch of my body that hadn't come under attack from a bramble or its thorns. These berries were so huge that it didn't take long before the milk pails were filled and we were on our way to the spring for a drink of icy spring water. You could usually tell which berries were in season by looking at the tips of my fingers, my mouth, and, not infrequently, my nose. When I was very little, I would shove berries by the fistful into my mouth. My grandfather thought it was funny, but Gram would have given anything to take a quick swat at the seat of my britches when the pail would come up half-empty and I very obviously was full.

Enough berries for a family of four to eat fresh as well as preserve can easily be grown in the home garden. Twenty blackberry plants, thirty red raspberry, six blueberry, and fifty strawberry plants would yield approximately 200 pints of berries a year. Eat half of them fresh in pies, shortcakes, and cobblers and freeze or preserve the rest for some good winter treats.

Strawberries

Strawberries are the most popular small-fruit crop grown in home gardens. They are easy to grow almost anywhere if you select a suitable site and varieties adapted to your area of the country. Fifty plants managed properly will supply a family of four. Plenty for eating fresh, and you can preserve surplus into jam or freeze for later use.

WHEN TO PLANT

Healthy dormant strawberry plants are usually set out in early spring as soon as the soil becomes workable. Runners start growing from July through early fall and form new plants, taking roots several inches from the original mother plant. Soon a succession of independent new plants is growing around the original plant. During the first year the mother plants often produce flowers that develop into fruit. These flowers should be removed so that the plant will develop and

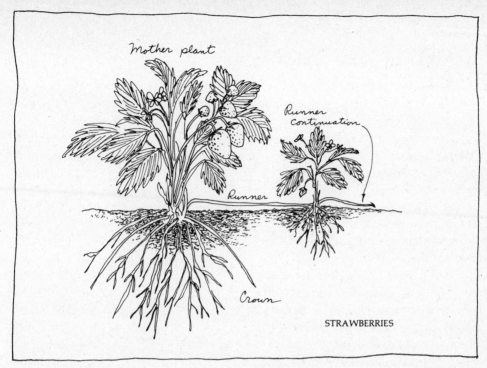

Mother plant

Runner Continuation

Runner

Crown

STRAWBERRIES

grow vigorously. As fall approaches, the growing points in each crown change into flower buds. New plants become dormant after the days become shorter and cooler.

The following spring the flower buds renew growth and develop into fruit blossoms that generally produce mature berries in about thirty days. The first flowers to open become the largest fruit, often called king berries. As later flowers develop, the resulting fruit is successively smaller.

Choose a sunny site for strawberries that has enough slope for good air and water drainage in order to minimize frost and soil disease problems. Avoid sites on which tomatoes, potatoes, peppers, or eggplants were grown within the previous two years.

Strawberries grow well in many soils, but they grow best in well-drained loams and sandy loams liberally supplied with organic matter. Very acid soils, soils testing below pH 5.5, will have to be limed. The best soil pH for strawberries is 6.0. If you are liming established beds, try not to spread lime on the plants.

Buy plants from local garden supply stores to make sure you have varieties for your area. If you want to send for new varieties, it would be wise to consult your local agricultural extension agent to find out if they are varieties that would adapt to your area.

If you are given plants from a neighbor's bed that has become overgrown, check the plants well for signs of disease and plant only the largest, most vigorous-looking crowns.

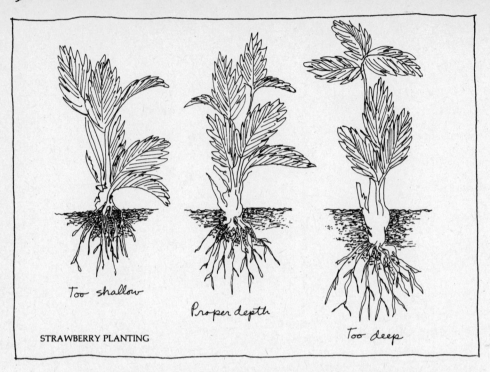

Too shallow

Proper depth

STRAWBERRY PLANTING

Too deep

We are not happy with the everbearing strawberries we planted. The first yields toward the end of June are fair, but the berries are not very large. The mid-summer and late-summer crops are very poor, with much smaller berries. Our plants that bear only once in a season produced larger yields and larger berries.

PREPARING THE SOIL

Strawberries grow best in a well-prepared soil that is relatively free of weeds. Plow or spade under a liberal amount of well-rotted manure or compost (about 4 bushels for 50 square feet). If desired, add a balanced commercial fertilizer (such as 10-10-10) at the rate of 1 pound per 25 feet of row.

Do not plant strawberries in newly plowed sod unless the land has been treated for white grubs (obtain U.S.D.A. booklet No. 1183, "Raspberry and Strawberry Pest Control for Home Gardening," from your local county extension office); these are very destructive to strawberry plants.

PLANTING

Set out dormant plants in early spring, as soon as you can work the soil (in the North, late April to early May is ideal). Keep the plants moist before setting. Prune roots to 4 or 5 inches in length. You may also want to remove some of the old outer leaves. Set plants with the crown flush with the soil surface (see sketch). If the soil is dry and hot, water immediately after planting.

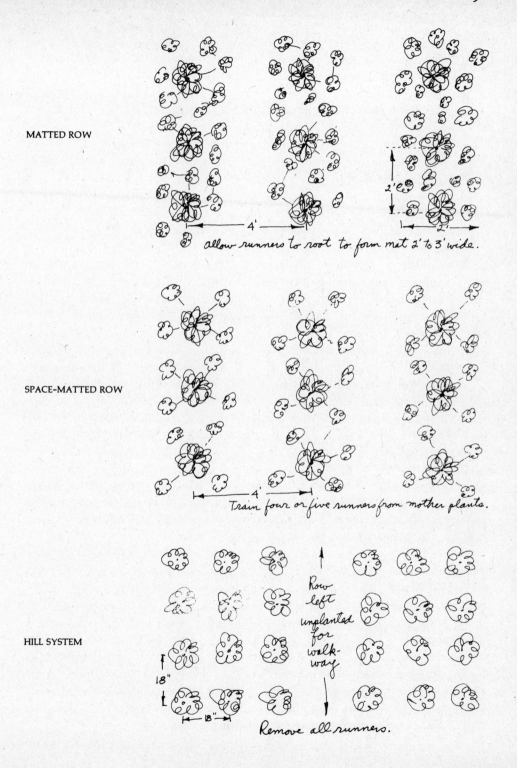

MATTED ROW

allow runners to root to form mat 2' to 3' wide.

SPACE-MATTED ROW

Train four or five runners from mother plants.

HILL SYSTEM

Row left unplanted for walk-way

Remove all runners.

SPACING

You can use any of three common systems to train strawberries in the home garden (see sketch). June-bearing varieties are grown most often in a *matted row.* Set the plants 24 inches apart in rows spaced 4 feet apart. Allow the runners to root during the summer to form a mat of plants 2 to 3 feet wide.

June-bearing varieties can also be grown in a *space-matted row.* Set the mother plants as in the matted row, but train four or five runners (when 12 to 15 inches long) 6 to 9 inches apart. Later remove other runners as they appear.

The hill system is often used with everbearing varieties. Set mother plants 12 to 18 inches apart within the row. Space rows 12 to 18 inches apart, and leave every third or fourth row unplanted to provide a walkway at harvesttime. Remove all runners, allowing only the original plants to grow and develop.

There is a fourth way of planting berries that I like best. Set plants 18 to 24 inches apart in rows spaced 4 feet apart. When the plants start to send out runners, take the runners and carefully move them so that they will grow between the rows. Pin the new daughter plants in place with wire hairpins. Harvest berries from the mother plants the second season after setting out. Then, after harvest, till the mother plants under, leaving the new row of daughter plants to establish itself as the fruit-bearing plants for the next year. This can be done year after year and, as long as you till in a large amount of well-rotted manure compost along with the old mother plants, you will maintain a healthy, vigorous-growing strawberry bed without all the work of preparing a new site each year. Other methods require that you change sites every two or three years. Watch for diseased plants and remove them quickly, putting new plants in their place.

Another way to restore vigorous strawberry plants is to renovate beds immediately after harvest. Rototill or hoe under each side of the row, leaving a narrow band of plants about 10 inches wide. Remove any diseased or weak plants. Cut the remaining foliage with a rotary mower, leaving plants 2 to 3 inches high. Thin the plants, leaving about four vigorous plants per foot of row. Space the runner plants that develop as previously recommended.

CARE OF NEW PLANTINGS

During the first season, remove all flowering stems of June-bearing plants. This strengthens the plants and also increases the number of daughter plants. Remove all flowers on everbearing plants up to July 1 of the first year. Flowers that develop after that date generally produce a fall crop.

FERTILIZER

Strawberry plants need adequate amounts of nitrogen and the other soil nutrients to build runners and strong crowns. As a general rule, apply fertilizers when you're preparing the bed and again during the first summer.

If using chemical fertilizer, apply a balanced fertilizer such as 10-10-10 at the rate of 1 pound per 25 feet of row when you prepare the soil bed. Repeat this amount as a side-dressing three to four weeks after planting, but apply the side-dressing only when the plant foliage is dry. When using organic fertilizer, one heavy application in the spring is enough.

MULCHING

In the North, you need to mulch strawberry plants to protect them from severe winter weather. Exposure of fruit buds to temperatures as low as 20 degrees F causes injury and reduces yield. Mulch is usually applied after the plants have been subjected to a few good frosts to help harden them. Normally early November is a good time to apply mulch in most northern areas.

Use materials that will not pack too tightly over the plants: straw, wood chips, sawdust, marsh hay, leaves, and pine needles are suitable. Apply mulch 3 to 4 inches deep over the row area. Rake all but a light covering of mulch into the alleyways between the rows as soon as the plants begin to grow in the spring. If some of the leaves start to turn yellow, remove the mulch at once.

WEED CONTROL

Remove weeds by cultivator or hand hoeing at intervals of ten to fourteen days throughout the spring and summer, or mulch heavily with newspaper and the same mulch material that you use for winter mulching, as we do here at Sunnybrook.

Blackberries

Blackberries grow best in temperate climates. They are not well adapted to areas in the Plains States or Mountain States where summers are hot and dry and winters are severe, but some varieties do well in most areas, including these states. Check with local agricultural extension services for adaptable varieties.

Choose types and varieties that are adapted to your area.
Prepare the soil thoroughly.
Plant only highest-quality stock.
Cultivate frequently.
Apply fertilizer every year.
Thin out all weak canes and suckers.
Protect plants from insects, diseases, and winter injury.

TYPES OF BLACKBERRIES

The two types of blackberries, erect and trailing, differ primarily in the character of their canes. Erect blackberries have arched, self-supporting canes. Trailing blackberries, also called dewberries, ground blackberries, or running blackberries, have canes that are not self-supporting; the canes must be tied to poles or trellises in cultivation. The two types also differ in fruit characteristics. Fruit clusters of the trailing blackberry are more open than those of the erect blackberry. Trailing blackberries generally ripen earlier and are often larger and sweeter than the erect type. Some varieties have canes that trail the first year after planting. Canes developed in subsequent years are more erect. These are called semitrailing blackberries, but they are essentially erect varieties.

PLANTING SITES

Availability of soil moisture is the most important factor to consider in choosing a planting site for blackberries. While the fruit is growing and ripening, blackberries need a large supply of moisture. During the winter, however, the plants are harmed by water standing around their roots.

Almost any soil type, except very sandy soil, is suitable for blackberries as long as the drainage is good. In areas where winters are severe, the slope of the site is important. Blackberries planted on hillsides are in less danger of winter injury and damage from late-spring frosts than those planted in valleys. In areas where drying winds occur frequently, the plants should be sheltered by surrounding hills, trees, or shrubs.

Plant blackberries as soon as you can prepare the soil—in early spring in the North, in late winter or early spring in the South. Our plants seemed to be slow in taking the first year. It was an especially dry, hot summer for Vermont, so even though our soil still tends to be slightly heavy, we decided to water more frequently the second month after planting. The plants tripled the first month's growth in the second month. We brought our mulch right up close around each plant and checked for moisture frequently, adding water as soon as the soil started to dry out.

PREPARING THE SOIL

Prepare the soil for blackberries as you would for strawberries. For best results, plow to a depth of 9 inches as soon as the soil is in workable condition. Loosen the soil again just before setting out the plants.

SETTING THE PLANTS

Plant erect varieties of blackberries 5 feet apart in rows that are 8 feet apart. Space vigorous varieties 4 to 6 feet apart in rows 8 feet apart.

In the Central States, set erect varieties 2 feet apart in rows 9 to 10 feet apart. Let the plants grow into hedgerows.

Do not let planting stock dry out. If you cannot plant the stock as soon as you receive it or if the plants are dry when you receive them, soak the roots in water for several hours before you plant them. When you are ready to set the plants in the garden, dip the roots in a thin mud made with clay and water or keep the plants in plastic bags. This helps to protect the roots from rapid drying while the plants are being set.

Before setting the plants, cut the tops back so that they are about 6 inches long. The 6-inch top is useful as a handle when setting the plants and will serve to show the location of the plants.

To make a planting hole, cut a slit in the soil with a shovel. Press the handle of the shovel forward to open the slit. Put the root of the blackberry plant in the hole. Set it so that it is about the same depth as it was in the nursery. Withdraw the blade of the shovel and pack the soil firmly around the root with your heel. If your soil is especially heavy clay, water a little more sparingly, but watch your plants carefully to prevent them from drying out.

TRAINING

Train blackberry plants to trellises. Erect blackberry plants can be grown without support, but many of the canes may be broken during cultivation and picking. Trellises will pay for themselves by reducing this damage. They can be constructed by stretching wire between posts set 15 to 20 feet apart in the row. For erect blackberries, use a single wire attached to the post about 30 inches from the ground. For semitrailing and trailing blackberries, use two wires, one about 3 feet from the ground and the other about 5 feet from the ground. Tie the canes to the wires with soft string—erect varieties where the canes cross the wire, trailing canes horizontally along the wires or fanned out from the ground and tied where they cross each wire. Avoid tying the canes in bundles.

PRUNING AND THINNING

The crowns of blackberry plants are perennial; new canes arise from them every year. But the canes are biennial; they live for only two years. During the first year they grow and send out laterals (side branches). The second year small branches grow from buds on the laterals; fruit is borne on these buds. After the laterals fruit, the canes die. Before growth starts in the spring, cut the laterals back to a length of about 12 inches. Fruit from pruned laterals is larger and of better quality than fruit from unpruned laterals.

Erect blackberries send up root suckers in addition to the new canes that arise from the crown. If all the root suckers were allowed to grow, they would soon turn the blackberry plants into a thicket. During the growing season remove all the suckers that appear between the rows. Pull them out of the ground; they will not regrow as quickly as suckers that are cut down. These can be used to start a new planting or replace diseased plants.

When canes of erect blackberries reach a height of 30 to 36 inches, cut off the tips to make the canes branch. Tipped canes also grow stout and are better able to support a heavy fruit crop than untipped canes. In summer, as soon as the last berries have been picked, cut out all the old canes and burn them. Also, thin out

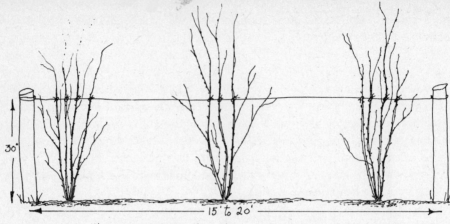

Tie erect plants where canes cross wire.

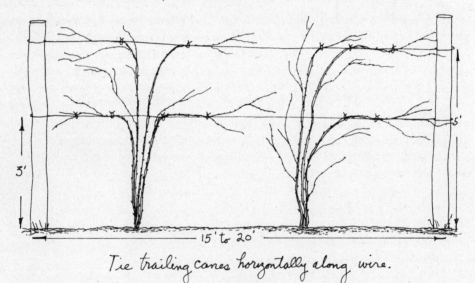

Tie trailing canes horizontally along wire.

TRELLISES FOR BLACKBERRIES

the new canes, leaving three or four canes of erect varieties, four to eight canes of semitrailing varieties, and eight to twelve canes of trailing varieties. In areas of the South where anthracnose and rose chafer are serious diseases on blackberries, cut out all the canes, both old and new, after fruiting. Then fertilize and cultivate to promote growth of replacement canes for the next year's fruit crop. If you let suckers form within the rows of erect blackberries, thin the suckers to about five or six canes per foot of row.

FERTILIZING

To get maximum yields from your blackberry plants, apply fertilizer every year at blossoming time. In the southeastern and south-central United States, make a second application after fruiting. Use well-rotted manure-compost or commercial 5-10-5 fertilizer.

CULTIVATING

If you are not mulching, blackberry plants should be cultivated thoroughly and frequently. If grass and weeds get a start, they are difficult to control.

Begin cultivating in the spring as soon as the soil is workable. Cultivate throughout the season as often as is necessary to keep weeds down. This may be as often as once a week. Discontinue cultivation at least a month before freezing weather normally begins. To avoid harming shallow roots of the plants, cultivate only 2 or 3 inches deep near the rows.

HARVESTING

Berries that are picked at the proper time, handled carefully, and stored in a cool place will stay in good condition for several days. If they are overripe or injured, they spoil quickly. Pick the fruit as soon as it becomes sweet; it should be fully ripened but firm. Pick often; for most varieties, pick berries every other day. The fruit of the Evergreen and Thornfree varieties remains firm longer than fruit of other varieties and may be picked less frequently—once a week is often enough.

Pick early in the day, and try to finish before the hottest part of the day. Blackberries do not spoil as quickly if they are picked in the early part of the day. Do not crush or bruise the fruit; place it carefully in the berry baskets. As soon as the baskets are full, place them in the shade.

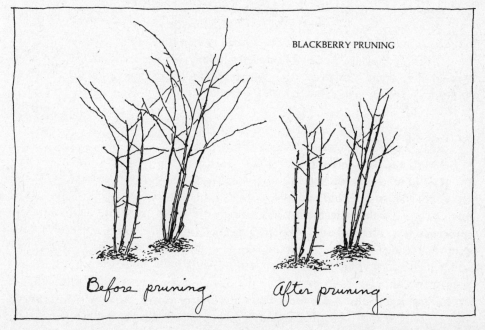

BLACKBERRY PRUNING

Before pruning

After pruning

PROPAGATING

Blackberry plants are easy to propagate, and most growers propagate their own planting stock. Erect blackberry plants can be grown from root suckers or root cuttings. The latter method yields the greatest number of new plants. The easiest way is to plant root cuttings in the location where they will fruit. Dig pieces of root from around established plants in early spring. The root pieces should be at least ¼ inch in diameter. Cut the roots into 3-inch lengths and bury them in trenches 2 or 3 inches deep.

Trailing blackberries and some semitrailing varieties can be propagated by burying the tips of the canes, which will then root and form new plants. You can also propagate tip plants from trailing blackberries in late summer by loosening the soil around each plant and burying the tips of the canes about 3 inches deep, pointing the tips straight down. Thornless Evergreen and Thornless Logan must be propagated by tipping, because the other methods produce thorny plants.

PREVENTING WINTER INJURY

Hardy varieties of blackberries can withstand still-air temperatures as low as −20 degrees F. Throughout most of the areas where they are grown, adapted varieties need no special protection in the winter. However, in areas where winter temperatures are colder than −20 degrees F or where cold, drying winds are likely to occur, the plants should be protected. In the fall, after warm weather has ended but before the ground is frozen, bend the canes over to the ground and cover them with a layer of soil, straw, or coarse manure. Uncover the plants in spring after severe weather has ended.

In western Oregon, where winters are mild and moist, canes of trailing varieties occasionally show a form of winter injury when they are allowed to lie on the ground. There they are best tied to trellises in late summer and allowed to stay up through the winter. However, if the winter has severe drying winds, considerable injury may occur when canes are on the trellis.

Red Raspberries

EVERBEARING RED RASPBERRIES

It's fun to grow everbearing raspberries. They produce an abundance of luscious rich red fruit not only in June and early July but also in August, September, and October—right up to frost! Everbearing raspberries are very hardy, vigorous-growing plants that require very little special care. The secret of success is in proper pruning to encourage fruiting. All you need to do is plant in well-drained soil, which you prepare as for other berries. Dig a hole about 15 inches deep, set your plants about 1 inch deeper than they were in the nursery and at least 3 feet apart. Firm the soil over the roots and water thoroughly.

Raspberries grow to about 6 to 10 feet high and then spread about 3 feet wide—even farther if you want to encourage them to grow as large bushes. They will grow out of bounds quickly if this tendency is not curbed as soon as suckers appear in the rows. The first raspberry patch we planted was the only berry patch that refused to be choked out by weeds. Though we lacked the time to give it good care, which caused it to become overgrown and reduced the quality of the berries, it seemed that nothing could stop its growth. When the addition to our home forced us to remove this patch of berries to make room for septic lines, the berries that were bulldozed out continued to spring up everywhere. Although you could get a small crop of raspberries the first fall, it's better if you sacrifice these few berries the first year for larger crops in future years. If you want to do this, cut the plants back to about 8 to 10 inches in height when planting.

The fall crop of everbearing raspberries is produced on the tips of new canes, which also produce the next spring's crop farther down on the same canes. Therefore, in order to get the maximum harvest, you should prune them back in late June or July after the spring crop is born. Just cut off all the canes that bore fruit, cutting them close to the ground. New canes coming from the roots will produce the spring crop the next year. Allow only the strongest, most vigorous canes to develop, removing all of the little canes. These new canes that started to grow in early spring should be pinched back in June and early July by about one third to encourage branching. Then keep your plants well watered and mulched during the summer months to assure a good fall crop.

In early spring (usually in early March) the canes that fruited in the fall should be cut back by one fourth; they are then ready to produce their spring crop. Because they blossom late, the blossoms are not in danger of frost kill.

REGULAR JUNE-BEARING RASPBERRIES

These are cared for exactly as described above except that they do not bear a fall crop on the new cane growth.

PEST CONTROL

You should learn to recognize common insects and disease problems of berries in order to control them as soon as they are discovered. Although good cultural practices help to reduce most problems, you may need to use sprays or dust. Information on pest control can be found in U.S.D.A. booklet No. 1183, "Raspberry and Strawberry Pest Control for Home Gardens," available at your local county extension office.

Blueberries

Interest in growing cultivated highbush blueberries in our area has increased considerably in recent years, and certain advantages make them a desirable crop for any home gardener: longevity of plants, few serious cultural problems, few insect and disease problems, good and consistent productivity, and adaptability of berries to preservation by freezing. But before you decide to grow blueberries, consider these factors: blueberry plants have special soil and moisture requirements; low winter temperatures may kill bushes or seriously reduce yields; and protection from birds is necessary during the fruiting season.

SOIL AND SITE

Plant blueberries in an area exposed to full sunlight most of the day. Acid soils (pH 4.0 to 5.5) that are sandy loams, well drained, porous, and high in organic matter are best. Blueberries are shallow-rooted plants and must either be irrigated, heavily mulched, or planted in soil with a high water table, but they cannot tolerate "wet feet." If the soil is not acid enough (determine by a soil test), you can modify it in either of two ways: Mix equal parts of acid peat and garden soil before planting or add sulfur at the rate of ¾ pound per 100 square feet (sandy soils) for each full pH point the soil is to be lowered (preferably six months before planting). For heavier soils, use 1½ pounds of sulfur. We worked several bushels of pine needles into our soil early in the spring and planted four weeks later. Our plants took well and are thriving.

Winter injury is one of the most serious limiting factors to growing blueberries in colder climates. Well-hardened blueberry bushes can withstand 25 degrees F with little or no injury. Bushes that are not well hardened or those that are planted in areas where the temperature goes below 25 degrees F may be killed back to the snow line. On the other hand, the flowers or developing berries will withstand spring frosts to 22 degrees F and still give partial crops.

VARIETIES

To improve productivity, plant at least two different blueberry varieties. Using honeybees during bloomtime can increase berry size and number. Bees are so important to blueberry production that Maine growers rent hives in the spring. Check with your local agricultural extension service to find the best varieties for your area. The best planting stocks are vigorous two-year-old plants 12 to 15 inches high.

PLANTING

Rooted cuttings and older plants are more difficult to develop. Set plants in the early spring as soon as the ground is workable. Space the plants 5 to 6 feet apart within the row and 9 to 10 feet between rows. Dig holes large enough to accommodate the plant's entire root system. Incorporate plenty of organic matter such as acid peat or sawdust into the soil around and into the hole. Set plants 1 inch deeper than they were grown in the nursery. Firm the soil mixture around the plants and water thoroughly.

CARE OF PLANTING

Limit cultivation to only shallow hoeing (1 to 2 inches deep). To eliminate cultivation, apply an acid peat or sawdust mulch 4 to 6 inches deep and 30 inches wide along the plant row (leaves, hay, or straw are second-choice mulches). Renew the mulch annually, as it helps control weeds, retain moisture, and eliminate potential root injury from cultivation and winter temperatures. We use pine needles covered with sawdust to help keep the acidity level lowered to between 4.5 and 5.

FERTILIZATION

When using a mulch, you'll need additional nitrogen fertilizer. If you are using commercial fertilizer, beginning the second spring after planting (before the buds break), apply 2 ounces of ammonium sulfate under the branches and in a circle around each plant. Increase this rate each year by 1 ounce until the bushes are mature or receiving about 8 ounces of fertilizer per year. Determine the desirability of high rates of ammonium sulfate or other fertilizers by soil tests. Don't fertilize more than once a year. We use well-rotted manure compost under the mulch; this breaks down slowly and can be added to each year according to need. As our acid-type mulch sinks into the topsoil, it keeps the soil's acidity high.

PRUNING

Do not allow the bushes to fruit during the first two years but instead rub off any flowers that appear to allow the plants to become well established. Blueberries

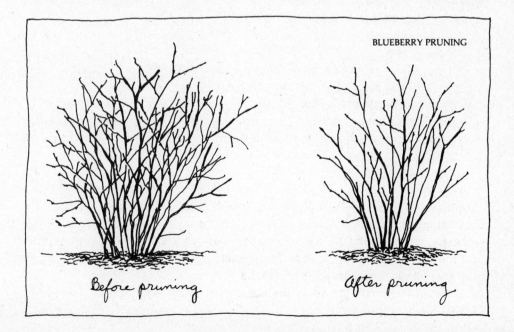

BLUEBERRY PRUNING

Before pruning

After pruning

need very little pruning for the first five to six years; simply remove a few low, dead, or diseased branches. The best time to prune is in late March to early April. A mature bush will consist of seven to nine main branches and two to three new branches. Regular pruning should consist of removing dead or injured branches, spindly or bushy twigs on mature branches, and low-spreading branches; also cut back all new branches by one third. Prune moderately each fall to maintain large berry size and consistent yields. Flower buds form near the tips of new shoots. Berries from the buds produced on thick shoots are substantially larger than those produced on thin shoots.

WINTER PROTECTION

In colder climates you must provide winter protection for blueberries, especially for younger plants, because temperatures below 25 degrees F can cause significant shoot and bud injury. To help reduce plant injury, cover the plants with straw or hay before severe winter temperatures occur in the fall but after the plants have been subjected to a few hard frosts. Some gardeners use a fence of wire or wood to keep the straw or hay on each plant.

PEST CONTROL

Blueberries are very attractive to birds. Cover the bushes with ¾- or 1-inch mesh netting during the harvest season to provide adequate protection.

Although blueberries are often attacked by insects and diseases, these problems seldom become significant in home fruit gardens. Use good sanitary and cultural practices, such as removing diseased branches and overripe fruit

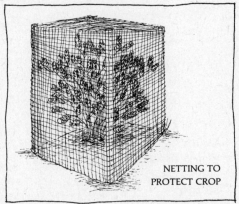

NETTING TO
PROTECT CROP

from the ground, to help minimize your pest problems. If a serious pest problem does arise, contact your county extension office for the latest recommendations on pest control.

HARVESTING

Berries are usually sweetest two to three days after turning blue at the stem end. A good year for a mature bush means a yield of 4 to 8 quarts, harvested over several weeks with an average of three to five pickings needed to harvest all the fruit. Allow five to seven days between pickings for the new berries to ripen.

Rhubarb

Rhubarb, like asparagus, needs cold winters with frozen soil, so it does well in northern climates. It is a hardy perennial that begins growth very early in the spring. The leafstalks (petioles) are used mostly for pies and sauces. A few hills will supply all that a family can use and provide enough to preserve for later use.

Any deep, well-drained, fertile soil is suitable for rhubarb. Sweet soils (pH 6.0 to 6.8) are best; if soil is acid, correct with lime or wood ash. Spade or till the soil as deeply as possible and mix in rotted manure, compost, decayed leaves, sod, or other organic matter. Prepare either a 2-foot-wide bed or individual 2-by-2-foot hills (one or two plants that are 2 to 4 feet from the next grouping).

Rhubarb varieties differ in size and stalk color. Ruby and Canada Red have small red leafstalks, while MacDonald's and Victoria's are broader. Valentine has broad pink leafstalks. Plants started from seed take several years to become established and are not always true to type. The best plants come from healthy crowns. Old plants may be divided into crowns or pieces of crowns dug from established hills.

Set healthy crowns, one to a hill, so that the tip of the bud just shows above the soil. Planting may be done either in early spring or in October. After six to eight years, when overcrowding produces small stalks, reset beds by digging up the plant crowns and dividing them. Slice right down through the plant and divide it into two or more new plants. Replant each section the way you planted the original crowns.

Fertilize rhubarb hills annually by top-dressing in fall or early spring with a heavy application of well-rotted manure or compost. Dark-colored compost in spring hastens growth. If you lack organic compost, sprinkle 1 cup of 10-10-10 or 2 cups of 5-10-10 fertilizer around each hill each year after harvest. Weeds are best controlled with organic mulches. Use 2 to 3 inches of wood chips or shavings, or 6 inches of hay over six sheets of newspaper. Place this on top of organic fertilizer early in spring.

Harvest rhubarb by pulling the stalks rather than by cutting them. During harvest season remove seed stalks as soon as they form. No leaf stems should be harvested during the first year and only a few during the second year for a week or two. After that you can extend the harvest to a period of up to eight weeks. Allow the leaves to grow on plants for the remainder of the summer to restore vigor to the crowns.

Use rhubarb as soon as possible after picking to preserve quality. Leafstalks can be stored for only a few days under refrigeration. Use only the leafstalk; trim off and discard all green leaf, and do not feed the leaves to your livestock, because they are poisonous.

Grapes

Principal grape varieties require an average growing season, from bud break, of about 150 to 165 days to mature their fruit properly. In colder climates the growing season ranges from 90 to 160 days, depending upon the locale. However, there are a number of grape plantings in home gardens that do succeed in these areas. In choosing a site for growing grapes, consider the average length of the growing season in your area and average minimum winter temperature. Too short a growing season may cause immature fruit at harvest as well as immature trunks and buds susceptible to winter injury.

SITE AND SOIL

The best site should afford a maximum of warmth and sunlight and a minimum of frost hazard. If possible, plant grapevines on sloping ground facing the sun (southeast to southwest) because these sites have higher night temperatures and afford good air drainage to protect against frost damage; avoid planting in frost pockets.

Select a deep, well-drained soil and fortify it with organic matter. Grapes will grow well on a wide range of soils, but sandy loams and gravelly loams are best. Avoid extremely wet or extremely dry soils. Grapes perform best on soils ranging in pH from 5.0 to 6.0. If the site is in sod, plow or rototill a 4-foot-wide strip well in advance of planting to give the sod time to break down. These strips will become the grape rows.

Gardeners are most apt to buy what nurseries describe in glowing terms and beautiful photos. The Concord variety is a good example. It is productive, hardy, and produces fruit of excellent quality. Unfortunately, it usually requires 155 to 160 days of growing to obtain optimum maturity. Vermont has only a few areas that can satisfy this growing requirement in most years; therefore, only very early to early midseason grape varieties can be considered for planting in our area. Fruitier types of grapes, grown for wines, can only be grown in warmer climates.

PLANTING STOCK

First-grade one-year-old vines with large, vigorous root systems are best. You can use two-year-old vines, but frequently they are culls from the year before and may be weak.

Two common methods for propagating your own plants are by layering and by hardwood cuttings. Layering is done in the spring to fill vacancies within the grape row. Extend a vigorous cane from a vine, placing the tip vertically upward and leaving two or three buds above the soil surface. Strip the old cane of growing shoots so that the new plant can develop rapidly. After two to three years the new vine should be well established and can be cut from the mother vine. The young vine can either be left in place or be transplanted in the spring to a new site.

Hardwood cuttings are the best method of propagation for large-scale use. Cuttings are made from dormant new wood, usually in late fall. Canes of medium size, usually 8 to 10 inches long with about three buds, are preferable. Tie the cuttings in bundles of fifty, with the butts turned in one direction. Store in moist sand, sawdust, peat moss, polyethylene bags, or other materials in a cool place; or bury the cuttings in a well-drained, sandy site and press at least 3 inches of sandy soil firmly against them, placing a heavy straw mulch over the cutting bed. In the spring, plant the cuttings 6 to 8 inches apart in nursery rows—areas where plants are grown for transplanting to a permanent site at a later date, usually when the plants have grown larger and their root systems have become better established. Be sure to leave only the top bud above the soil surface. Cuttings are best grown in the nursery for one year before transplanting into the grape rows the following spring.

PLANTING THE VINES

Plant vines in the spring as soon as the soil can be properly prepared. Keep the roots moist from the time the plants arrive until they are planted. Space the vines 6 to 8 feet apart in the row and 9 to 10 feet between rows. Before planting, remove all but the most vigorous cane from each plant; trim off any broken or excessively long roots; set the plants about 1 inch deeper than they grew in the nursery. Dig a hole large enough to spread the roots without twisting or bending them. Fill the planting hole with a good topsoil mixture, and be sure to pack the soil firmly around the roots and water thoroughly. After planting, prune back the remaining cane to two strong buds.

WEED CONTROL

Hoe or cultivate enough to control the weeds throughout the season. Weeds will deprive young vines of nutrients and water. As with all fruits, we fertilize with well-rotted manure compost and top this with six layers of newspaper and sawdust mulch. If you do not choose to do this, do not cultivate after August, so that weeds will grow back to help insulate the roots against winter injury. If you've no objection to herbicides, they can effectively be used for weed control. For the latest information on herbicide usage, contact your local extension service office.

FERTILIZING

A young grapevine needs and responds well to fertilizer applications. Usually the fertilizer or organic matter applied in the initial soil preparation at planting is sufficient for first-year plants. The year following planting, apply a bushel of well-rotted manure along with ¼ pound of superphosphate per plant in the early spring.

If you use commercial fertilizer, the following kinds and ratios are suggested: 33-0-0 (ammonium nitrate), ¼ to ½ pound (½ to 1 cup) per bearing vine; or 10-10-10, 1 to 1¼ pounds (2 to 3 cups) per bearing vine. Use half the rate of these materials for nonbearing vines. When buds begin to swell in the spring, apply the fertilizer directly to the soil in a circle 1 to 2 feet from the plant.

TRELLISING

Construct the trellis during the first growing season or the following spring. Two wires are adequate for the umbrella Kniffin system and four-arm Kniffin system, the most commonly used training systems. The top wire should be

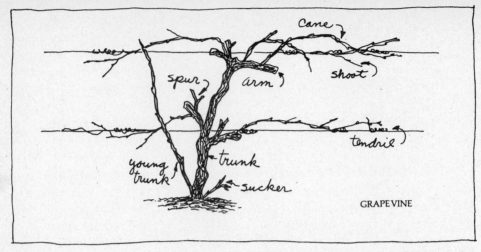

GRAPEVINE

5½ to 6 feet above the ground and the bottom wire 2¼ to 3 feet above the ground. Use treated posts 8 feet long with a top diameter of 3 inches. Set the posts 2 feet into the ground at a distance of 20 to 24 feet apart. The end posts, which function as anchor points, should be railroad ties 8½ to 9 feet long set 4 feet deep at an angle 30 degrees from the vertical; brace each end post to an anchor set in the soil, or you can build an arbor of slabwood as we did. Three sizes of wire are commonly used for the trellis: numbers 9, 10, and 11. Number 9 is used for the top wire. Each spring tighten all loose wires and drive down all loosened posts.

TRAINING

It will be easier to understand training and pruning procedures if you're familiar with the basic parts of the grapevine.

TRUNK: The main stem of the vine. There may be one or more per vine.

ARMS: The main branches attached to the trunk.

SHOOTS: New succulent growths from the buds of a cane, spur, arm, or trunk. They produce leaves, tendrils, and fruit. After the leaves fall, they become the fruiting canes for next season.

CANE: A mature, woody shoot after leaf fall.

SPUR: A cane pruned back to four or fewer buds. A renewal spur—one or two buds—is selected to produce canes at a particular location on an arm or trunk. A fruiting spur—three or four buds—is selected to produce fruiting shoots.

SUCKER: A shoot from a bud below ground.

TENDRIL: A slender, curled structure that can firmly attach the shoot to a support.

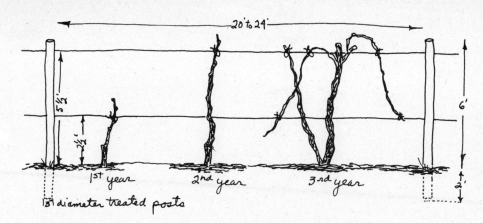

TRAINING OF GRAPEVINE

Training involves arranging the canes on the trellis to position the leaves for greatest exposure to sunlight and the fruit for ease of harvest.

The two common methods of training grapevines suggested for northern growers are the four-arm Kniffin system and the umbrella Kniffin system. Two trunks are recommended for all northern grape plantings involving European varieties because one trunk is likely to be lost from either winter injury or disease.

During the first growing season maintain the young canes in an upright position and remove fruit clusters as they develop. Since winter protection is necessary, lay the vine on the ground in November (if attached to a trellis or a stake) and mulch 4 to 6 inches deep with hay, straw, or sawdust. The following April remove the mulch from the vines and tie the strongest and largest cane to the trellis. If vine growth was very weak the first year, start over again by pruning back to two buds. A second cane, preferably a sucker, should be pruned back to two or three buds. It will become the second trunk, added insurance against winter injury. In the second year retain only four to eight buds per vine for the larger cane and two buds on the smaller cane. Remove all flower clusters to ensure greater development of the vine's roots and top.

FOUR-ARM KNIFFIN SYSTEM: This system provides strong support to the vine and crop while allowing for good exposure to sunlight and air circulation. It is most often used for native American varieties. Tie the trunk loosely (so as not to cut off circulation) to the bottom and top wires. Run canes in both directions from the trunk along both wires. Ideally there should be a total of four fruiting canes and four renewal spurs for next year's fruiting canes. Wrap each cane around the wire and fasten tightly at the end before buds swell in the spring. At each pruning, retain the required bud number on two to six canes. (If you need more than four canes, it is best to leave these on the top wire, where they will be more productive.)

UMBRELLA KNIFFIN SYSTEM: This system is commonly used for both European (including French hybrids) and American varieties. A mature vine consists of a

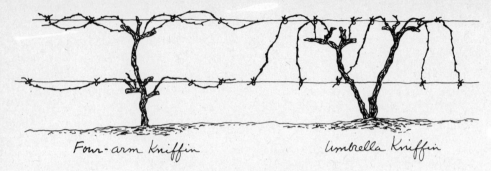

Four-arm Kniffin   *Umbrella Kniffin*

FOUR-ARM KNIFFIN AND UMBRELLA KNIFFIN

single or double trunk with numerous canes headed 6 to 10 inches below the top wire. Ideally there should be a total of two fruiting canes per trunk. Spread and bend the canes sharply over the top wire so that the outer bark cracks, and tie them to the lower wire. Leave the same number of renewal spurs as fruiting canes at the head(s) of the trunk. Shoots that arise at the bend will be vigorous and will be excellent to retain for fruiting the following year.

PRUNING

Prune in March or early April in colder climates, anytime in midwinter elsewhere (before buds swell), so long as the vines are still dormant. A grapevine is pruned to control the quality and quantity of both fruit and vine growth. Pruning also promotes uniform distribution (80 to 90 percent) over the entire trellis.

Fruiting buds on medium-size (diameter of a lead pencil) fully exposed one-year-old canes with dark brown bark are the most productive and are the only buds that you should count on for fruiting. Avoid leaving excessively long, large-diameter canes, called bullwood. Pruned canes may vary in length from eight to fifteen buds, depending upon varieties, weight of prunings, and vine spacing.

RENEWING OLD VINES

A vine unpruned for several years has a low reserve of food in its roots and trunks. In the first year only, retain the best-quality canes and no more than eighty buds, along with renewal spurs at points where you want canes the following year. Remove all flower clusters before bloom. Starting the second year and thereafter, balance-prune and leave all flower clusters. Because trunks of neglected vines are likely to be injured, retain one or two suckers for renewal when they appear. Good weed control and liberal fertilization with nitrogen will speed the recovery of neglected vines.

HARVESTING AND HANDLING

Most grape varieties change color long before they are mature enough for harvesting. For table use (dessert), grape maturity is best judged by taste; but the color of seeds, which change from green to brown, will help. Maturity of wine or juice grapes is determined by the sugar content, or Brix. The Brix test is performed with a hand refractometer, or Balling hydrometer. It is often desirable to harvest a vine more than once over a two-to-three-week period.

Ideal conditions to keep grapes for a long period are similar to those for apples, namely, temperatures of 30 to 33 degrees F and a relative humidity of 85 to 90 percent. For storage periods of only a few days, temperatures between 35 and 45 degrees F may be satisfactory.

PEST CONTROL

One of the major pests of grapes is birds. Netting is the only practical control and can either be used on an overhead trellis (large-scale planting) or be drooped over individual vines during the harvest season.

The other principal grape pests are black rot, downy mildew, grape-berry moths, Japanese beetles, and rose chafers. Contact your local extension service for the latest control recommendations.

Fruit Trees

When I was eight and just barely old enough to drive the team of draw horses Nellie and Jessie for haying, my grandfather Bachand and I would take a break at the height of the afternoon sun. We'd sit under the gnarled old apple trees that stood neatly in a row right in the middle of the meadow. While he would peel away at the hard old calluses on his hands, he would tell me how different things were when he was growing up. As we talked, I often picked up some of the fallen fruit surrounding me and was always disappointed at not being able to find an apple that was not worm-ridden. These trees were huge and had not been taken care of for many years. After all I have learned these past years, I can't help but wonder if they couldn't have been reclaimed.

Because dwarf fruit trees are the easiest type of fruit tree to adapt to the small-scale homestead, giving an opportunity for a larger variety of fruit in a small area and needing only a minimum of care, I will address myself in this section to their care. Some varieties of fruit trees grow naturally small, and the basic principles I will discuss can be applied to them as well.

Dwarf trees are trees that have been propagated in such a way that the mature size of the tree is smaller than standard varieties. They are developed from a small branch of a fruit tree that has proven its ability to produce good fruit, plus a rootstock. The rootstock could have been grown from seed, or it could be a root division from another tree, in which case you can usually see where the graft was made. In examining the trunk of the tree, you will find a little knob toward the bottom; it's more pronounced on some trees than on others. On our dwarf apple trees, for instance, it was hardly visible, but our dwarf pears had very large knobs.

Be sure not to let any branches develop below the graft on the rootstock. These rootstocks are usually from inferior trees and will not be good producers.

Fully dwarf trees usually have such small central stocks that they must be staked until well established. Fruit trees such as plum, peach, apricot, and cherry are normally small in size and less upright than apple or pear; however, there are dwarf varieties of these fruits available too. Most dwarf varieties require a growing space of only about 8 feet in diameter, so an entire orchard containing six fruit trees could be planted in an area as small as 10 by 20 feet, the same amount of space that is required for one standard-variety apple tree. While you will not harvest as many fruits per tree on the dwarf variety, you can plant so many more in the same area that in the long run you may well harvest more total fruit. These trees are much easier to prune, and as an added bonus they do not require as much pruning as larger standard varieties. It is much easier to apply fungicides and pesticides if the need arises, too, as these trees do not grow very high. Special care must be taken at planting time, however, to make sure that dwarf trees are not planted too deep. If they are planted much deeper than they were in the nursery, an inferior type of tree may take root. More on this later.

Most dwarf trees grow rapidly when they are young, and these trees bear at an earlier age than standard varieties. They will usually start to bear the second year after planting, while standard varieties take up to five years or longer to bear.

The biggest disadvantage to dwarf trees is their poor-quality rootstocks. These rootstocks are not usually hardy enough to withstand very cold winter temperatures, especially in areas that tend toward many below-zero days in January and February. If you decide to use dwarf trees, you should check with your local agricultural extension agent for varieties that do well in your area, or try to obtain some that were grown by local nurseries. Large chain stores tend to order all their trees from the same supplier, shipping them to their various stores at planting time. Because of this, these trees are not always varieties that are suited to your area.

Dwarf trees need extra protection from high winds and deep snow. The main trunk on these trees is not very large, and high winds can often cause breakage. The branches on these low-growing trees can be severely damaged by deep snow in the winter, but with extra care these little trees can survive. There are certain varieties of fruit trees that are not winter-hardy, but because they can be grown in large tubs and taken into the cellar in the winter, you could try some of the more exotic types of fruits.

PREPARING TO PLANT

Trees need the same kinds of rich, humus soils that are needed for a vegetable garden. Before you plant your trees, take the time to prepare your soil well. For instructions on soil preparation see Chapter 3. Tree roots spread rapidly and they need room to grow. Heavy, wet soils hinder this root development and can destroy your trees. On the other hand, loose, sandy soils that will not hold moisture are not good either, so it pays to take the extra time required to make sure that soil conditions are at their optimum.

Fruit trees should be planted in early spring or late fall in the North, or anytime from fall through winter in the South. When you order trees, time their arrival for the proper planting dates in your area. Local nurseries usually have good healthy stock of the varieties of trees that adapt best to your area.

Most fruit trees need to be pollinated. Without adequate pollination, they may blossom abundantly but will never bear fruit. Some species of fruit trees have perfect blossoms. Both the anthers, which contain the pollen, and the pistils, which develop into the fruits, are in the same blossom. There are, however, many other types of fruit with perfect flowers that can't produce their own pollen. These trees require pollen from another variety of tree to become fruitful. Trees such as persimmon and date have male trees that produce pollen and female trees that produce fruit. To achieve success with these types of trees, a male tree must be planted near a female tree. Almost all citrus trees are self-pollinating. Other self-pollinating trees include quince, sour cherry, some varieties of apricot, some figs, and a few varieties of peach. Trees needing more than one variety for pollination include apple, pear, sweet cherry, and plum. You must plant at least two of these trees, and they must be two different varieties of the same species, such as a McIntosh apple and a Delicious apple, or a Bartlett pear and a Duchess pear. Bees normally pollinate fruit trees, though other types of insects help too. To ensure adequate pollination, it would be wise to keep a hive of bees yourself, unless of course someone within a mile of you has bees.

Plant at least two varieties of apple trees near one another. Golden Delicious, a self-fruitful type, is one of the few exceptions to this rule. Poor pollen-producing types, such as Baldwin, Gravenstein, Staymen, Winesap, and Rhode Island Greening, need to be planted with at least two other varieties to ensure adequate pollination of all. Sweet cherry trees such as Bin, Lamber, and Napoleon (Royal Ann) do not pollinate one another. Plant a pollinating variety such as Black Tartarian, Republican, Van, or Windsor, or a sour cherry, such as Montmorency, nearby. Many varieties of pear are completely or partially self-unfruitful. For adequate pollination, plant at least two varieties together. Bartlett and Seckel pears will not pollinate each other and must be planted with another variety. Most varieties of Japanese and American plums are self-unfruitful; plant two or more varieties together. You will find catalog descriptions of new varieties that are advertised as being self-pollinating, especially peach and apricot, but in most cases you are taking a risk by not planting two varieties of any fruit tree together.

When your trees arrive, they may come balled, which means that the roots will still be enclosed in the clump of soil they were growing in and all will be wrapped in a burlap bag or will be in a container. Or the trees may come barerooted, which means that they have had the soil removed and the roots will be surrounded with either some form of moist mulch material or moist peat moss. These trees are usually wrapped in plastic. If it is balled, just make sure that the soil is kept moist until planting, but if it is barerooted, remove the wrapping and place the tree in a pail of water to keep the roots from drying out before you plant it. We like to soak ours for twenty-four hours before planting. Keep the mulch material the trees come packed in and add it to the topsoil as a conditioner when you plant. If the trees you ordered arrive on a very cold day and are frozen, place them in a cool area and let them thaw gradually before placing them in a bucket of water.

Keeping in mind that your trees are going to stay in the same place for many years, choose an area that gets sun all day and is not shaded by taller trees or buildings. If you have made plantings of landscaping trees nearby, you must also take into consideration how tall they are going to grow. One large maple could conceivably block out all the sun to your entire small orchard.

PLANTING

Remove 4 to 6 inches of topsoil from a circle 30 inches in diameter and set it aside. Mix this soil with the soil conditioners that came with the tree and some well-rotted manure compost (half and half), adding 3 cups of lime. Dig the rest of the soil out until you have a hole large enough in diameter to accommodate the roots of your tree. Make sure that it is large enough to spread out all the roots without bending any of them, or they will break. Place a couple of shovelfuls of the topsoil mixture in the hole and carefully place your tree roots down in the hole. Do not put it any deeper than it grew in the nursery. Look for the graft ring at the base of the trunk and do not plant any deeper than this. You must take care not to plant the trees too shallow, either, or the roots will dry out. Very gently separate all the roots and spread them out. Be careful not to damage the fine little feeder roots. If you are going to stake the tree, put the stake in place now so that you can see where it is going, or you might damage the young tree's root system later when you drive the stake into the ground. Pour a gallon of water containing a good starter solution, such as Miracle-Gro or liquid manure tea, into the hole. Let the water soak in and, using the topsoil mixture, carefully refill the hole, leaving a depression to catch the rain. Pack the soil firmly around the roots with the heel of your shoe (if you use the toe of your shoe, it might make a sharp depression, which could easily damage the feeder roots).

If the tree wasn't pruned in the nursery, prune away excess branches. Prune strong healthy branches to one-half their original length, and the central trunk back to three-quarters of its original height. Make the cut about ½ to ¼ inch from the bud. Cut above a bud that is growing in an upward direction, otherwise new growth will create a poorly shaped tree with some branches crossed and others growing down and then curving upward and outward. The top of the tree and the root system should be in balance. Water again and mulch with old hay or straw.

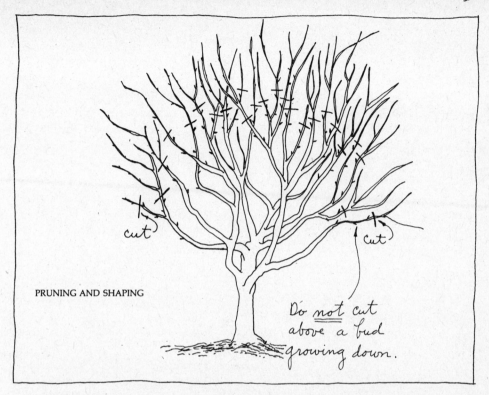

PRUNING AND SHAPING

Some type of tree wrap or wire protection should immediately be put in place around the trunk for rodent protection.

I like to tie my trees to the stakes with old strips of nylon stockings. These do not rot, and they expand easily enough so as not to cut into the tender bark of the tree. Tie one end securely around the stake and then wrap it around the tree trunk. You can use strips of burlap bags or pieces of plastic wrap too. Never use strong twine or wire that can cut into the bark and damage your trees. After a year or so, even dwarf trees become well enough established to enable you to remove the stakes.

Keep a record of the type and variety of each tree or plant, the date purchased, and where it was purchased. If the tree or plant does not do well, you won't forget what type it was and will be able to replace it with another similar tree to ensure good cross-pollination. Many companies will replace trees up to one year from the purchase date.

FERTILIZING

As with all growing things, young trees need most of their nourishment in the months that they make their most rapid growth, late spring to early summer. Most fruit trees prefer a slightly acid soil, with a pH from 6.0 to 6.5, so there isn't much need for liming unless you are trying to reclaim an old orchard that has long been depleted of all nutrients. If a soil test indicates that the pH is too low, you will have to make an effort to bring it up, because otherwise the fertilizers you apply could become chemically locked into the soil and be of little use to your trees. Too high a pH could retard the growth of your trees and cause fruit to drop. Trees need nitrates, phosphate, and potash. We fertilize with well-rotted manure compost. When we fertilized our first fruit trees years ago, we would pour water-soluble fertilizer right by the tree trunk, not realizing that the large roots of the tree were the closest to the trunk and the feeder roots that actually took in the nutrients were more spread out at the tips of the roots. Small wonder that our efforts failed to show any resultant healthy growth.

Trying to grow trees using chemical fertilizers those first few years gave us enough experience to know that if there is one area of gardening where organic fertilizers really come into their own, it's in the small orchard. One good thick application of well-rotted manure compost early in the spring is all you need for an entire season. It breaks down slowly and feeds a constant supply of nutrients to your trees throughout their growing cycle, and you don't have to worry about chemical burn from overfeeding. We use about a 6-inch layer of compost spread from a few inches of the trunk to the area beneath the tip of the outermost branches. Make your heaviest feeding toward the outside of the circle. Remember, that's where the feeder roots are located.

If you are using commercial fertilizers, you should use about 5 pounds of 5-10-10 per 100 square feet, spread in the same area as the manure compost. It is a waste of fertilizer to fertilize outside the perimeter of the longest branches of the tree, since the feeder roots only extend underground as far as these branches extend above the ground. If you are using commercial fertilizers, never overfeed your trees. This causes rapid growth and weakness in the tree. Nor should you fertilize past midsummer; this will cause new growth to start, and this tender new growth will not have enough time to harden off before cold weather comes, causing serious damage to your trees. But when you fertilize only once early in the season with manure compost, this does not present a problem.

WATERING

Newly planted trees should be watered at least three times a week, using at least a 5-gallon pailful each time. Continue watering this amount for at least the first season after planting unless you have a good soaking rain. It is a good idea to use a weak fertilizer solution, such as Miracle-Gro or manure tea, during the first month. After that make sure that the trees have an adequate amount of moisture for the rest of the growing season. Mulching after a good soaking helps to maintain moisture at the proper level throughout the growing season.

MULCHING

We mulch our trees at the same time that we fertilize early in the spring. Once we're sure that the frost is out of the ground, we put down our manure-compost fertilizer, cover this with six layers of newspaper, and add to the top of this 3 to 4 inches of sawdust. You could also use wood shavings, old hay, straw, peanut hulls, leaves, and so forth. Mulching and fertilizing the way we do allows the organic material to break down slowly, constantly feeding the root system just what it needs for proper growth. The newspaper over the compost discourages weed seeds from growing, and the sawdust finishes the job by holding down the paper and giving the orchard a neat appearance. In addition, mulch prevents frost heaves during the winter.

Besides nourishing the trees and preventing loss of moisture, mulch provides a healthy climate for earthworms. They do a wonderful job of aerating the soil, and the castings they throw off add additional nourishment for your trees. This is especially important if you have heavy clay soil, because well-aerated, friable soil is a must for proper root development.

In the fall we add a little hen manure to the top of the sawdust. Sawdust breaks down slowly and uses a great deal of nitrogen. In order to prevent a nitrogen deficiency in our soil, we add the hen manure, which is high in nitrogen; this helps the sawdust to decompose faster and prevents nitrogen loss. A sprinkling of bone meal would be just as effective.

Each year thereafter, *as soon as the frost is out of the ground*, we follow the same process. With the exception of the peaches, pears, and plums, which tend to blossom too early in the North, this is especially important, otherwise you might retard the start of your growing season. For those trees that require as long a growing season as possible for your area this could prove to be dangerous.

WINTER

Today's weather patterns fluctuate so drastically in all parts of our country that weather damage is a major factor in growing fruits. Most hardy fruit trees need a certain amount of cold winter weather to end their dormancy and to promote spring growth. When winters are too mild, spring growth is delayed, irregular, and slow. These factors extend the period of blooming and thereby increase the possibility of frost injury. Hardy fruit trees grown in climates considerably warmer than their native ones often bear poorly because of insufficient winter cold. This problem can occur in areas with mild climates such as southern California and within two hundred miles of the Gulf of Mexico.

On the other hand, extreme cold during winter dormancy may kill the fruit buds. Winter weather rarely threatens hardy apple, pear, plum, and sour cherry varieties. Sweet cherry trees, however, are relatively sensitive to cold until they become dormant. Peach trees are very vulnerable to cold weather. Their buds can be killed by midwinter temperatures of around 10 degrees F.

Here in Vermont on a clear, sunny day in March, the temperatures could go as high as 60 degrees F, but if the night remains clear of overcast, the temperatures could go down to 10 degrees F. This sudden heating of the tree during the daytime might start the tree growing, only to have that new growth shocked by the rapidly falling low nighttime temperatures. It could even kill the trees. Very young trees could be protected the first year or two by building light removable A-frames that have a light plastic covering that can be put over them during the coldest parts of the winter. Just be careful to build them in such a manner that exposure to the heating rays of the sun in late January and early February can't cause overheating in your miniature greenhouse. A good way to prevent this is to put cardboard under the plastic on the eastern and southern sides. As soon as temperatures moderate in the early spring, loosen the plastic to allow for good ventilation, and remove the plastic completely as daytime temperatures get above freezing. The frame is left in place until all danger of hard frost is over. As your trees grow, it will not be as easy to cover them this way, but by then they will have become better established and will tolerate the extremes in temperature changes with less risk.

Don't be fooled by mail-order nursery advertisements that state that certain fruit and nut trees are hardy to 20 degrees F. We sent for and planted two Carpathian walnut trees three years ago, and neither survived. A young forester whom I met last year explained why. Many trees can withstand cold temperatures *if* they have completed their growing cycle. These trees must have enough of a growing season to set out their new growth and then for that growth to have time to harden off before cold weather comes. If your growing season is too short and cold weather sets in early in the fall, the new growth is still too tender and will be killed by the cold temperatures. This is why I can't emphasize enough the importance of checking with a knowledgeable nurseryman or county extension agent before buying fruit or nut trees for your area of the country. We've lost a considerable sum of money over the years because of mistakes of this nature.

In preparing your trees for winter, you should take care to protect the trunk, from a couple of inches below the ground level up to about 2 feet off the ground, from rodents and deer who love to nibble at the tender young bark of these trees. Once a tree is completely girdled (the bark eaten away all around the trunk) by these nibblers, it is almost impossible to save the tree. Painting the trunk with dried blood meal mixed with water to form a paste or with white latex paint will prevent some of the nibbling, but to be on the safe side the trunk should also be wrapped with some form of tree wrap, screen, or at least tinfoil. Tree wrap is available in most garden supply stores and nurseries. Check trees early in the spring as soon as the frost is out of the ground. Repair any damage caused by animals and weather that you missed in late winter. Be sure to check down close to the soil or beneath the mulch if you mulched your trees. Paint any breaks in the tender bark with Tree Kote or a similar preparation, and pull any weeds that can choke out the new growth.

This past winter we had one limb of a small apple tree that was badly damaged. Just below where that limb grew from the tree trunk there was a long split in the bark. When spring came, the bark loosened and fell off. I was telling our problem to a friend of ours who grows dwarf trees, and he suggested that I cut the damaged branch and paint the injured part of the tree with Tree Kote, which I generally use at pruning time. In hopes of saving this tree, I followed his suggestion, and the tree thrived this summer, even if it did look a little lopsided. It's important to prune back any damage that you notice early in the spring before the weather warms up.

Peaches, plums, and pears tend to blossom earlier than apples and are apt to be damaged by late frosts. A good way to help prevent this is to use a heavy mulch throughout the winter. Because the frost will go out of the ground more slowly under mulch, your trees will start to grow and blossom later, hopefully missing a late hard frost. Once the tiny fruit is set, a frost is less likely to damage your crop, because the blossom is less hardy than the tiny little fruit. However, the open blossoms of practically all fruit trees may be killed if the temperature drops below 27 degrees F. When a heavy frost is expected, covering the trees will sometimes prevent bud or blossom injury, provided temperatures do not fall too low and the cold weather is of short duration. Protective covering may be effective, and such things as cheesecloth or old blankets may be used.

PRUNING

After planting and until they begin to bear fruit, trees need very little pruning other than to cut off an occasional damaged branch or do some minor shaping. Once trees start to bear, they should be pruned yearly to ensure good fruit production. Always make sure to prune branches growing too near to the ground. After dwarf trees start to produce, shaping is usually all that is necessary. Standard trees need more care.

Pruning should be done in the late winter or early spring in the North and can be done anytime during the winter in the South. It should be done on a mild, sunny day when the temperatures are above freezing. You will need a pair of hand clippers, a pair of long-handled pruning shears for high places, and a good handsaw. Do not use electric saws, because they could slip and injure the tree.

We found the whole subject of pruning to be rather awesome for many years until the vast amount of reading I had done on the subject finally convinced me that it was really just a matter of common sense. You have to keep in mind what fruits need to grow and ripen in addition to good soil, moisture, and nutrients. Fruits need healthy branches to carry nutrients to them, so you would remove any broken or diseased branches or branches that cross and rub on one another. Remove the least vigorous branch or the one that is poorly shaped or growing in the wrong direction. Fruits need room to grow, so remove branches that crowd out the growing surfaces of the strongest branches. And fruits need sunshine, both for good growth and to ripen, so make sure to remove branches that block the rays of the sun to large areas of the tree. If you are pruning stone fruits (plums, peaches, apricots, etc.), be careful not to cut too many branches with spurs. These fruits grow on spurs, whereas apples grow along the branch. The only other pruning needed is to keep the tree well shaped. Be sure to cut above a bud that is growing upward or outward and paint the cut with Tree Kote. This is hardly what an orchardist would call a scientific method of pruning, but it's a practical method, and if it is used, it's pretty hard to make a serious mistake.

Do not allow dwarf trees to produce fruits the first two years, and allow a rest of four years or more for standard varieties. Producing fruit too early will weaken young trees, and weak trees are very prone to diseases that might be fatal in their weakened condition. Remove any small fruits as soon as they appear. By the third year you should be able to harvest your first fruit from the dwarf trees; it takes up to five years for standard varieties to bear.

RECLAIMING AN OLD TREE

When my brother Ron and his wife, Renée, bought their present home, there were two old crab apple trees, plus a McIntosh and a Baldwin apple tree in their backyard. These trees were old, overgrown, and had produced nothing but small wormy fruit for many years. After they had lived there a few years, Ron read some material on reclaiming old fruit trees. Deciding he had nothing to lose, he pruned them back severely that year in the late winter and began a regular spraying schedule, starting with a dormant spray in the early spring. That first year the trees were so loaded with beautiful, large disease-free fruit that the tips of their branches touched the ground and had to be supported.

While I don't guarantee that kind of result with every old tree, it's worth a try if you have one or more trees that are old and worm-ridden. Ron's method of pruning that first year was somewhat drastic, though he certainly made out fine. Experts recommend that old trees should be pruned back over a period of at least two years, so that they will not be too severely shocked. Don't worry about the size of the branch. If it needs to go, cut it out, even if it's a foot in diameter, using a handsaw. Follow a good spraying schedule and make sure that the tree is well fed. It's a good idea to check the pH of the soil around the tree and adjust it if necessary.

INSECTS AND DISEASES

You will have to use common sense when it comes to the use of pesticides and fungicides. Fruit and plants cost money, and their care requires time. It hardly makes sense after investing all this time and money to just sit back, chew your fingernails, and mop your brow while you watch bugs and disease devour your trees. There are many organic aids to help prevent problems in the first place, such as keeping your trees well nourished to keep them healthy. Healthy trees are more disease-resistant. Buy disease-resistant varieties. Place bird feeders in the orchard; the birds will eat the bugs. Plant marigolds, mums, calendula, garlic, onions, and other plants known to ward off insects. Keep the orchard free of disease-carrying weeds, and quickly dispose of these and any pruned branches by burning them. Clean up fallen fruit from the ground; don't leave it to decay and attract insects. If there are wild fruit trees close to your orchard, treat them as you would the culti- vated trees and you won't have insects and diseases spreading from these trees to your cultivated trees. This might bring the added bonus of some pretty good fruit trees to your efforts.

After you have taken all these precautions, if you still have problems, then you must act at once to stop them or risk losing your trees. In each area of the country there are different varieties of insects and diseases that affect both fruit and nut trees, along with various methods of control for each area. It would take too much space to try to describe them all in a book of this type, so instead I will give you information on what to do in an emergency until you can have your local county extension agent check your problem and advise you what to do. The most widely used pesticide sprays that are relatively safe are liquid Sevin and Malathion. In- structions for their use on various types of fruit trees and plants are on the bottle. Read and follow these instructions carefully. Captan is the most widely used fun- gicide on the market, and it's toxic. Unfortunately, there isn't a really safe fungi- cide on the market at this time, so read the instructions for Captan *very* carefully.

This past summer I was given a copy of Lewis Hill's *Fruits and Berries for the Home Garden* (published by Alfred A. Knopf, 1977). What I wouldn't have given for a book like this ten years ago. It tells you everything you need to know, in a style that makes reading it fun for everyone. I can't begin to include all the interesting and more technical information that he includes in his book. The present chapter will help you to get started, but for the serious self-sufficiency gardener I can't rec- ommend the book highly enough.

5

KEEPING BEES

Honey has often been called the nectar of the gods, but as much as we all enjoy eating honey, I feel that the most important reason for homesteaders to keep bees is for the amazing amount of work bees do in making our gardens and orchards more productive. They increase the yield on all cucurbits (plants of the gourd family: cucumbers, squash, melons, and pumpkins) and on all plants that flower before setting fruits or vegetables. Ninety percent of the productivity of strawberry plants is created by bees (this is why our bees are located right beside our strawberry patch).

When I started writing this book, I wanted to include a chapter on bees because of their importance. At the same time I had many reservations about it due to my intention to write only about the experiences we have learned from here on our own homestead, and at that time our experience with bees was limited to two short disastrous weeks two years ago. But in the course of writing the book we have started to keep bees again.

Honey-making is the process of gathering nectar from the blossoms of fruit and flowers and depositing it in the foundation combs, where, by means of evaporation, the nectar turns into honey. The moisture in the nectar evaporates about 25 percent in the first twenty-four hours. How soon it will actually be thick enough to be called honey will depend on daytime temperatures and the type of blossoms from which it came. Some blossoms produce high-moisture nectar, making it very thin. Other plants, such as fuchsia, produce very thick nectar, and the evaporation time is much shorter.

In the course of our new beginning with bees, John Tardie, a very fine local beekeeper, cautioned me about the work ahead: "There are many who become enchanted with the idea of keeping bees and harvesting the honey for their own use and to sell, and believe that the only requirements needed are to obtain a box [hive], throw in a package of bees, then wait until fall and harvest the big crop of honey. For anyone with this notion, there is a sad awakening due. The art of bee-keeping is a very complex undertaking. Anyone can own a hive of bees and be a bee-haver, but it takes knowledge to truly be a beekeeper." It isn't that keeping bees requires a lot of time; in fact, it's the opposite. Very little time is needed to take care of your bees, but if you don't know what you are doing, you can invest a considerable amount of money and lose it all.

Once we began setting up our own hives again, I discovered a multitude of questions that needed answers. Taking out my beekeeping books, I found that the two books I had, both written by professional beekeepers, were not explicit enough for a novice. Either the language was too technical or the material, in some cases, seemed to assume that we already knew the answers. This sent me running to my uncle, Jules "Chic" Chicoine, a former apiarist, and also to John Tardie. I was going to need help getting off to a good start this time, and I knew it. My uncle, a self-styled naturalist, traveled throughout Vermont several years ago lecturing on beekeeping. John Tardie has been a beekeeper for the past twenty-seven years; he is a past president and current board member of the Vermont Beekeepers Association, a past member of the board of directors of the Eastern Apicultural Society of North America (EAS), and is slated for the presidency of EAS in 1980. He has done a vast amount of research on bees and teaches courses in beekeeping here in the Burlington, Vermont, area. These two men were able to give me commonsense, down-to-earth answers to my questions. Now I realize that I couldn't have picked a better time to write this chapter. If I had these questions, then maybe you have them too. Hopefully, my initial inexperience and subsequent learning process will be of help to you.

Our first attempt at beekeeping was quite disastrous. For Christmas the children gave me a beginner's beekeep-

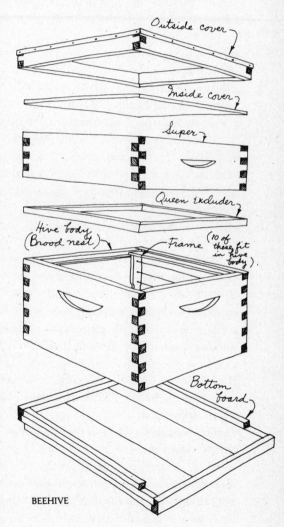

Outside cover

Inside cover

Super

Queen Excluder

Hive body (Brood nest)

Frame (10 of these fit in hive body)

Bottom board

BEEHIVE

ing kit consisting of the main parts of the hive: the bottom plate, the hive body (called the brood nest) where the queen lays her eggs, ten deep frames, ten pieces of foundation wax, the queen excluder, an inner cover, a telescoping top cover, and an entrance reducer. Also included were the feeder board, gloves, veil, smoker, and hive tool, and a book on beekeeping. Ray added to my equipment by giving me an extra super. My family was not as enthusiastic about my beekeeping project as I was. They informed me that they didn't intend to go within 100 feet of my bees, so I could expect that their contribution to my beekeeping efforts ended when they bought me my equipment. Everything came boxed and had to be put together. I didn't mind putting the hive and super bodies together, but I have to confess that assembling the foundations and frames was something of a pain. Now I understand why. The instructions that came with the kit were quite clear, except for the foundation-wax assembly. They did not show that you were to loosen and remove one section of the split board from the top of the frames to install the foundation wax, then tack the little board back on, so it was difficult for me to slide the foundation into the existing slot. All in all, it took me about two weeks of puttering around evenings to get all the parts assembled and painted, but it was a good use of some dreary winter evenings.

When spring came, I ordered my first package of Italian bees from Montgomery Ward. The package consisted of a queen and thirteen to fifteen thousand bees. They arrived in exceptionally good shape, with only three dead bees in the package. They were still so full of honey that I was able to open the package, remove the queen cage, and set the rest of the bees down between the frames in the hive without using gloves. The rest of the family wasn't about to come anywhere near the hive, and I was relieved not to have had an unpleasant experience. I could just hear the "I told you so's" if I had been stung.

I fed the bees daily and was watching them as carefully as a mother hen. One day after they'd been installed about two weeks, a former neighbor came up to see us. Boasting that he'd raised bees as a youngster, he asked if he could go and see the hive. I couldn't imagine anyone harming a hive by just looking at it, so I told him to go ahead. He decided that he wanted to see the queen, so he took the hive cover off, and when he couldn't see her, he took a stick and prodded the bees in the hive between the frames. It's a wonder they didn't attack him, but apparently their fear made them fill with honey. Then they just swarmed from the hive. I didn't know what to do, so I ran for my book. It said that they usually land on a nearby tree. Alas, they didn't. They took off for the woods, and we couldn't find them. I learned later that because this was an unnatural type of swarming, one caused by fear, they most probably flew farther than normal. Also, it was possible that the stick used in the hive had killed the queen. I was too discouraged to start again that year, and I didn't have the time or money to get started again until this past spring. This time I promised myself that I would try to get all the extra help that I could find.

Starting Your Hive

To get started again this time, I took my hive body to John Tardie, and he installed the package of bees right into the hive and fed the hive until it was well established. Then we brought it home. It cost a few more dollars to do it this way, but as a beginner I felt more secure about the success of my new hive. Next year I hope I will have learned enough to start another hive or two myself. The following information is based on what John Tardie told me about getting started with packaged bees. He feels that it is the fastest and best way to install your bees. There are many other ways, but trying to learn too many will only confuse you as a beginner.

Mix 10 pounds of granulated sugar with 1½ gallons of warm water, or a 1-to-1 mixture by volume (example: 1 quart water to 1 quart sugar). Feed the bees soon after they are received. Mr. Tardie prefers spraying the solution on with a Windex sprayer or any similar sprayer because you can cause the bees to injure their tongues against the screen if you brush the syrup on the screen. If the weather is too bad to install the bees, put them in a dark, cool, well-ventilated place and feed them twice daily. Spray sugar syrup on both sides of the cage with a coarse spray until syrup starts to drip from the cluster. Repeat at least three times at fifteen-minute intervals for each feeding. You can keep them a week or longer this way. Install the bees at any convenient time of day, but late afternoon as the sun is setting is best. Feed them heavily for thirty minutes before proceeding as follows: Place your nailed and painted hive in its permanent position, off the ground to prevent rotting, not too near the street, neighbors, or house, and where it will have a light shade from abut 10:00 A.M. to 3:00 P.M. Hives should be placed where they will get winter protection from northerly winds, and the hive should be painted white or aluminum to reflect the heat of summer. It is important for the hive to receive some shade during the hottest part of the day, but remember that no shade is better than too much shade. Fill the feeder jar with sugar syrup and place it near the hive. Now put the entrance reducer in place with the smallest opening in use and shove some green grass loosely into the entrance, loose enough so that air can enter freely and the bees can remove it the next day. This is to keep the bees from rushing out.

Pry off the short top board on the package and remove the nails from it, setting it nearby. Now pick up the package and slam it down on the ground or the top of the hive with a solid, sharp bang. Don't worry, you won't injure the bees. This will drop all the bees to the bottom of the cage. Quickly remove the feeder jar and the queen cage. If the queen cage is suspended by a piece of screen or metal in the same hole as the feeder jar, you'd better hang onto the screen or metal while removing the feeder jar. If you don't, the queen cage can drop to the bottom of the package with those ten to twelve thousand bees. Then you've got a problem. If this happens—and you should prepare yourself for this—use a pair of ice

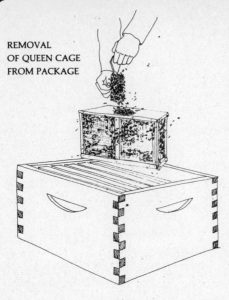

REMOVAL
OF QUEEN CAGE
FROM PACKAGE

tongs or vegetable tongs (the kind you use to take sweet corn out of the water) and go after the cage immediately before the bees swarm all over it. If the queen is suspended by a metal disc to one side of the feeder-jar hole, then remove the queen cage first and then the feeder jar. As soon as the feeder jar and queen cage have been removed and before the bees have had a chance to climb back up, place the short top board, which you set aside earlier, over the hole so that no bees can escape. This whole process should not take more than a very few seconds.

Don't be afraid of the bees; they will not sting you even if they light on you. Don't slap at any flying bees. With the package closed up again, you now have time to examine the queen and to make sure that she is alive. If a number of bees are adhering to the screen on the cage, just brush them aside gently with your hive tool. The queen is longer, yellower, and is bald on the middle part of her body where the wings and legs attach. If she is dead, notify your supplier immediately and they will replace her. Meanwhile, continue to feed the bees with the feeder jar. The queen must be replaced within ten days. Workers will kill any new queen introduced after that time, and the colony will die off.

Queens furnished in packages can be in either of two different types of cages, and each must be handled differently. If the queen is in a candy cage (a cage with two or three compartments, one of which is filled with sugar candy), after ascertaining that the queen is alive and well, remove the cork or the perforated metal covering from the candy end of the cage. CAUTION—There is a cork at both ends of the cage; *remove only the one at the candy end.* Then make a small hole through the candy with a 10-penny nail and hang the cage between the third and fourth frames of your hive with the candy end up.

The second type of queen cage is a dry cage. This cage has only one or two compartments, the queen is alone in the cage, and there is no candy. This cage should be suspended in the hive the same as a candy cage, but the cork should not be removed for a couple of days. Then remove the cage and brush off all the bees. Remove the cork, being careful not to release the queen. This can be done by placing your finger over the hole as soon as the cork is removed. Now fill the hole full of candy made with powdered sugar and a little water to make a thick paste. Push the candy into the hole until you can see it about level with the edge of the compartment. Replace the cage in the hive. The queen will be released in a few

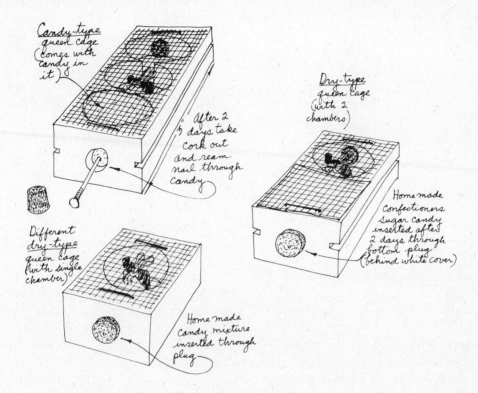

Candy-type queen cage (comes with candy in it)

After 2 3 days take cork out and ream nail through candy

Dry-type queen cage (with 2 chambers)

Home made confectioners sugar candy inserted after 2 days through bottom plug (behind white cover)

Different dry-type queen cage (with single chamber)

Home made candy mixture inserted through plug

hours. If you have had the package of bees for a couple of days before installing, you can eliminate the two-day wait before removing the cork and putting in the candy.

If you are installing bees on foundation wax, you will need to staple a piece of thin metal or screen approximately 5 inches long to the back of the cage on the candy end to be able to hang the cage between the frames. Make sure that the screen on the front of the cage is in a position that will allow free access to it by the bees so that they can keep the queen warm and feed her. If you are installing on drawn combs,* press the queen cage into the combs with the screen side facing the front of the hive. Do not install the cage with the screen toward a comb; the bees cannot get at it, and you will end up with a dead queen. For foundation-wax or drawn-comb installation, the cage should be placed approximately 1 or 2 inches down from the top of the frames and in the middle, from front to back, of the hive. If the queen comes in a candy cage, the bees will chew through the candy and release the queen in the quiet of the hive in approximately one to three days, depending on the weather and the size hole you made in the candy.

---

* Drawn combs are combs that have been worked using the wax foundation together with the wax the bees produce with their mandibles and work with their feet and mandibles into beautiful combs of hexagonal cells in which the bees rear their young and store their honey. When honey is extracted with a mechanical honey extractor, these combs can be reused.

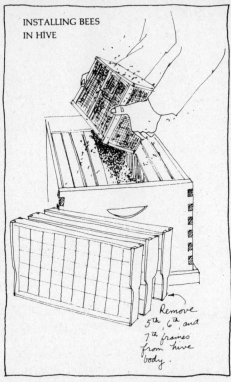

INSTALLING BEES
IN HIVE

Remove
5th, 6th and
7th frames
from hive
body.

With your queen now installed in the hive, remove the fifth, sixth, and seventh frames and set them against the hive. You have reached the point where you can call yourself a beekeeper: You are now ready to release your bees. Spray the bees again with sugar syrup on both sides until it drips from the cluster, then bang the package down again, as you did to remove the feeder jar and queen. This is to free the bees from the screen and make them easier to dump out. Remove the top board and immediately turn the package upside down over the space made by the removal of the three frames. Shake all the bees out, banging the sides and the bottom with the palm of your hand or your fist to dislodge as many bees as possible. If you are not able to get all the bees out, place the package at an angle in front of the hive with the opening near the hive entrance. With all or most of the bees now in the hive, spray them again to wet down any that are trying to fly. With your hive tool gently spread the pile of bees on the bottom board, pushing a good amount under the area where the queen is. Don't worry, you won't hurt them.

Now gently replace the three frames. Bees have a natural tendency to crawl up and in a very short time will all be up off the bottom board and forming a cluster around the queen cage: It's important to put your cluster near the exact center of the hive right under the inner-cover hole, where it will be easy to feed them. Place your inner cover on the hive, deep side up, or if you made a candy board, place it candy side down. Invert the jar of syrup over the hole, place your empty deep super or empty hive body on top of the inner cover and the telescoping cover over that.

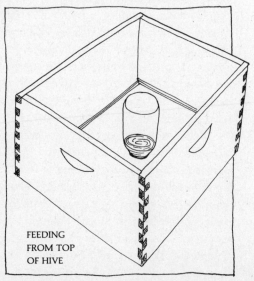

FEEDING
FROM TOP
OF HIVE

You did it—you installed your bees! If there were any bees left in the package, make a small hole in the green grass that's blocking the entrance, just large enough to allow them to enter. You should be able to do all of this without gloves and without a single sting. *Do not hit at any flying bees, EVER.*

Now leave them alone until the next day, at which time you should gently remove the telescoping cover. If you see plenty of bees around the bottom of the feeder jar and in the remainder of the hole in the inner cover, all is well. Make sure there is still plenty of syrup in the jar; if not, refill it and replace the cover. Check this jar *daily* and never let it run dry. It's a good idea to have an extra feeder cap; that way the exchange of jars is much faster. Use an extra Mason jar.

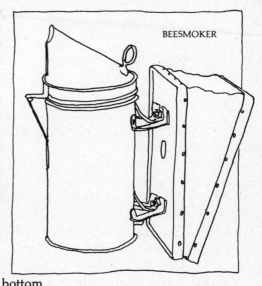

BEESMOKER

Do not open the hive until two days later, then lift out the queen cage. If she is out, throw the cage away and close the hive. (To check the hive, give the bees a puff or two of smoke at the entrance before opening the hive, then another puff or two after the hive is opened. This causes the bees to fill with honey, and they become more docile to work with. Dried pine needles make a good fuel for the smoker, or torn pieces of cardboard box.) If the queen is still in her cage, shove a match or stick through the candy and ream it out so the queen can get out in an hour or so. If the bees are hanging on to the inner cover, shake it and they will fall to the bottom.

Open the hive three days later and the bees should have drawn part of two or three sheets of the foundation wax into a comb and stored a little sugar syrup, and the queen should be laying in the cells. The eggs are small and white but can be seen with average eyesight. After three days of incubation, the egg hatches into a grub and grows rapidly. After your queen starts to lay, you can examine the hive daily, and the beginner should do this, if it is convenient, so as to learn to find the queen and to study the development of the colony.

Continue to feed your bees daily until all of the combs in the brood nest are drawn out and there is a reserve of 25 pounds of honey and syrup. In unfavorable seasons, when the spring remains cool and damp, as much as 40 pounds of sugar may be required. To stop feeding earlier is to endanger your success. Use only granulated sugar in making your syrup. In areas where spring weather is unpredictable, John Tardie suggests feeding your newly hived package of bees from the top instead of through the Boardman feeder at the entrance. If the weather turns cold and remains below 50 degrees F, the bees will not break cluster and go down to the Boardman feeder for food. In fact, they can't go down; therefore, your new bees will die of starvation at the top of the frames around the queen cage, with a full jar of sugar syrup sitting out there in the Boardman feeder. To feed from the top, invert the jar of syrup with the Boardman feeder cap over the hole in the inner cover, place an empty deep super or hive body over the main hive body on top of the inner cover, then top with the telescope cover. You are now feeding inside the hive, and the cluster of bees is only ¼ inch away from the food; they will quickly readjust the cluster and be able to take in food no matter what the weather turns up. A towel or clean rag can be placed around the jar if you don't want the bees to come up into the empty deep super, or you may leave it as it is. You may feed through the Boardman feeder placed at the entrance in approximately three weeks, when you will have to put frames in that super and place it under the inner cover to form the second brood chamber.

The following is not necessary, but John recommends it for giving your new colony an added boost. Before installing your bees, make a candy board out of your inner cover as follows: In a canner put 1 pint of water, bring to a boil, then add 5 pounds of sugar. Heat to 240 degrees F or the soft-ball stage. Remove it from the heat, stir the temperature down to 210 to 215 degrees F, or until the mixture takes on a milky look. Just as it is showing signs of beginning to set, pour it into the deep side of an inner cover and let it set. This recipe can be made in as many multiples as necessary. It takes 4 to 5 pounds of sugar to fill an inner cover. Make sure that your inner covers are on a level surface before pouring sugar candy in. Tape a piece of cardboard or anything suitable to the underside of the cover to block the bee escape hole. After the candy has hardened and cooled, remove the block over the bee escape hole and cut out the candy from the entire bee escape hole. Place the inner cover with the candy side down on the hive body.

Many problems can, of course, develop. John Tardie has supplied me with the following list of potential problems and remedies:

PROBLEM: Bees don't take the syrup. The cluster has formed to one side and not under the feeder jar, and they are too cold and hungry to move.
REMEDY: Remove enough frames from the side opposite the cluster, gently sliding the remaining frames so that the cluster is under the bee escape hole; replace the frames on the other side. If the bees are not moving, sprinkle warm syrup on them. Use the feeder jar as a salt shaker to sprinkle them with.
PROBLEM: The bees appear to be dead but move a little if cupped in your hand and breathed on; they are starving and very cold.
REMEDY: Screen the entrance so that no bees can get out, sprinkle them with warm syrup, and close the hive. Then bring the hive inside where it is warm until you can hear bees inside putting up a good roar; then bring the hive back outside. If the cluster was not in its proper place in the hive, wait until the bees cool down and recluster, then rearrange the frames as in the first problem.

PROBLEM: On opening the hive, you find a large ball of bees on the bottom board or on one of the frames. The queen was released too soon; or she is a nervous, "running" queen, and the bees are "balling" her—they could kill her. Occasionally a queen that is nervous will drop down from the comb foundation where she is laying a new brood in the cells. She might drop to the bottom of the hive or just run from one side to the other. Looking into the hive, the beekeeper will note that the other bees are running around and back and forth. If the beekeeper is not able to spot his queen where he thinks she should be, he is apt to think that he has lost his queen. This usually causes him to buy a new queen needlessly. Careful inspection will usually locate the queen, and if she is left alone she will return to her work in the comb. She is referred to as a "running" queen. Sometimes a queen will become very nervous and start to run around in the hive. The other bees of the colony, thinking that she must be an outsider, quickly form a dense cluster around her. This cluster can be as large as a golf ball. This will suffocate the queen and she will die. This phenomenon is referred to as "balling."

REMEDY: Sprinkle the ball liberally with syrup and break up the ball gently with the hive tool while constantly sprinkling syrup. A few drops of vanilla extract will help to confuse the bees because it obscures the hive scents. Close the hive and do not reopen for a couple of days.

PROBLEM: A large piece of comb is attached to the bottom of the queen cage; the comb has been built somewhere that it shouldn't be; the comb has been built away from the foundation with a bridge or bridges attaching it to the sheet of foundation. These are all things that often happen.

REMEDY: Cut it all out as soon as you see it. The longer you wait, the worse conditions will get. Inspect all frames regularly to make sure that comb building is going on as you want it, straight and solid.

PROBLEM: Queen cells within a few weeks after installing your package.

REMEDY: Look for your queen; if she looks okay and you have several frames of good worker brood in all stages including capped, then you have the problem that often occurs in newly installed packages. An excessive amount of brood for the amount of nurse bees. To allow your colony to superseed needlessly at this point will weaken it. Superseedure instinct is the instinct of a hive of bees to allow a greater number of queen and worker bees to develop than the nurse bees (drones) can feed and care for. Destroy all queen cells and keep an eye out for new ones for the next few weeks. As soon as some of the capped brood emerge, the superseedure instinct will stop.

PROBLEM: The queen cage is empty when removed from the package; the queen was released either because the screen did not completely cover the top of the cage or because the cork fell out.

REMEDY: Install the bees as previously described, then examine the frames very carefully the next day and try to find the queen. Repeat this examination daily until the queen is found or eggs or larvae are seen in the cells. If the queen, eggs, or larvae are not seen in five days, chances are that the queen was killed. Notify your supplier for a replacement.

Supers

Study your beginner's book and give the bees additional room as required. A good queen will require two of the ten frame hive bodies for a brood nest as well as several supers on top of this. Therefore, one super is not enough for any colony of bees. If you wait until the honey is sealed in a super before giving them another super, you have lost one and probably several supers of honey. When the bees have drawn the comb out about halfway on all of the frames and stored honey in them, it is time to raise up the super and place an empty one under it, which should be next to the brood nest. Repeat this process as often as necessary.

Do not remove any honey from the hive until it is completely sealed over, or it may make you sick. However, all honey that is to be sold in the comb should be removed soon after it is sealed over, or it will become travel-stained. Comb honey should be removed from the supers as soon as they are sealed over, or the combs will become stained as the bees walk over them. You can remove a foundation that has been sealed over and replace it with an empty one. This saves adding another super to the hive.

Frames of extracted honey should be removed at the end of the flow season; however, do not mix white clover honey with the darker and heavier fall clover honey if you want to sell it. It's best to remove the sealed foundations of white clover honey at the end of the white clover season. That way it won't mix with the darker, strong-flavored sweet clover and buckwheat honey. If it's just for home consumption, mixing the qualities may not be that important to you.

Unsealed honey is not good to eat. If you must remove foundations that were not sealed, you can ripen the honey by air-drying it at room temperature until the honey thickens, or save these foundations to start your next season with. If the honey is gathered on a cool day in late fall, it's easy to brush away any bees remaining on the foundation.

For those of you starting with packaged bees, there is a rule of thumb to follow for adding to your hive: When the bees cover seven frames of the first brood chamber, it is time to add the second deep brood chamber. Never add a shallow super until the bees are covering at least seven frames of the second deep brood chamber. If the weather favors good production—a wet April, dry May (good building-up period), rainy June (gives the main honey plants, clovers, etc., a good soaking), July and August hot and dry (best honey-producing conditions if plants have had ample moisture)—be prepared to give those bees some room. In ideal conditions, bees can bring in 6, 8, or even 10 pounds of cured honey per day during the main honey flow. That's one full shallow super every three to five days. Under these conditions, you should have at least two or three empty supers on at all times. They need the room to spread out the incoming nectar to evaporate the excess water. If you have 6 to 8 pounds of honey per day, it means that the bees brought in twenty-four to forty pounds of nectar per day.

Varieties of Bees

There are several varieties of bees: Italian bees are fairly even-tempered, good honey producers, hardy, and the ones used most often in our area of the country. Starline bees are an Italian hybrid; they are good-tempered and good honey producers. Caucasian bees are large black bees that are very gentle; they're heavy propolizers (propolis is a brownish resinous material of waxy consistency collected by bees from the buds of trees and used as cement to close openings in their hives) and fairly good producers, but they tend to swarm quite readily. Carniolan bees have a temperament about like that of Italian bees or gentler; they are large gray bees that use very little propolis, are good honey producers, and are winter-hardy. Midnight bees are a Caucasian hybrid, a black bee that is supposed to be very gentle and an average honey producer. Mraz bees are a combination of Italian, Caucasian, and Carniolan; they are dark bees with a sometimes peppery disposition developed by Charles Mraz of Middlebury, Vermont, and used in his one-thousand-plus hives; they're hardy and good honey producers. Contact your local extension service or beekeepers association to find out what variety of bee is best for your area.

A good healthy hive is composed of 30,000 to 40,000 bees. The queen is the only perfect female. Worker bees are imperfect females, and they are the only ones that gather honey. There are many worker bees, but their life-span during

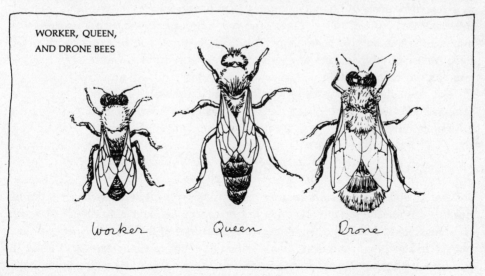

WORKER, QUEEN, AND DRONE BEES

worker   Queen   Drone

the working season is only a few weeks. They literally work themselves to death. In the winter, when all they have to do is move about the hive, they will live for several months. They are constantly being replaced by the 2,000 to 3,000 eggs a day that are being laid all the time during the peak build-up period in the main body of the hive. Worker bees are also the guard bees for the hive. You will see them near the entrance of the hive, and they will gang up on intruder bees near the hive opening. Occasionally you will see 15 or more bees with their backs to the hive opening and their wings spinning. They are sending cool air into the hive on hot days to cool it down. Drones are useless except for mating with the queen on her maiden flight. The drone is a larger bee than the worker bee, his big round head is larger with whiskers, and he has no stinger.

At a certain time each spring the bees will start raising a new queen through a process of special feeding. Queens are raised in long, dark cells like nipples, where they are surrounded by a special fluid called royal jelly. There are usually five or six of them. The first queen that is born will destroy the others before they have a chance to be born. She remains the only true queen. Then she leaves on her maiden flight. A drone flies up with the queen, and in the reproductive act he attaches

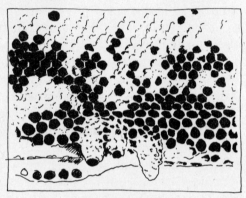

QUEEN CELLS

himself to the queen. She retains his reproductive organs, and the drone dies. She becomes fertile for life. The queen mother stays in the hive body, and when the new queen returns, the new queen starts laying eggs. If the hive should become overcrowded, the old queen leaves with her old bees; this is called swarming. If you want to prevent this from happening, you must pull out the frames and cut off the nipples with the new queens before the new queen has a chance to be born. If you do this, the old mother will continue to produce and will not leave the hive. A queen's life-span is about three years. For greatest success, gentle bees, and a minimum of swarming, requeen your colonies every year, preferably during the fall honey flow.

Swarming

If you would like to start another hive, you should allow the new queen to be born, and when the old queen and her bees swarm, you can use this swarm to set up a new hive. Usually when the bees swarm, they fill themselves with honey enough to last them two to three days. They seldom go farther than 100 yards from the hive if there is a nearby tree with low-hanging branches. From there the worker bees go scouting for a hollowed-out tree or log in which to set up a new hive. This is the time to pick them up. If it's a small branch that you can cut off, first dress in your veil for protection, though at this time the bees are very docile because they are so full of honey. Place your new hive body with its frames on a white sheet on the ground nearby. Shake the bees toward the opening, and soon, as if in one great mass, they will enter the new hive. It's a sight to see, thirty to forty thousand bees all swarming at once. If it's an old hive that has been used before, you will soon see them going in and out cleaning up every bit of old debris from the inside of the hive before they start to fill it up. Place the hive in its permanent location and put the branch on the top of it so that the workers will know where it is until they have become more accustomed to the new hive location. If you can't reach the branch they're on, place a new hive as close as possible to the swarm and try to hose them down. Try to locate the queen and place her in the hive; hopefully the bees will follow into the new hive.

The swarming of bees became quite a topic of conversation recently here in Vermont. First of all, the state had voted to name the honeybee as its state insect. Not long after that, a swarm of bees attached themselves to the State House in our capital, Montpelier. A bee expert was called in to solve the problem, and he made several attempts to hive the bees before he successfully got them relocated. Our poor governor and legislators suffered many a pun about the state's official new insect paying a call on the legislative members to thank them.

New hives of bees should be started in the spring after it has warmed up in your area to temperatures that remain above freezing, with daytime temperatures of at least 50 degrees F but before the blossoms appear on the trees and plants. Up here in Vermont, that's usually sometime between the last week in April and the first week in May. In 1978 it was so cold in the East and Northeast that bees were shipped from the South much later than usual.

Winterizing Your Hive

Once you have established your hive of bees and have gotten through your first summer of beekeeping, you must give thought to protecting your hive through the winter. Unless you had a very productive hive, you will not be able to harvest any honey for yourself that first year. All that is gathered is left in the hive to feed the bees through the winter. A hive should weigh at least 120 pounds including honey when it is ready for winter. This includes the weight of the hive body. If there isn't enough honey left in the hive or if the spring is exceptionally long and cold, the hive will have to be fed in the spring until the flow is good again.

My uncle thinks that the best way to winter over your hive is to put a box or plastic bag around it, fill it with leaves, adding a layer to the top, then tie the plastic down in place, leaving only a 3-inch opening in the bottom for air. Make sure that this hole remains open. Worker bees take the dead bees out during the winter, and sometimes in doing so, they plug the hole and the bees in the hive suffocate and die. Another method is to wrap the hive in black tarpaper. One winter my uncle tried moving his hives into an old chicken coop, and he lost several hives that winter. He thinks that the closed building held too much moisture. Unwrap the hives early in the spring as soon as the weather warms up and start feeding them. If you live in a moderate climate where temperatures do not fall below 50 degrees F, the only precaution you will need to take is to make sure that there is sufficient honey to feed the brood throughout the winter when bees become dormant. There should be a minimum of 45 pounds in the upper brood chamber and half that much in the lower brood nest. Check periodically and feed through the feeder jar if necessary.

A word of caution about overwintered colonies: If we have a nice warm May, then a rainy June (good colony buildup, after which the bees are forced to be inside), these are the prime swarm buildup conditions. Watch your overwintered colonies closely if this weather sequence occurs. Swarming will be excessively heavy just as the weather turns warm and clear again unless swarm-prevention methods are followed very closely. You may even want to split the colonies in early May to prevent this.

Don't be fooled into thinking that you can stop feeding your overwintered colonies when you see bees flying in the spring. Most of the time they are only bringing in pollen, and bees cannot live on pollen alone. If your bees are short of food at this time, don't stop feeding until dandelions are in bloom.

Pollen

Pollen, which is gathered from the flowers at the same time as nectar, is mixed with honey to make what is known as bee bread. This is used as food for the developing larvae (brood) and is important to the healthy growth of the hive.

Diseases

NOSEMA DISEASE. This is a very detrimental disease that is often overlooked or goes unnoticed because there is nothing you can visibly see in the hive unless it is a severe case. Canadian bee inspectors have found so much of it that they treat all colonies as if they were infected. Though not as common in small home apiaries, it can be detected by taking five or six live bees from the landing board of each hive in the spring, or anytime for that matter. Squeeze their heads to kill them, put them in an envelope, and number each envelope with the hive number. Send these to the U.S. Department of Agriculture, Entomology Research Division, Beltsville,

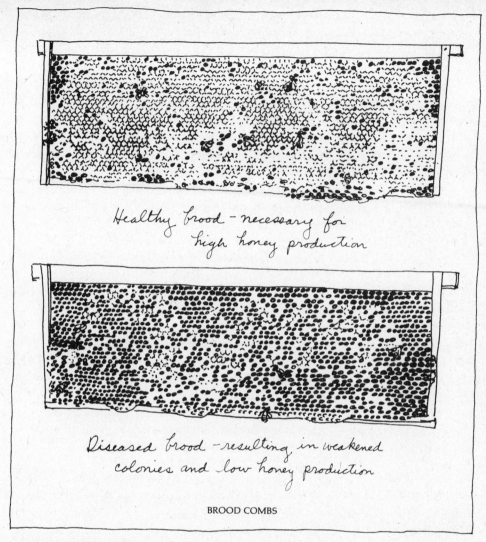

Healthy brood — necessary for
high honey production

Diseased brood — resulting in weakened
colonies and low honey production

BROOD COMBS

Maryland 20705, and ask them to check the enclosed bees for nosema disease. You will have your answer in a week or less. (Make sure to include your return address.) The cure for nosema is feeding Fumidil-B at a rate of 2 gallons of sugar syrup with Fumidil-B per colony once each year.

FOULBROOD. This is a topic that is getting to be controversial. John Tardie has his own thoughts about it, and this is how he explained it to me: Foulbrood is a spore disease and can be harbored in some hives for long periods of time, even years, without any physical signs because the spore count is too low to kill larvae. When these hives are subjected to stress conditions (confinement due to long adverse weather conditions, scarcity of food, etc.), the spore count will increase to a point that will kill larvae. At this point you have physical evidence of foulbrood.

Other colonies have a very low resistance to foulbrood, and when they are subjected to the spores, they become highly infected, and the colony must either be burned to destroy the disease or treated. Both Terramycin and Sulfathiazole have been used for years but these drugs do not attack the spores, which are immune to the effect of medication. The drugs will kill the bacteria when they enter the vegetative stage, but the spores could lie next to drugs for many years without being affected. At this time, Terramycin is the only chemical allowed for use in controlling bacterial diseases of honeybees. Contact Dr. H. Shimanuki at the Bioenvironmental Bee Laboratory, Plant Protection Institute, USDA, Beltsville, Maryland 20705, if you have any question about disease treatment.

The best way to combat honeybee diseases is to prevent the diseases from occurring in the first place. The following methods will help keep the colonies dry and less susceptible to disease.

• Elevate each hive off the ground by using bricks or other types of support. This will let air circulate underneath and keep the bottom board off the moist ground.

• The entrance to the hive should face south or southeast, and the sun should not be blocked from hitting the hive entrance. Bees start to work earlier and harder if they get the morning sun.

• Tilt the hives slightly forward so that moisture inside will run out along the bottom board to the entrance.

• Do not place hives in wet areas. They should be put in locations where the air will drain downhill away from bee colonies.

If your state bee inspector finds severe cases of diseases in your hives, consider requeening the colony. This gives the bees a more prolific queen and allows for a time lag in brood rearing for the bees remaining in the hives to clean out the disease.

Honey and Beeswax

Strained liquid honey is obtained by taking a heated uncapping knife and sliding it over the top of the sealed combs. This uncaps them; then they are slid into the honey extractor, and the honey is spun out. The extracted combs are placed back in the supers and reused again year after year, replacing only those that are damaged as needed.

If you're lucky, you live in an area such as ours that has a public canning center. We can go there and have our honey extracted for a few pennies per pound, and we don't have to buy a honey extractor. For beginners who cannot afford an extractor or do not have access to one, the simplest way to extract honey from the comb is to mash chunks of comb honey in a double boiler. Place the top part of the double boiler over boiling water and heat the honey to 143 to 145 degrees F; at this

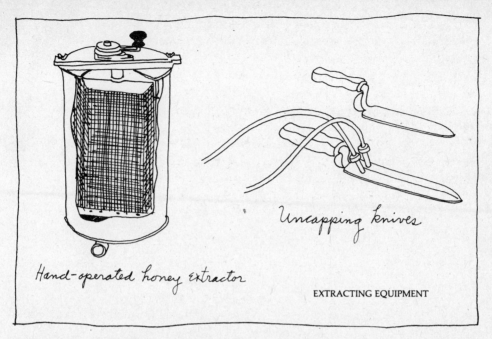

Hand-operated honey Extractor

Uncapping knives

EXTRACTING EQUIPMENT

point the wax will melt. Quickly set the pan containing the honey in cold water to cool. The wax can then be lifted out.

Honey can be stored in moderately warm rooms or storage areas so long as they are dry (possibly a spare room or a closet) for any length of time. In fact, some was found in Egyptian tombs when they were opened after thousands of years, and it was still good. Montgomery Ward carries a complete line of beekeeping equipment and honey extractors, as does John Tardie. You can write him for his price list at 79 Center Road, Essex Junction, Vermont 05452, or call him at (802) 878-4500. You might also ask to be placed on his newsletter mailing list. I know of no one better informed or with a better supply of the newest in beekeeping supplies. (To keep up-to-date, you should take a good bee magazine and learn how other beekeepers are overcoming some of their problems and of the new methods and equipment that they are using.)

Capping wax is said to have certain medicinal properties, and it's the wax most often used for making the finest candles. Unless the queen excluder is put in place above the brood hives, the wax in the supers will sometimes be quite stained. (A queen excluder is a thin sheet of perforated metal that has openings in it large enough to allow worker bees to go up into the supers and fill them, but that is at the same time too small for the queen to gain access to these supers and lay eggs in the drawn cells.) Clean, rendered beeswax brings a good price. A good way to save a lot of beeswax that is otherwise thrown away is to carry a little pail with you about half filled with water when opening any hive. As you scrape away burr comb or bridge comb, or any out-of-place beeswax from the hive, rather than just throwing it away on the ground where it can cause robbing or spread disease, put it in your pail. Burr comb is comb built in out-of-the-way places, such as between supers. It is also referred to as bridge comb when it is built between foundation frames. The water will dilute any honey present, therefore eliminating any robbing, and it also cleans your wax.

As my Uncle Chic would say, "Raising bees is a honey of a hobby."

6 RAISING GOATS

Goats are the most winning little animals you could ever hope to own. They each have a special personality of their own, and they should have a place on every small homestead. Today, as I'm writing this, our four youngsters have made a little carrying pack for Jebediah, our little six-month-old wether. (A wether is a male goat that has been altered.) They are going on a picnic in the woods, and Jeb is going along to carry their lunch and play with them. We own many small animals, but the children have made our goats their special playmates. Even without all the practical reasons for raising goats on small acreage, we would have them around just because they're so much fun.

Now for the practical reasons: Goats have all the advantages of dairy cows and more. They require simple housing, little or no pasture, and only about one-half as much feed or less. They are freer of disease than our bovine friends, yet they produce enough milk for the average family. An average of 3 to 5 quarts of milk daily for ten months of the year is what you will get from a good grade doe. Two good grade does would be about right for a family of four. This would provide you with 6 to 10 quarts of milk a day, the higher amount right after freshening (giving birth to her young) and the smaller amount as it decreases in a few months. This amount would provide milk for drinking plus enough left over to make butter, cheese, yogurt, and ice cream. You can give any extra that you don't use to the other animals. This milk is more digestible than cow's milk because the fat particles in goat's milk are very tiny and are therefore more easily digested than the large fat globules in cow's milk. Furthermore, goat's milk is naturally homogenized. Otherwise, goat's milk is the same as cow's milk in composition. Now add all this to the fact that a good grade doe can be purchased for as little as one-fifth the cost of a good milk cow and you've got yourself a first-class bargain. More people drink goat's milk throughout the world than cow's milk, especially in European nations.

Furthermore, it would be economically impracticable to attempt to raise a dairy cow on a small homestead. Each cow requires 2 acres of good pasture, 2 tons of dairy-quality hay per year, and 2 to 3 tons of grain per year. Unless you have the pasture and the ability to produce your own hay, owning a cow would be just too costly. You might get some static from people who claim that as a dairy animal goats aren't worthwhile. These people are thinking of a money-making proposition, and I agree that you do not get the volume of milk that you get from a cow. On the other hand, you're not out to make money, and the amount of milk you will get from your goats will be plenty for your family.

Other people will tell you that goats stink. This isn't really true either. Female goats (does) do not have any odor and are very clean little animals. Male goats (bucks) kept for breeding do have an offensive odor during the breeding season, from late August till late January; this is how they attract the does. Much of the odor can be eliminated by keeping their quarters clean and cutting their beards. Our vet has told us that there is a small node on the head that can be cauterized when the buck is a baby kid, at the same time that he is dehorned, but there will still be a slight odor during the mating season. We have never had this done because we do not keep a buck.

You will surely hear remarks to the effect that goats will eat anything, such as clothes, tin cans, and so forth. This is not true either. They do prefer leaves, twigs, bark, and weeds to good grains and hay, but they will not eat anything dirty, nor will they eat food that has been in the pen on the floor if the floor is wet and dirty. The can-eating story comes from the fact that they will eat the paper labels off cans. After all, this is a wood product, and wood is one of their favorite foods.

Goat's milk is very rich and sweet. It will taste bad only if you allow your doe to run loose where there are some strong-tasting weeds. This is usually a danger only during the summer months, and when it occurs, if you take care to get rid of the offensive growths in your small pasture, you shouldn't have any more problems.

Buying goats is a far easier task than it was even ten years ago. The goat population in this country is steadily rising because of the increase in the number of people who want to become self-sufficient. If you do not know of any goat breeders in your area, I would advise you to contact your state extension service. The dairy divisions of these extension services are beginning to carry information on the dairy goat population in their respective states. I do recommend two does for the small homestead. Goats, like other animals, do best in pairs. They are much happier this way, and a happy goat produces more milk. This will also give you a constant supply of milk.

Housing

Housing for your goats should be ready before you bring your goats home. If you have a barn, stalls, or pens that are each 4 feet square, this will be more than

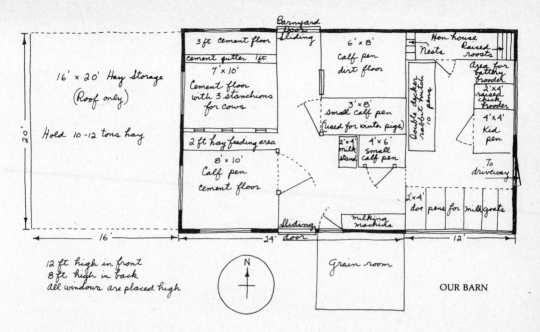

16' x 20' Hay Storage
(Roof only)

Hold 10-12 tons hay

20'

16'

Barnyard
Door
Sliding

3 ft cement floor
cement gutter 1 ft
7' x 10'
Cement floor
with 3 stanchions
for cows

2 ft hay feeding area

8' x 10'
Calf pen
cement floor

6' x 8'
Calf pen
dirt floor

3' x 8'
small calf pen
(used for winter pigs)

2' x 4'
milk
stand

4' x 6'
small
calf pen

Hen house
Nests

Raised
roosts

Area for
battery
brooder

2' x 4'
raised
chick
brooder

4' x 4'
Kid
pen

Double decker
rabbit hutch

10 pens

To
driveway

2' x 4' doe pens for milk goats

12'

24'

Sliding
door

milking
machine

Grain room

N

12 ft high in front
8 ft high in back
All windows are placed high

OUR BARN

adequate. Actually, our new pens are each only 2 feet wide and 4 feet long, with a larger pen for kidding (the does' giving birth to their young) and another large one for the kids (goat offspring) after we take them away from their mothers. If you do not have a barn, a small shed should be constructed. It doesn't have to be fancy, but it should be free from drafts. A building that is 10 by 12 feet and only 8 feet high would give you enough room. This would give you space for two stalls, 2 by 4 each, for your milk goats plus one 4-by-6-foot kidding pen. The baby kids could be left in this pen after they are born. Along the wall outside the kidding pen you could place your milking stand, with one corner about 4 by 6 feet for hay storage, which is more than enough for ½ ton of hay, plus 2 barrels of grain. This amount of feed will last two goats approximately three months.

A pole barn is the least expensive type of structure to build and is more than adequate. Walls and roof are built of plywood and rolled roofing. It doesn't have a poured-concrete floor. The posts that support it do not have to be fancy so long as they are good and straight. They can be made of hemlock or cedar trees that are about 6 inches or more thick and should be set down into the ground about 3 or 4 feet.

We have tried both cement- and dirt-floor stalls, and we prefer the dirt floors, especially in our cold northern climate. During the winter an unheated barn freezes. The cold does not harm your goats, but lying on a wet, frozen floor can make them sick. We use dirt-floor pens with a few inches of fine crushed stone covering the dirt and bedding covering the stone. The urine runs down through

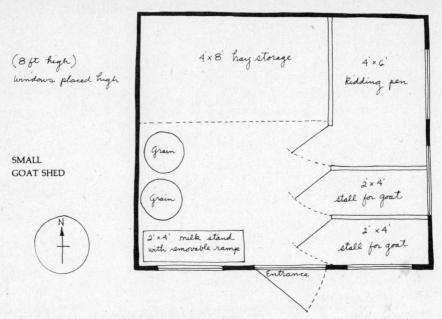

(8 ft high)
windows placed high

SMALL
GOAT SHED

N

4 x 8' hay storage

4' x 6'
kidding pen

Grain

Grain

2' x 4'
stall for goat

2' x 4'
stall for goat

2' x 4' milk stand
with removable ramp

Entrance

the bedding and stone and into the dirt, keeping the goats dryer and warmer in the winter and cooler in the summer. In the winter the bedding should be allowed to build up for warmth, so make sure that the walls of your stalls are high enough. The floor can actually get to be 2 feet higher in cold weather.

In very cold climates it is a very good idea to insulate at least the ceiling of your barn. Make sure, though, that the ceiling is high enough so that the goats can't stretch up and eat it. Goats can stretch their necks up quite high. A ceiling 8 feet high is just high enough to prevent problems while at the same time being low enough to retain heat. If you decide you can afford to insulate the side walls too, be sure to cover the insulation with heavy plywood or slabwood. Goats love to nibble at wood, and they will soon demolish anything lightweight. Planning your barn so that you can stack your hay against the north and west inner walls in the winter also helps to give added protection against the coldest northwest winds.

Bedding for the pens can be made of almost anything. Hay is expensive, and straw is beginning to climb. We find sawdust to be the most economical, at just a few dollars a truckload if you haul it yourself. Depending on your location, you could also use peanut hulls or crushed corncobs. Whatever you use, pile it neatly near the barn and cover it with black plastic to keep it fairly dry. If you are going to use goat manure in the garden, sawdust has the advantage of not having weed seeds in it. It tills in well and is especially good material for loosening heavy clay soil.

We also find that a small hay manger made of slabwood over the top of the stalls saves a great deal of hay. Goats are picky eaters and will waste most of their hay if it is placed on the floor. They will pick out what they like best and trample the rest. Whatever they leave uneaten in the manger we give to the rabbits, so nothing is wasted. Eating off the floor can also cause worms, the one disease to which goats seem prone.

The next thing you will need is a milking stand. It's not absolutely necessary, but your little milk goats are so short that even the few minutes it takes to milk them can be backbreaking. Ours is made of 2-by-4's and ¼-inch lumber and is simply constructed.

It is not necessary to put goats out to pasture, and on the very small homestead of just one or two acres, you might not have the room. Goats should, however, have a small exercise yard outside their barn. A *well-fenced* area the width of the barn, say 12 feet wide by about 20 feet long, would be enough. Whether you intend to fence them in or pasture them, remember that goats need good fencing.

MILKING STAND

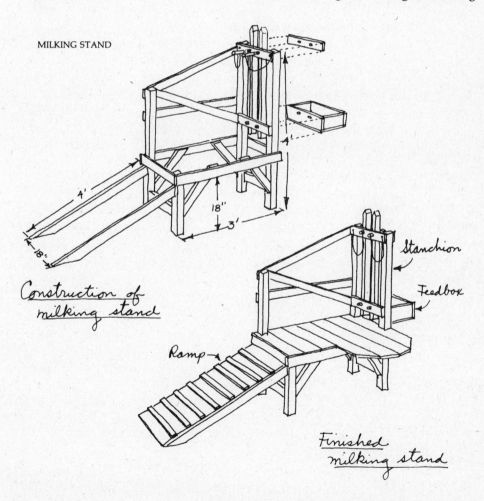

Construction of milking stand

Stanchion

Feedbox

Ramp→

Finished milking stand

They love to jump and they can jump high. All it would take is one afternoon of two goats loose in your garden to make you realize that the time and money you spend on good fences is well worthwhile. If you are using barbed-wire fencing, your fence should be at least 4 feet high, with several strands of barbed wire placed horizontally about 8 inches apart.

We have been successful in keeping our older goats fairly well corraled (they still jump out occasionally) by using three strands of electric wire. The electric wire with small barbs works best. To be successful with electric fencing, you must train your goats to understand what it is. The best way to do this is to put them out in the pasture the first day and wet the ground along the fence. Then offer them grain outside the fence. As they push against the fence to reach the grain, the combination of the wet ground and the electric current gives them a good shock. After that they stay in pretty well. This is not effective for baby goats. They need wide-mesh fencing, otherwise they will be out all the time. We don't bother to put them out to pasture; we keep them in a fenced exercise area.

The one thing that will make a goat jump or run through any fence is a thunderstorm. Goats are skittish little animals and they are terrified of storms. Take care to put them in their pens when you know one is brewing, especially if you are going to be away from the homestead. If your pasture has no trees for shade, you should build them a little three-sided building with a roof to protect them from heat and rain. Build it with the protected side on the south, because in the spring and summer months the winds usually come from the south or east during storms.

Feeding

You must also consider how you are going to water your goats. They should have access to water at all times. In the winter their water should be warmed at least a couple times a day. Goats are just as fussy about clean water as they are about clean food, and they will not drink water that is dirty or that has droppings in it. The ideal, of course, is an automatic watering system, such as dairy barns have. That is quite expensive, though, and not usually practicable for the small homestead. We find that tall, straight-sided buckets work best. When you fill them, they are heavy enough not to be tipped easily and they are tall enough so that they are not as apt to catch droppings. In the pasture we use an old oil drum cut in half and burned out. We use a garden hose to fill it.

In addition to water, you must provide a salt block for goats. We use mineralized blocks to make sure our goats are getting the proper nutrients. Salt also increases the quantity of water a goat will drink, and they require a large amount of water in order to be good milk producers.

I think you should have your feed on hand before you bring your goats home. The more prepared you are, the less confusion there will be getting started. For each pound of milk your goat produces (a pound of milk is equal to 1 pint), your milking goat will require about ½ pound of grain. So if she is giving about 1 gallon of milk a day, or 8 pounds, she will require about 4 pounds of grain. When your goat is dry, 1 pound of grain a day is all she will need. This is plenty for kids too. Most feed dealers now carry grain especially for goats, but if your area feed dealer is not sure what you should have, tell him that you need a coarse ration, preferably one coated with molasses, that contains about 16 percent protein. Little kids do well on calf starter. Dry milk goats do very well on 14-percent protein rations, but try to get the coarse ration for them.

A homesteader can supplement commercial grain rations by raising extra vegetables for the animals, such as carrots, beets, potatoes, kale, and comfrey. About 4 pounds of these vegetables equal 1 pound of grain. The carrots, beets, and potatoes are high in carbohydrates, and the kale and comfrey are good sources of extra protein. A word of caution, though. Cut the vegetables up into small pieces and, as with all food, feed it clean. When feeding vegetables, always feed after milking, because strong tastes and colors can change the taste and color of the milk. No matter how good a pasture area you have, goats need some hay daily. Grass only turns to water in their stomach and causes bloat. Unlike cows they do not derive adequate nutrition from grass. Be very careful that your pasture or dry hay does not have any poisonous weeds in it. Milkweed, wild cherry, locoweed, or whatever poisonous weeds are common to your area must be removed; they are toxic to both cows and goats.

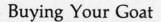

DAIRY GOAT FEED NEEDS FOR ONE YEAR

You will need for each goat: ½ ton, or about 25 large bales, of good hay (plan on more if you are without pasture, at least twice as much), two mineralized salt blocks, and ½ ton (1,000 pounds) of grain and forage crops. If you want to pasture your goats, each will require slightly less than ½ acre of land. (Again, let me say that this is not necessary.)

Buying Your Goat

There are several breeds of goats available in the United States: Saanen, Nubian, French Alpine, Swiss Alpine, and Toggenburg. Two breeds beginning to gain more popularity are the La Mancha and the Black British Toggenburg. Purebreds will cost more, but a good grade doe (three-quarters purebred and one-quarter of another breed) is also an excellent second choice. We prefer good grade does to purebreds for the simple reason that they are not as nervous and highstrung. We feel that the more placid an animal is, the better her production.

Saanens are the highest milk producers in the dairy goat field, though their butterfat content isn't the highest. Our Saanen gives us 6 quarts (12 pounds) per day after freshening. Within a month she is down to about eight pounds and maintains that amount of production for quite a while, usually dropping down gradually about four months from freshening until she dries off in about eight and one-half to nine months. A goat's highest production period is in the first two months after she kids again. Saanens are pure-white goats.

Nubians are strange-looking goats. They have long, droopy ears like those of a beagle hound and a blunt nose that is often said to look like a Roman nose. They can be any color. Their milk production is low, but their butterfat content is very high.

Alpines, both Swiss and French, are many colors, though the French is the most common, and they do have some markings. All of this breed that I have seen are only part Alpine, and they seem to carry the markings of whatever other breed their genes carry. We have two French Alpine Toggenburg goats, and the Toggenburg markings are the most predominant.

Toggenburgs are a smaller breed than either Saanen or Nubian, but they are very good milk producers. Ours have been giving us an average of 8 pounds of milk daily. They are usually colors of brown with white markings on their faces and backsides. They so much resemble deer that we keep ours in the barn during deer-hunting season.

La Manchas are never purebred, but they are at least seven-eighths pure. They are very odd to look at because they have no ears. They are known for their gentleness, and they are excellent milk producers, with a very high butterfat content to their milk.

Black British Toggenburgs are new in our area, and there are not enough production figures available yet for me to comment. However, a local breeder is converting his entire herd to this breed and is very happy with them. I'm quite taken with the looks of this breed; they are very beautiful little animals.

All goats, male or female, may have horns, beards, and wattles, but there are naturally polled (hornless) goats in each breed. The Toggenburgs are most apt to have wattles, which are nothing more than a decoration. They serve no special function.

You should know what to look for in a good milk goat whether it be purebred or grade. Goats are easiest to obtain in the spring, when kidding multiplies most herds beyond their owners' capacity to house them. Prices vary, so ask around and get a good idea of price range before you buy. Buying from a breeder with a good reputation is your best bet. A good rule of thumb to follow is that a good grade goat should cost no more than one-fifth the price of a good grade cow. Purebreds follow the same rule.

The younger the goat, the less she should cost, because it is going to cost you more to raise her until she is old enough to kid and begin paying her own keep. If you want to get into production quickly, without waiting approximately thirteen to fifteen months, try to buy a bred doe late in the fall or early winter. There is a good solid reason for buying shortly after a doe is bred. It gives the new owner time to make friends with the new goat and to help her through her first kidding. She will repay you for your friendship with good production. One of our Saanens was given to us just after she kidded and her kids had just been taken away from her. She was almost impossible to milk. She would kick and jump around so much that the milk pail was forever being spilled. To make matters worse, she held back on her milk. This poor animal was just terrified of us; we were complete strangers to her, and she had had too many changes in too short a time. It took almost a month to win her over.

Look for a goat with a good barrel. This means one that has plenty of room in the stomach area and between the rib cage. She needs room to carry her kids, and having a good barrel means that she can eat more food and digest it well, which is important to good milk production. She should have well-spaced hipbones and straight legs. Look at her feet. If her toenails are long and have turned under, she has not been well cared for, and her feet will surely hurt her. This will keep her from browsing and will cut down on milk production. If she's healthy, she will have a nice coat and bright eyes.

Treat your animals with kindness; they will respond. Goats love treats of pine needles, apple tree twigs, pieces of clean fruit, and berries. It's a good way to get to know your new animals and to win their confidence in you. If the goat is still a kid, be sure not to overfeed her; it could kill her.

When to Breed

There is much controversy over the age at which to breed your does. When we bought our first pair of twins, they were eight months old. We intended to breed them at eighteen months. As it turned out, somehow the former owner's buck had gotten loose, so they were both already bred. Each was a healthy little doe, so we watched them carefully and stayed with them when they kidded. They made wonderful little mothers, each producing a healthy kid with no difficulty. Further reading on this matter convinced us that young healthy does can be bred at about eight to ten months. They will seem small, but they will continue to grow as they carry their kids and will be large enough by the time the kids are born.

Goats cannot be bred year-round like dairy cows. They come into heat sometime late in August and, if not bred, will continue to come into heat again every twenty-one days until late January. A doe stays in heat for a period of from a few hours to three or four days, though that long a time is unusual. Young goats can breed as early as four months, so if you have young kids of both sexes and unaltered males in the group, be sure to separate them by this time.

If you don't have a buck on hand, it's very important to learn how to recognize a doe in heat. It takes careful watching for the beginner. Make sure that you have your source of either buck or artificial insemination lined up ahead of time. (The nice thing about goats is that a goat in motion will not make a mess in your car; just be sure to get her out quickly when you stop.) There are several things to watch for. A goat in heat will become talkative. By that I mean that she will blat at you all day. She will pace around, not being able to lie still any length of time. If you check, you will be able to note a slight mucous discharge from the vulva. She sometimes refuses her feed. If she is already milking, having freshened in the spring, her milk production will take a sudden drop. Occasionally one goat will ride another the way cows do. In this case, it is the goat being ridden that is in heat. Many breeders will allow you to rent a buck for a month or so for a very small fee. Others will board your doe for you, though this method is usually more costly. This fee is generally based on whether your goat is dry or milking. Milking does require more grain and care.

Once you have attempted to have your doe bred, watch her closely throughout the next heat period. If she shows no symptoms, you can assume that she has been bred. Within a couple of months a doe that has been bred for the first time will begin developing a little bag, and it is easy to tell that she has been bred. A doe that has freshened before is not as easy to be certain of. The average length of time for gestation is 155 days. If your doe is dry, feed her a minimum of 1 pound of grain a day, but don't go over 2 pounds. A fat doe has a more difficult time having her kids than a lean, healthy one. If your doe is already milking, she will usually dry herself off by her third month, but if she hasn't, you must do it. She needs all her strength to go toward the proper development of her young.

Drying your goat off is very simple. Our method is to take all grain away from her for one week. At the same time milk her only once a day. After that week, return a small amount of grain to her diet, about ½ pound twice a day, and milk her every other day. The third week, continue the same grain ration and don't milk her at all unless you can see that she is uncomfortable. This latter will be very unusual, but it occasionally happens in a high-producing doe. Just milk out enough to relieve her discomfort. When she is dry, continue with the twice-daily grain ration until she is ready to kid. A week before she is due, you can raise her grain ration slightly to about 1 pound twice a day. We also give our does a small dose of cider vinegar this last week, about 1 tablespoonful twice a day, to prevent mastitis when she freshens.

Keep your goat well groomed, paying special attention to her toenails. If you check them often, they will be easier to control. We use pruning shears to clip their nails. It's easier to do if you put her in the milking stand, then stand behind the leg. Bend it up toward you at the knee and hold the hoof firmly so that you won't slip and injure her. This is also a good time to get out any burs or stones lodged in her hooves. Just before it is time for her to kid, you should clip the long hairs on her udder; also watch for engorgement. Occasionally a doe will fill up so fast just prior to kidding that you will need to milk her out enough to relieve her until she has her kids.

Kidding

The arrival of our kids is always exciting. We make it a rule to be on hand to help our does when they kid. About a week before a doe is due, we assemble some old clean towels, a pair of scissors that has been boiled (to cut the cord if necessary), a bottle of iodine with which to paint the cut cord, and some strong twine with which to tie the cord off. We make sure that her pen is clean and that fresh bedding is put in daily. Usually your doe can deliver her young without any help, but there are times, especially when she is having more than one kid, that she might run into trouble. Some problems you can learn to handle yourself; others require a veterinarian. The first time your doe kids, you should call a vet if you suspect that there may be a problem. Watch him carefully so that you will know what to do in the future.

Signs that your doe is ready to kid will be a sudden refusal to eat, a pacing around in her pen, a continuous bleating, and heavy mucous discharge. Even if it means losing a night's sleep, be sure to stay with your doe. When she is ready to kid, she will usually cry quite pitifully. This is normal; do not make any effort to help her other than to talk gently to her and soothe her. If she goes several hours and is obviously in a great deal of pain, check to see if you can tell if the kid is in a normal position. The kid should come with its front feet first, followed by its head. If you can tell that the kid is not in this position, wash your hands well, preferably with an antibacterial type of solution, and carefully work them into the uterus; then feel for the position of the kid and carefully and slowly turn it around to the proper position.

Often when having more than one kid—and two or more is not unusual—your doe will tire after delivering the first kid. It is a kindness if you help in easing the second or more out. Be sure not to pull, because you might rip the afterbirth, causing hemorrhaging. She will usually break the cord herself by cutting it with her teeth, but if she doesn't, wait until the bleeding stops and tie it off with twine in two places, about 2 inches apart, and 6 inches from the kid's navel. Then cut between the two sections that are tied off. Wipe the mucus from the kid's mouth and nose so that it can breathe, and paint the cut end of the cord with iodine. As soon as you can see that all is going well, clean only the messy area of the pen and put fresh bedding over it. If the kid hasn't found its mother's teats yet, show it how. It's very important that it nurse immediately. Nursing helps to contract the mother's uterus quickly and prevents excessive bleeding, and the rich colostrum of her first milk is full of antibodies that the little one needs in its first weeks of life to fight off infections.

After your doe has kidded, you should give her a bowl of warm water mixed with a bran cereal. This is a special treat, and it will help to prevent her from becoming constipated after kidding. It will usually take your doe about twelve to twenty-four hours to clean out well. During this time you will note that large pieces of bloody tissue, some even forming sacks, will hang from her vagina for a few hours. This is normal and nothing to be concerned about. I wish someone had warned me of this; I panicked the first time I saw it. But if there is heavy bleeding of bright red blood, there is something wrong, and you must call a vet immediately.

Kids

Kids are the most delightful little creatures ever born on the homestead. They are the only animals born with all their teeth and with their eyes open. They are bouncing around within an hour of their birth. The doe usually takes very good care of her kid from the moment it is born, but as with all things on this earth, there is an occasional exception to the rule. Once in a great while you'll find a doe who has delivered more than one kid rejecting the smaller or weaker one. She won't even bother to clean it off. You'll have to be prepared for this emergency with towels and a blanket. As soon as you can see that in spite of your efforts to get it to nurse, this little kid is being rejected, take a towel and dry it off, roughing up its fur as the mother would with her tongue to stimulate circulation of its blood. Wipe the mucus out of its nose and mouth and try again to get it to nurse.

If the mother will still not nurse the kid, wrap it up well in the blanket and bring it to the house. Put it in a box in a warm place and go back and milk out of the doe enough colostrum to protect the kid from infection. It needs this colostrum even more than its brother or sister, because its resistance to infection is lower. Put the milk in a baby bottle, and with the kid on your lap, try to teach it to drink from the bottle. (Milk should always be fed warm.) Usually this is very easy because natural instinct will teach it to suck right away. If you should have a kid that is terribly weak (that is, it can't hold its head up or stand), it may be too weak to nurse. In that case, take a plastic syringe without a needle and force-feed the kid by squirting a few drops at a time onto the back of its tongue. Feed the kid 1 ounce each hour in this way until it is strong enough to nurse. We thought for sure that we would lose one little doe kid last spring. She was so weak, but we all took turns feeding her and keeping her warm, and in twenty-four hours she was managing to hold her head up and walk with a wobbling gait. This little doe proved to be one of our fastest gainers after she got going, so it was worth the effort.

Another occasion that might warrant bringing a kid into the house would be if a particularly tiny kid were born in the late winter when it is still very cold in the barn. It's natural for a kid to shiver for a little while after it's born; this helps it to get its blood circulating. But if you notice that after several hours it is huddled in a corner shivering and is making no attempt to nurse, it would be wise to bring it to the house for a couple of days until it is stronger. Put it in a box lined with plastic and newspaper. Change the papers frequently, because little kids wet a lot. After a couple of days in a box, a frisky little kid will figure out how to jump out, and then the situation can get somewhat hairy. Try to get it back into the barn as soon as it seems reasonable to do so. It doesn't make sense, though, to take a tiny kid from the warm house and put it into the barn on a bitterly cold day, so try to make the change on a day that is as warm and sunny as possible for that time of the season. After returning the kid to the barn, keep an eye on it for several hours to make sure it doesn't develop a chill. If it remains cold, you could try to take it up to the barn in midday for an hour or so a couple days in a row to give it a chance to adapt to the colder temperatures.

There is controversy about when to take kids away from their mother. Some breeders say immediately because that way it's easier to teach them to drink from a bottle. Others say three days, after they have had all their colostrum. Still others will leave the kids with their mother for months. When you are keeping goats because you want the milk, it isn't practical to let them nurse for a long time. We have tried the first two ways and have settled on a method of our own. We let kids nurse for seven days. Our experience has taught us that this gives them a great start; it is healthier for the mother's reproductive system; and their constant demand affords us a greater milk supply when we do take them away. As for having trouble getting them to drink from a bottle, you don't have to worry about it. After a day or two they will be wolfing it down in a matter of seconds.

To teach them to drink from a bottle, you must warm their milk to your body temperature. Then, holding them securely on your lap, slip your finger into the side of their mouth between their teeth. Follow immediately with the bottle. If they don't start sucking right away, move the bottle in and out slowly a few times as you work the nipple over to the front of their mouth to give them the idea. I must admit that the first few times both of you will most probably get pretty wet, so protect your clothes if you need to. After a couple of sessions they'll go right to it. Kids should have whole milk for the first month; skim milk or milk replacer is fine after that. Start with 6 ounces four times a day the first week, then 8 to 10 ½ ounces three times a day the second and third weeks, and by the fourth week you can feed them 16 ounces twice a day followed by as much warm water as they will drink. They can be started on a little grain within the first week; we use calf starter. Never overfeed; it will cause them to be sick or have scours. When they are three months old, we stop giving milk unless we plan to butcher them. In this instance, we go on giving milk until it's time to slaughter them.

Hay should be freely fed from as early as they will take it, but it should be fed in a manger. Little kids wet a lot and waste most of their hay, but that isn't the only reason to feed from a manger. Reaching up for their food is a more natural way for goats to eat, and their feed is digested better. This is also the reason why it's best to give milk out of a bottle instead of a pail at first. Kids tend to gulp their milk from a pail so fast that they develop digestive problems. If you want all the milk for your family, after the first month you can switch to reconstituted skim milk or calf-milk replacer.

At one month you can switch from feeding from a bottle to feeding from a pail if you want to, but it isn't necessary; they will learn to drink their water out of a pail just the same. To switch to a pail of milk requires a little effort. The easiest way to do it is to take the nipple from the bottle and hold it over the pail. As the kid lowers his head for the nipple, slowly slide the nipple down into the milk. After a day or two he will get the idea of drinking with his head down, and you can put the nipple away.

Goats with horns can injure other goats by butting them in the udder. So kids should be dehorned when they are less than a week old, before the horns have a chance to start growing. There are two ways to do this. There is what is known as a debudding iron; and there is a caustic paste, which we use. Both can be purchased at farm supply stores. The debudding iron is easy to use. It is heated for a few minutes, then held against the horn buds for a few seconds.

Caustic paste, which costs less, is a little more difficult to use. It must be applied carefully, otherwise it isn't effective and it can cause burns to both the kid and the person using it. To use the paste, you must first carefully shave the area of the horn button down to the skin, an area about the size of a nickel. With scissors trim the long hairs around this area and then coat them with Vaseline. This will help to prevent the caustic paste from running and causing burns. You should have someone help you with this. Little kids like to bounce around, so it's hard to do it alone. Now, holding the kid securely, coat the area with caustic paste, using a Q-tip or Popsicle stick. Be very careful not to get any of the paste on your skin. If you do, wash it off with cool water immediately and then rinse the area with vinegar. The kid will get upset, so plan to hold him and rock him or walk with him for about half an hour. Make sure that during this time he doesn't rub his head on anything, or he will get it in his eyes. After a while he will forget all about it. If he is drinking well out of a bottle, it's a good time to give him one. Caustic paste is not effective after the horn buds have started to grow.

Another thing you must decide is what you are going to do with your buck kids. You can't even consider keeping them for breeding your herd, because breeding related goats produces unhealthy kids. The alternatives are to sell them for breeding purposes or to butcher them for meat. We butcher ours, and they are delicious.

Young chevon properly raised is very tender and sweet, but the young bucks must be neutered by the time they are six weeks old or they will have a strong taste. We do our own neutering with a band castrator. This can be purchased at a farm supply store and is well worth the money. The principle is simple. A heavy rubber band is placed on the castrator, which is then stretched to slip up over the testicles and up close to the body. When the band is released, it shuts off the blood supply to the organ and atrophies the nerves. After about a month the testicles just dry up and fall off. Make sure that the testicles have fully descended before you do this; otherwise you might end up with a kid that is not neutered. Older kids have to be castrated by a vet. You can do it yourself, but it is painful to the young animal, and if it is done wrong, you can injure your kid badly.

Milking

For milking you will need certain equipment. As I stated earlier, milking a short-legged little goat can be back-breaking, and, though not necessary, a milking stand will certainly make your job easier. You will also need a milk pail, milk strainers, strainer pads, and storage containers. All of these items (with the exception of the pads) should be of stainless steel, aluminum, or glass. Stainless steel is the most expensive, but it lasts for years and is worth the investment. Aluminum pails are less expensive, easily cleaned, and just as sanitary, but they do not hold up as well. Glass is cheap and makes good storage containers. It is important to strain and cool milk quickly to avoid the growth of bacteria. You should also be careful not to put the lids on the jars too tightly while cooling, to avoid giving the milk an off-taste.

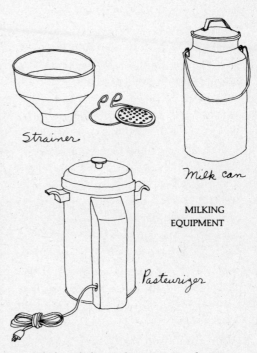

Strainer

Milk can

MILKING EQUIPMENT

Pasteurizer

In addition, you will need some sort of a bucket (plastic will be fine here) and some clean rags to use for washing and drying the udder before milking. Plastic pails should not be used for anything else besides this purpose because they can't be properly cleaned or sterilized. There are people who use plastic pails for milking, but I'm sure that the bacteria count of their milk must be very high, especially in warm weather.

Never use household cleaners and bleach for cleaning milking equipment. Household detergents leave a film on milk pails that gives a taste to the milk, and bleach is not strong enough for a sterilizer. Farm supply stores carry good alkaline and acid detergents for washing your equipment and iodine and chlorine compounds for sterilizing it.

Everyone develops his or her own system after a while. Ours is to rinse out all containers with cold water as soon as they are emptied of milk in order to remove any liquid milk residue. (Don't use hot water, because it sets the milk.) Then we wash them in an alkaline detergent and rinse, followed by a ten-minute soak in an iodine compound. Then we empty out the iodine solution and, without further rinsing, turn the containers upside down in a clean place to air-dry. Make sure to read the instructions that come with the iodine solution that you use. It's important to use enough, but it's costly to use too much. Occasionally the alkaline washing detergent will leave a white film on your milk pail, especially in hard-water areas. This is a mineral buildup. To clean this, occasionally use an acid solution. Though you can buy such solutions, we find that vinegar works fine.

For the sake of both the cleanliness of your milk and the comfort of your goat at milking time, the long hairs on and around the udder should be clipped. You might find a local farmer who will be willing to lend you his cow clippers a couple of times a year to do this. We use a small pair of sharp scissors and clip very closely.

Now, obviously, in order to be able to do this, to milk, and to clip toenails, it goes without saying that you should be good to your goats. Never yell at them or hit them. It frightens and confuses them, and whatever behavior has made you upset will only get worse. Talk gently to them, stroke them, bring them treats (a few raisins, a carrot, some apple tree twigs). All these things will make them gentle and manageable. When it comes time to milk, you won't have your goat kicking over the milk pail.

If you are using a milking stand, you will have to lead the goat up the first few times, but after that she will jump up with no encouragement at all. We feed our goats their grain ration while they are being milked. It helps to keep them occupied and happy while you go about the business of milking them. In cold weather we also give them a drink of warm water just before milking. It seems to help keep their production high.

The goat's udder should be washed before and after each milking with warm water that contains an iodine solution. This keeps the udder and teats clean and helps to heal any small sores on the teats or udder. It is important to dry her well, otherwise she will become chapped and sore. Never milk with dirty or wet hands. All the sanitary procedures that you use will be worthless if you milk with dirty hands, and if your hands are wet, it will cause chapping and pain to your goats.

If you've never milked before, you will most probably end up with more on you and on the walls of the barn than in the pail at first. But it doesn't take long to get the hang of it. The whole idea is to drain the teat of milk without sending it back up into the udder, then to allow the teat to fill again. With this process in mind, grasp the teat at the top between your thumb and forefinger, squeeze together, and hold. This prevents the milk from backing up into the udder. Now, with the next three fingers, close them one at a time in order, finally forming a fist around the teat and forcing the milk down and out. Then release the pressure of the whole hand to allow the teat to refill. Repeat. At first you will be convinced that you have five thumbs on each hand and that it's going to take hours to finish. Before you know it, though, you'll feel as if you've been doing it for years. My twelve-year-old daughter milks out each goat in five minutes or less.

Make sure to empty the udder. Gently massaging it toward the end of milking will encourage the goat to let down all her milk. When she seems empty, grasp each teat between your thumb and forefinger, sliding your fingers down the length of the teat. This is called stripping, and it's important, since it gets the last of the milk, which contains most of the cream. Do not attempt to strip her more than once or twice, for this will cause damage to the teats. Goats that are not milked out at each milking develop mastitis. This is an engorgement of milk in the udder, leading to inflammation, pain, and infection. Don't be afraid to use a certain amount of firmness in milking. If you watch the baby kids nurse, you will realize that, within reason, a firm pressure will not hurt the goat.

As I stated earlier, it is very important to strain and cool the milk immediately after milking. Cool it quickly in ice water or running cold water with the covers left slightly ajar. Besides all the good reasons for straining milk immediately that I have already given you, there is the additional one of being able to notice if there are any signs of mastitis present. The sooner treatment is started, the less of a problem it will be. A symptom of mastitis is the presence of a thick, chunky, or stringy white substance in the milk. Do not use any milk that contains these substances. If only small chunks the size of grains appear, you should cut back on your doe's grain to one-half her ration for a few days. Add 2 tablespoons of cider vinegar to each feeding and make sure that you milk her out completely. At least twice a day put hot packs of Epsom salts and water on the udder, only be sure that they are not too hot or they will burn her. Follow this treatment with a good bag balm (a special ointment for treating sore teats and udders), available at any farm supply store. Massage this onto the udder to reduce the inflammation. If after one or two days she is not free of symptoms, or if she is worse, call a vet. And anytime that the chunks are not very tiny, you should call a vet right away.

If you feel that you might want to sell your older does as young stock comes along, you should keep track of how much milk they produce over the period of each year. This tells the prospective buyer what kind of a milk goat he or she is buying. Even if your goat is not a high producer but produces a consistent amount over a long period of time, she might be a better buy than a goat that starts off high in the spring but dries off early. Good records are the best asset you have when it comes time to sell your goat. Milk is usually weighed and recorded by the pound. If you do not have a dairy scale, you could keep track fairly accurately by measuring it. (Again, each pint is equal to 1 pound.)

Because goats rarely catch diseases such as tuberculosis or brucellosis (Bang's disease), it is not necessary to pasteurize the milk. My own feeling about this is that if the Lord wanted us to drink pasteurized milk, he would have pasteurized the cow or the goat or what have you. However, I realize there are some people who feel differently, and if you want to pasteurize your milk, you can do so by heating it quickly to the point of skimming over, then cooling it just as quickly in cold running water. I will give you recipes for making butter, cheese, ice cream, and yogurt in Chapter 11.

Chevon

The meat from goats is called chevon. If you have two milk goats, you can expect anywhere from two to four kids per year. Unless you've decided that you want to raise more does, you will have to decide what to do with the extra doe and buck kids. Selling some is a possibility. There is a greater demand year after year for goats because they are the ideal milk producer for the small homestead. Or you could butcher them for meat. If you decide to do this, your bucks should be castrated, as suggested above.

Kids kept for butchering should be kept penned and should be fed milk and grain until they are six months old, then butchered. There is little purpose in keeping them any older, since they do not gain after that in proportion to what it costs for grain. At six months our average kid dresses out to about 35 pounds of meat.

Goats are butchered much like lambs. You will need a good sharp knife and a .22-caliber gun that shoots long rifle shells. Shooting them is the most merciful way to slaughter them. Our animals are never allowed to suffer, and this goes for slaughtering time too. Animals to be slaughtered should not be fed for twenty-four hours prior to slaughtering. This helps the carcasses to cool down more quickly. Pen them up with plenty of water and avoid getting them excited. If ours get too upset at not being fed, we give them something like a few pieces of green vegetable leaves, but not any milk or grain.

To shoot them, you should stand behind them, tie them up, and shoot down from behind the ears toward the nose in a straight line. The bullet will go right through their brain, and they will die instantly. Once the animal is dead, slit the throat from ear to ear and hang upside down, allowing the carcass to bleed freely. We cut the head off at this time; it makes the rest of the job easier. Now cut a slit in one of the hind legs, insert a garden hose, and run cold water into the hide. This serves two purposes: It helps to cool the carcass quickly, and it helps to separate the hide from the flesh, making it easier to skin.

Written material on the home slaughtering, cutting, and processing of chevon seems to be nonexistent. However, we found most helpful Bulletin 2153, titled "Slaughtering, Cutting and Processing of Lamb and Mutton on the Farm," put out by the U.S. Department of Agriculture and obtainable through your local agricultural extension agent. Lamb and chevon are very similar except that the carcass of the latter is somewhat smaller. You can also send the carcass to a local butcher for processing.

Cutting these small carcasses is a quick and easy job. It requires a good sharp butchering knife, a boning knife, and a meat saw. A good clean hacksaw works well, too. All of these items can be purchased at any restaurant supply house or from specialty suppliers. One source is the Garden Way Catalogue, 1300 Ethan Allen Drive, Winooski, Vermont 05404. Write and request information about what you want and their nearest supply store to you.

Be sure to save all trimmings from the butchering to make sausage with, adding some pork fat to make it more moist and tasty. If you want to use it like hamburger, add ground-beef suet to it for moisture and flavor. From each carcass you can plan on two leg roasts; two shoulder roasts; four or more meals of chops, depending on how you cut them; stew meat; and trimmings for sausage or hamburger. We use the ground meat in spaghetti and casserole dishes. I have even made hamburgers out of it, and no one knew the difference. Those that do notice that it isn't beef think that it's veal, and it does taste very much like it. Chevon is very sweet and moist. We take the little riblets that come off the chops and saw them into 2-inch pieces, then coat them with a good barbecue sauce and bake or grill them. They make a great snack.

Many people of European descent buy newborn kids and roast them whole like suckling pigs, with a stuffing, for Easter. If you should decide to try this and you enjoy it, you might want to look into a market for kidskin. It is in demand for gloves and pocketbooks and brings in a good price.

7 RAISING HOGS

Raising hogs for pork is one of the easiest, least time-consuming jobs on the homestead, and the amount of meat and by-products it provides is so great that it is also one of the most rewarding projects. Though most farmers breed their sows to farrow (give birth to their young) in the early spring, piglets are usually available from early spring through fall. Timing and raising of your pigs to coincide with surplus garden produce is of the utmost importance to the small homesteader.

We feel that trying to raise pigs through the winter in an unheated barn is a big mistake. When we first started off with all of our animals, they all arrived the Saturday before Christmas, December 23, except for our pigs, which arrived one week earlier. Our piglets, named Sooner and Later (their destinies having already been foretold), were just five weeks old, and I must tell you about their arrival. This story deserves a book by itself, but I will try to condense it here for you. They were ready to be picked up a week before our larger animals were to arrive, and we knew we couldn't put them in that cold barn alone, so we pleaded with the farmer to keep them the additional week, but it was useless. He assured us that many people kept piglets in a box in the house; in fact, he told us, "Some even raise pigs as house pets." I wasn't convinced, but there didn't seem to be anything we could do but bring them home in a box and put them in the bathroom. We put a screen over the box and a piece of firewood over the screen, but by the time evening came, it was obvious that this wouldn't hold, so we added another piece of wood and went to bed. Sometime around 1:00 A.M. Ray poked me awake and in a hoarse whisper informed me that he thought my little "friends" were loose. We got up to investigate, and sure enough, two frisky little piglets were scampering around the living room. The chase was on! Ray went one way and I the other, and amid many squeals and shouts the piglets managed to evade us. By now our kids were all awake and choking with laughter as their dad stumbled over furniture and I tripped on my long flannel nightgown and went sailing flat on my stomach trying to reach for a hind leg of the nearest escaping piglet.

Finally, with everyone's help, he managed to get them back into the box. We added two more pieces of heavy firewood (we were up to four pieces by now) to the screen. Back to bed only to wake up a couple of hours later for a repeat performance. Two more pieces of firewood this time. By the time we got up for the third time, as dawn was approaching, we'd had it. When we got them in their box this time, we put on all the firewood the screen would hold and wound masking tape around the box. It was a ridiculous sight. They could have escaped from a bank vault more easily than they could have gotten out of that box. With just a few more minor incidents we got through the rest of the week. I'm not sure what excited me most that Saturday, the arrival of all our other animals or the departure of Sooner and Later from the house.

It was very cold at that time of the year in our uninsulated barn, even though we had many other animals. We used a heat lamp to keep our piglets warm for a few weeks and fed them warm milk and water. They grew, but it took so much of their energy to keep warm that growth was very slow. Early growth is important. A young pig that does not do well in the early stages of its growth is apt to remain stunted. Our spring pigs arrived about four months later in mid-April, and by the fall, when butchering time arrived, they all averaged out at the same weight. Obviously, we had fed the first pigs for four months for nothing. We do raise winter pigs now, but we start them in September so that they will be good size before cold weather. And now that the ceiling of our barn is insulated and we have many more large animals, the barn stays much warmer.

It would be ideal to time your piglets to arrive around the first week of June. By then the goats have weaned their kids, and you'll no doubt have extra skim milk and whey for them from your cheese making. Add to this the root crops that you have planted early with the piglets in mind, such as carrots, beets, early potatoes, and all table scraps, and you'll get your young pigs off to a very good start. When fall arrives and your pigs are large enough to require large amounts of food, you'll have garden surplus plus pumpkins, squashes, and late potatoes for them. Adding cornmeal to their diet for the last six or seven weeks will give you some of the finest pork you have ever eaten. They will be ready to butcher about the last week of November, an ideal time of the year to handle these large carcasses since outside temperatures will have cooled down considerably by then. You'll be able to serve your own roast pork for Christmas.

Housing

Before buying your first pigs, you must give some serious thought to their housing. While they do not need anything fancy, they do need pens that are sturdy. When they get to be about five months old, they're no easy task to catch if they get loose. The following are some of the important things to keep in mind about hogs when you design their housing.

The first thing to be considered is where to locate the pigpen. You can include it in your barn plans, but if your barn is close to the house, the odor in the summertime can be overwhelming. There are ways of controlling offensive odors, but even with the best of efforts, at the height of the summer heat it can get pretty bad. The most effective ways to control odors are either to build the pen and divide it into two sections so that you can move the hogs every other week, covering the ground in the unused side of the pen with slaked lime, or to add a layer of hay or straw to the pen every few days. This last method is effective if you have access to enough old hay or straw. It would be very expensive if you had to buy it.

Ideally, housing should be located in the area of your homestead where the odors will be least offensive to your neighbors and yourself but that at the same time is reasonably accessible by truck or tractor. At slaughtering time a 200-plus-pound hog, deadweight, can't be picked up like a sack of flour and carted off to the truck, even if it's just a matter of a hundred feet. Pigs will root deep into the soil, so if the bottoms of their pens are not secure, they will dig under the boards or fencing and get out. There are a few ways to prevent this. You can lay a concrete floor for their pen or construct it of very heavy boarding. You can also run several strands of barbed wire around the bottom of the pen, right down into the dirt. They will not root where there is barbed wire. Another very important thing to remember is that a pig's normal body temperature is 110 degrees F, so a pen that does not adequately protect your hogs from the hot summer sun can cost you your hogs. They could die of heat exhaustion.

The very best type of housing is a pen built of sturdy slat sides, with 4-by-4-foot corner posts set in cement and a cement floor that slopes to the front of the pen. This type of pen stays dry, and it's easy to scrape it down every couple of days. If you put this manure into your compost pile, cover it with a little slaked lime or bone meal and a light covering of mulch. At the same time that you are keeping your hogs clean, dry, and odor-free, you are also providing yourself with a pile of compost that is rich in organic matter and nutrients, which means another benefit from your hog-raising project.

We have kept our hogs penned with just electric wire, but we don't recommend it. This year we will construct new pens with cement floors similar to the one shown in the sketch. Actually, the biggest drawback to electric fencing is the danger of power outages in your area. Very stubborn hogs will occasionally go through an electric fence anyway, and once the current is interrupted by the broken wire, the others will all get out.

One of the funniest experiences we ever had came late one August after a wild thunderstorm had knocked out our power. Our four hogs, each weighing about 200 pounds by then, headed right for the garden. My two little girls and my sixteen-year-old son were with me at home. We chased those crazy pigs all over the place trying to get them back into their pens. In desperation, I called my husband home from work. It was a twenty-mile drive from town, and when he finally ar-

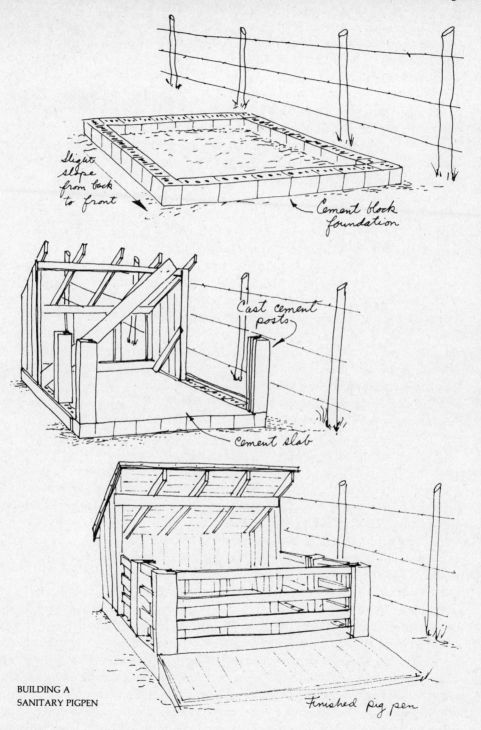

Slight slope from back to front

Cement block foundation

Cast cement posts

Cement slab

BUILDING A
SANITARY PIGPEN

Finished pig pen

rived, I was exhausted. He went out with the children, and the chase started all over again, but to no avail. The two little girls weren't about to let the hogs get the best of them, so they figured out a solution of their own. The youngest, Kim, climbed on the hog's back and grabbed hold of its ears to steer, and Mary got behind and pushed. After all our efforts, it took the two girls just ten minutes to have them back in their pen. As tired as we were, we had to laugh; it was the funniest sight you could ever imagine.

To sum up your housing needs, your pen must be removed from the area of your living quarters, it must have a "hog-tight" bottom, and it must protect them from the sun. Keeping these things in mind, you should be able to build yourself a good pen, ranging from one that can run you almost nothing in cost to one that could be more costly because of the cement but would be longer lasting.

What to Look For When Buying Your Pigs

Keeping a sow is just not practical for the small homesteader. You would have to buy grain year-round, invest in farrowing equipment, and then if you ended up with twelve or more piglets once or twice a year and were not able to sell them, you would have lost all your profit and more money besides. If you want a way to defray the cost of raising your own pigs, it would be more practical to contract with someone you know to raise a pig for them with the understanding that you will sell it at whatever is the going price of pork, hanging weight, at slaughtering time. Raising one or two hogs this way pays for all your costs and then gives you a little profit besides.

Pigs are usually sold when they are six to seven weeks old. Be sure to buy from a farmer you can trust. It's a good idea to make a couple of trips to see your piglets before they are weaned. Healthy piglets usually come from good mother sows. If the sow isn't taking good care of her babies, the chances are high that her piglets will not do well. A young female pig is called a gilt; she becomes a sow after she has had a litter of piglets. A male pig is called a boar and becomes a barrow after he has been castrated. An old boar that is castrated just prior to slaughter is called a stag.

In spite of the fact that some people have raised only one pig at a time with "moderate success," it still remains a proven fact that two pigs raised together do much better. If you are going to raise one alone, be prepared to make a pet of it so that it will be happy and grow well. This will bring you some additional problems when it comes time to butcher your pet. Any homesteading family can certainly make use of two hogs. Make sure when you buy your piglets that the males have been castrated and those of either sex have been wormed. A male pig that has not been castrated will be tough and have strong-flavored meat, and piglets that have worms do not grow well. We make it a practice to worm our hogs once around three months old, just to be on the safe side. We use Piperazine wormer solution. Instructions for use are on the container.

Feeding

Young pigs require at least a gallon of water a day each. As they grow, they consume more and should be given water a couple of times a day, but not with their food. Too much water mixed with their food, especially in the wintertime, is very wasteful of the young pigs' own body heat. So give them plenty of water between meals, but only enough at mealtime to moisten their food.

Before getting into what you should feed your pigs, I will tell you about the few things you should not feed them. Do not give them peels of citrus fruits, rhubarb tops, and tea and coffee grounds. Do not give any food that has soapy water in it, and be especially careful not to feed anything that has glass in it.

The following foods are considered the best quality, and 1 pound of any of these foods alone or in combination equals 1 pound of grain. The following are classed as grade 1 foods:

1 gallon of milk

All table scraps (as long as there are not too many raw vegetables or peelings in them), breads, cakes, pies, fruits in small amounts

Meat trimmings: bones, scraps, fat, offal from slaughtering homestead animals (Make sure that any pork trimmings are well cooked, just as they are for human beings.)

Fish and fish trimmings

Whey

Acorns

The following foods are considered to be of very high value, but must be fed in larger quantities to equal a pound of grain. It takes 4 pounds of the following foods to equal 1 pound of grain; they are classed as grade 2 foods:

Boiled potatoes

Sugar beets

Jerusalem artichokes

Carrots

Corn on the cob

Fresh clover, alfalfa, or grass clippings

The last group of foods is fine for feeding to your hogs after they have reached about 140 pounds, somewhere around twenty-one weeks old. Little pigs couldn't consume enough in one day to replace the amount of grain they need. It takes 10 to 12 pounds of the following foods to equal 1 pound of grain; they are classed as grade 3 foods:

All garden wastes: cabbage and cauliflower stalks and leaves, broccoli plants, vines

Vegetables such as turnips, rutabagas, kale, chard, beets

Vegetable peels, tops, and trimmings

Fruit pulp from juice making

By then the extra pumpkins and squashes you have grown just for them will be ready too.

If you haven't a scale, you can figure that solid kitchen waste such as bread, gravy, pies, cakes, and so on weigh about 1 pound per pint. Solid fruits and vegetables such as sugar beets, carrots, potatoes, and so forth weigh about 1 pound per quart. Leafy vegetables such as spinach, chard, kale, vines, and grass clippings weigh between 10 and 12 pounds per bushel.

If you can make friends with bakery or restaurant owners and they are willing to save their food garbage, your pigs will eat royally and it won't cost you a cent to raise them. Another good source of high-quality food garbage is child-care centers. In some areas there are cheese factories, and you should investigate the possibility of getting free whey from them. In most areas of the country, whey disposal is a serious problem, so they would probably be happy to give you all you want. Be sure to supplement the whey with some extra protein, because unless it contains a lot of cheese solids, it won't take the place of milk completely.

The first two years we raised pigs, we were able to obtain a great deal of whey for them. But now the whey is being shipped away to be processed as a food supplement, so we have solved our problem by using extra skim milk from our goats and whey from our own cheese making. When we don't have enough, we give our pigs some calf-milk replacer. Though the calf-milk replacer is quite expensive, one 50-pound bag goes a long way. We add this to the ton of potatoes that we grow for them, and along with the abundance of other extras around the homestead, it has raised some very nice pork and for as close to nothing as you can get. I should add here that when the pigs are little, under 100 pounds, we prepare the potatoes for them by cooking a cannerful over a wood fire outside every couple of days. As they grow, we feed them the potatoes raw. Six weeks before slaughtering, we add 5 pounds of cornmeal per hog to their daily ration.

We tried an experiment this past year to help us get our young pigs off to a good start, and it worked fine. As the winter went along and the freezer began to empty out a little, we rearranged what was left to give us room for a large garbage bag. From then on until our new piglets arrived, we kept all food scraps that fell into the grade 1 group. We packaged these in 2½-pound packages and just threw them into the larger bag. When the young pigs arrived, anytime we didn't have enough grade 1 food, we would take out a package. This not only gave the piglets a good start, it also helped to keep our freezer full and cut down on the cost of running it. If you have a lot of space available, you could even freeze plastic jugs of extra milk and whey.

Little pigs should be fed three times a day. When they reach 100 pounds, we switch them to twice-daily feedings.

HOW MUCH TO FEED
Using a minimum of commercial grain:

Weight of pig (in pounds)	Approximate age (in weeks)	Amount to feed
30	7	2½ pounds of any grade 1 food
60	12	3½ pounds of any grade 1 food
100	17	2 pounds of grade 1 food, plus the equivalent of 3 pounds of any grade 1 or 2 foods
140	21	2 pounds of grade 1 food plus the equivalent of 4½ pounds of any grade 1, 2, or 3 foods
180	24	2 pounds of any grade 1 food plus the equivalent of 6 pounds of any grade 1, 2, or 3 foods
200	26	5 pounds of cornmeal plus all of the grade 1, 2, or 3 foods they will clean up

Use your head when feeding your hogs. If after twenty minutes they still have food left in their trough, they are being fed too much, but if they gobble it right down in less than ten minutes and are looking around for more, they are not getting enough. When feeding grain, we put it in a bucket and add just enough warm water to be absorbed by the grain, so that it is moistened but not soupy. Letting it sit a few minutes will give the grain time to absorb the water before you feed it to the hogs. This should also be done with table scraps that contain breads of any sort.

When building a hog-feeding trough, be sure to anchor it solidly to one side of their pen. I was amazed to watch our first pigs literally toss their trough in the air with their nose, even though it weighed plenty. From then on we bolted it down. When the pigs are small, all food should be put in a trough, but when they are old enough to start trampling around in it, it doesn't pay. Unless it's milk or something very wet, just throw it on the floor of their pen. Large fruits and vegetables should be chopped coarsely.

Occasionally your hogs might get loose bowels from too much of something they ate, such as fruits. Treat them with the same medications you would use for a member of the family who had diarrhea. Use the same amount that you would use for a person of the same weight.

Our hogs, fed as I've just outlined for you, dress out to an average of 200 pounds hanging weight, with just enough fat on them to make the meat tasty and give us nice lean mixed bacon and a fair amount of lard. One year we tried to give grain for just two weeks prior to slaughtering, and though we had beautiful meat, we were disappointed in the bacon. It was too lean to be tasty, and we didn't have enough lard.

You will come up against people who will scoff at what you are trying to do. For instance, someone got very upset with me because I made the remark that good-quality pork could be raised with a minimum of grain. A commercial farmer pointed out that his pigs were about 30 pounds heavier than ours, and at a month younger, because they had been entirely grain-fed.

What this farmer said was absolutely true, but let's take a good look at what our pork-raising venture accomplished for us: Though it took us one month longer to raise the same size hogs, our pork cost us 2½ times less per pound than this farmer's did. Along the way, we made good use of the earth's resources. We didn't use up several hundred pounds of grain that could be used to feed many starving people. We returned good rich organic matter from our project to the soil, in an effort to replenish the resources that we drew on. And, in the end, we achieved the same results: good-quality protein with which to nourish our family.

It doesn't do any good to argue with these people. Just know in your heart that you are achieving something good and that you are doing it in a responsible and conscientious manner.

When to Slaughter

Pigs should be ready to slaughter at about seven and one-half to eight months of age. As I said earlier, if you bought them at six weeks, early in June, they should be ready about the end of November and should weigh about 225 to 250 pounds liveweight. This is a very good time of the year to butcher, because the outside temperatures have cooled down considerably by then.

A good way to determine your hog's weight is to provide him with something to eat to keep him busy and, with a measuring tape, measure him around his body just behind the front legs. This is his heart girth. Then measure his length from the base of his tail to the middle of his ears. To determine his weight, use the following formula: heart girth ‾ heart girth ‾ length, and divide by 400. If the answer is under 150 pounds, add 7 pounds, and that is your hog's weight.

Butchering

I am not going to tell you how to slaughter your pigs in this book. It would require more equipment than would be practical for a small homestead. You would have to have a gambrel, hooks, barrels for water, heaters to heat it with, bell scrapers, a tractor or truck, and a tall, sturdy tree or beam to haul the carcass up on. If you would like to read more about doing it yourself, I recommend that you obtain the U.S.D.A. Bulletin No. 2138 from your county extension agent. It's put out by the U.S. Department of Agriculture and it's called "Slaughtering, Cutting, and Processing Pork on the Farm." It sells for about 65 cents.

We do not attempt to slaughter our own pigs. We have a local farmer come to our homestead. He shoots the hogs and then quickly bleeds them here. Once he is certain that they have bled out well, he takes them back to his farm to finish dressing them out there. Some farmers will bring their equipment over to your homestead to do the job. We give the farmer a couple of hours, and then we drive over to pick up the organ meats and leaf fat. Leaf fat is the fat that surrounds the organs (not the offal) on the inside of the carcass. Usually this makes the finest-quality lard. The fatback, which is the layer of fat that covers the rib cage, is more commonly used for salt pork, though we use it for lard too. We chill this leaf fat quickly and then render it immediately. Recipes for rendering lard and making sausage and headcheese will be found in Chapter 11.

The carcass is allowed to hang and cool for twenty-four hours, and this is why it's so important for temperatures to be down below 40 degrees F. Otherwise, there is a high risk that the warm pork will start to develop bacteria, which will cause your meat to spoil. If temperatures in your area do not fall low enough, it would be worthwhile to rent locker space for twenty-four hours to chill the carcass properly.

Cutting the Carcass

There is very little waste on a pig; almost everything is utilized. Our two winter pigs dressed out to about 220 pounds hanging weight each. We had an end product of about 400-pounds-plus of usable products. Most families of four can easily make use of this much meat per year. This amount of meat breaks down to:

4 hams averaging 20 pounds each
45 pounds of bacon
4 butt-end shoulder roasts, 6 pounds each
4 smoked shoulders, 6 pounds each
4 rib-end roasts, 3½ to 4½ pounds each
4 loin-end roasts, 3½ to 4½ pounds each
32 to 38 pounds of pork chops
20 pounds of sausage
10 pounds of fresh side pork
5 pounds of salt pork
8 pounds of ham hocks

4 pounds of trimmed pigs' feet for pickling
40 pounds of top-quality lard
20 pounds of rendered trimmings for making soap
8 pounds of pork liver
2 to 3 pounds of pork rinds for frying or scrapple
2 hearts to stuff and bake
2 sweetbreads
4 kidneys
2 tongues (we pickle them and serve them cold sliced with crackers)

We do not happen to like kidneys of any kind, so we freeze them and later cook them with potatoes for our next batch of pigs. This provides some first-class feed for them.

The most important point I want to emphasize here to novice butchers is that no matter how inexperienced you are, you can't possibly cut the pork so that it can't be used. So don't be afraid to try. You might possibly cut your hams a little too large or too small, or your chops a little too short, but if you have ever bought these cuts of meat, you already know what they are supposed to look like, and if you follow the charts included in extension service booklets, you will have a pretty good idea of what to do. You'll find yourself getting more and more professional with each passing year. Just make sure to wrap and refrigerate each piece as it is finished. Freeze all pieces that you are not going to have smoked, and if you are going to send your hams and bacon to be smoked, be sure to keep them refrigerated until you bring them to the processor.

If you are going to smoke them yourself, I suggest that you again refrigerate them overnight before you go on to get them ready for curing and smoking. There is a good reason for this. While you have been cutting the carcass, the internal temperature of the meat, especially in the larger pieces, has had a chance to rise, and meat that is to be brined or salted should be well chilled first. Salting does draw heat from the meat, but in the larger hams the meat closest to the bones and joints takes quite a while to cool down.

Curing

Pork can be cured in a salt brine and just left in crocks in a cool root cellar for several months. This is commonly known as salt pork. Or it can be cured with a dry-cured or a sweet-pickle brine cure and then smoked or not, as you prefer.

The U.S. Department of Agriculture recommends dry cure for the southern states because it is faster, but you must still maintain cool temperatures. If you have enough refrigerator space, you can dry-cure hams and bacon in plastic bags in the refrigerator. I am going to give you the Department of Agriculture instructions for using dry-cure, since I have not had any personal experience with it myself. We prefer the sweet-pickle brine cure. Regardless of which method you use, you must remember the following:

Chill the meat and keep it cold.

Use the amount of salt called for in the recipe.

Give the meat enough curing time to absorb the salt thoroughly.

Smoke cured meat long enough to drive out excess moisture. (If you are going to freeze the meat immediately after curing, this is not as important.)

Weigh meat and curing ingredients carefully. Too little salt may cause spoilage; too much salt makes hard, dry, oversalty meat.

Keep the meat cold while in the cure. Hold curing meat at a temperature near 36 to 40 degrees F. Higher temperatures increase the chance of spoilage. Lower temperatures slow salt penetration. If curing temperatures drop below freezing for several days, add the same number of days to the curing time.

Frozen meat is difficult to handle. If fresh meat freezes, thaw it in a chilly room or in cold water before putting it to cure. Figure curing time carefully. Too few days in the cure may cause spoilage. Too long a cure in heavy salt results in loss of quality.

Dry Cure

Check the internal temperature of the heaviest hams. Be sure it is below 40 degrees F. Weigh the trimmed meat and the right amount of curing material. For 100 pounds of ham or shoulder, use:

Salt (coarse), 8 pounds
Sugar (brown, white, or maple syrup), 2 pounds
Saltpeter,* 2 ounces

For bacon and other thin cuts, use only half these amounts.

Mix curing ingredients thoroughly, and be especially careful to mix the finely powdered saltpeter throughout the mixture. Divide the mixture approximately in half, one part to use at once and the other to save for resalting. For bacon and other thin cuts, use the required amount all at once; do not resalt. Rub one part of the curing mixture on all surfaces of the meat, packing some into shank ends. Pat about a ⅛-inch layer on the lean face of the ham. Pat a thin covering on the shoulders. "Frost" the thin bacon strip with the mixture; the heavier the cut, the greater its share of the mixture.

Fit the salted meat into a clean barrel or crock, being careful not to shake off the curing mixture. Or put the pieces into individual plastic bags in the refrigerator. Hold it at temperatures of 36 to 40 degrees F. Figure out the amount of time in the cure (a minimum of twenty-five days for hams and shoulders, four days to the pound). Bacon takes 1½ days to the pound. Check the curing time on a calendar and record when the meat should be removed.

Six or eight days after the meat has been put into the cure, take it out of the barrel and resalt it with the other half of the curing mixture. Salt the hams and

---

*At the time of this writing, there is still much controversy over the use of nitrates and nitrites in curing meat. However, the U.S. Department of Agriculture still includes it in their recipes for curing meat, so I include it here. You may exclude it if you are concerned about its safety as a food additive. Its main purpose in curing meats is to intensify the red color of the meat and to prevent this color from fading, though it does have some preserving qualities as well. It isn't really necessary.

shoulders as before, but add nothing to the bacon and thin cuts. Repack and keep cold. Give the salt plenty of time to penetrate to the center of the cuts and to distribute itself evenly throughout the piece. Each piece will take three or even four days to the pound. All the surface salt may be absorbed into the dry-cured meat before the curing time is up. Give it more time to work down into the center of the cut. On the farm, meat often has to be cured at temperatures above 40 degrees F. Under these conditions, speed up salt penetration. Salt lightly and spread the fresh warm cuts. (Never pile warm meat or blanket it with salt.) Poke salt into all the joints. Bone or slice the cuts into smaller, more quickly salted pieces. All these methods help and may save the meat, but none are so satisfactory as curing at the proper temperature.

If you find after curing your own meat the first time that it was too salty, the next time try using just 6 pounds of salt. It's enough and will make the meat less salty tasting, but be very careful to pack the cure mixture well into the shanks and rub well onto the face of the hams.

❀ Sweet-Pickle Cure

Fit the cold, smoothly trimmed cuts into a clean barrel or crock (plastic works well, as long as it has been well scrubbed) and cover with cold solution.

This is the recipe I use, but some recipes call for other spices:

> 6 pounds coarse salt (We like our hams lightly salted; you may use up to 8 pounds.)
> 1 quart grade B or C maple syrup (Grade A is too mild for a nice flavor.)
> 2 ounces saltpeter
> 4½ gallons water

Divide all the ingredients evenly among two canners. Bring the solution to a boil and simmer for 5 minutes. Remove from the heat and cool. Pour into five or six gallon jugs and refrigerate overnight until very cold.

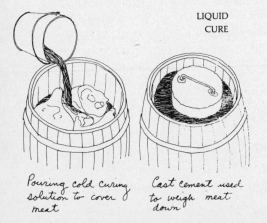

LIQUID
CURE

Pouring cold curing solution to cover meat

Cast cement used to weigh meat down

To make sure that large hams are cured properly, you should buy a pumping needle. We bought ours from Garden Way Center here in Vermont. Pump extra brine along the bone and into the joints, because this is where bacteria builds up the fastest. The reason that we prefer the sweet-pickle brine is that we find it less salty and more uniform in cure. There are no pockets that get saltier than others.

We have developed a way of maintaining cold-enough temperatures for our brine. On the day we slaughter our pigs, we put six to eight gallon plastic jugs full of water in the freezer to freeze solid. Those with wide mouths, available from restaurants, fast-food counters, snack bars, and so on work best. Once our pork is in the barrel and we have poured the chilled brine over it, we weigh it down with a large crock cover. (A large clean flat stone will do.) Then we put three or four of the frozen jugs of water in a standing position on top of the crock cover, with just the bottoms resting in the brine. These jugs are changed every twenty-four hours, with the ones taken from the barrel returned to the freezer. Even though the temperatures in our root cellar stayed as high as 50 degrees F most of the time, the temperature of the brine remained a constant 38 degrees. If you slaughter in very cold weather and your root cellar stays between 36 and 40 degrees, this is not necessary.

A few words of caution on this whole process. We like the taste of maple-syrup-cured hams, so when I did my first ham, I decided that it might give a nice flavor to the meat if I added some extra maple syrup to the pumping brine. This was a big mistake because it caused the meat closest to the bone to sour. I called an old friend of ours to ask what I had done wrong, and this elderly sage, who has been a meat cutter all his life, informed me that too much sugar in the meat or brine will cause the meat to sour and could be a cause of the brine turning ropey. Also, before you put your plastic jugs of water into the crock, make sure that the plastic jug hasn't split in the freezer, otherwise the melting ice will go into your barrel and give you too much water for the amount of salt in your brine; this could cause your pork to spoil. You must also be careful not to let the jugs fall on their sides. Actually, with a little care this method works very well. This method also works very well in keeping your meat well down in the solution. Just make sure to use enough solution to submerge the meat, and keep the brine cold throughout the curing time. It is very important that you keep the temperature of the brine between 36 and 40 degrees F.

Overhaul the pack about the seventh day after putting it in the cure by removing all the meat, pouring out the sweet-pickle brine, repacking the meat, and covering it again with the same, restirred mixture. Overhaul two more times, about the fourteenth and thirty-eighth days.

Curing time for hams and shoulders should be about four days per pound, according to all the instructions I have read, with a minimum of twenty-eight days for the lightweight cuts. But I used a pumping needle and pumped the brine well into the joints and along the bones, and I found that my hams were ready in less time than that, about three days per pound. Recommended curing time for bacon is only 1½ days per pound. If you do not use a pumping needle, make sure that you follow the recommended curing time for hams and shoulders.

If the sweet-pickle solution sours or becomes ropey or syrupy, discard it, scrub the meat in hot water, scald and rechill the barrel, repack the meat, and cover with new, cold curing solution. Use 5½ gallons of water to make this second solution instead of the 4½ gallons recommended before.

Preparing for Smoking

Remove pieces from the dry or brine pack when their curing time is up. Brush the lighter cuts to remove any excess dry mixture, or lift them from the brine and hold them in a cold place until the heavier pieces are ready to smoke. Soak fully cured meat in cold, fresh water to remove some surface salt, about fifteen to twenty minutes. String the meat for hanging it in smoke: hams and shoulders through the shanks, bacon reinforced at the ends with hardwood skewers or clean galvanized wire to hold it squarely in the smoke. Scrub the strung meat clean with a stiff brush and hot water, 110 to 125 degrees F, so that it will take on a brighter color in the smoke. If a smoked flavor is not desired, hang the cured meat to dry for about a week before bagging it.

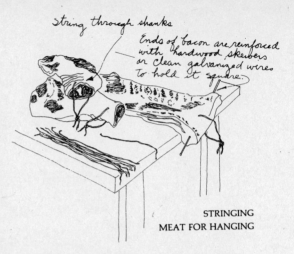

string through shanks

Ends of bacon are reinforced with hardwood skewers or clean galvanized wires to hold it square.

STRINGING
MEAT FOR HANGING

Smokehouses

Smokehouses can be constructed of many things. The basic requirements are a closed unit that will hold the pork in a hanging position with none of the pieces actually touching, though they can be hung closely. You must be able to control ventilation in it. You will also need a separate unit that will contain the wood chips or corncobs, plus some way of controlling the amount of smoke and the temperature. The temperature of the smokehouse should not get any higher than 110 degrees F, just hot enough to melt the surface fat. Otherwise, you will cook your meat instead of smoking it. This is why it's a good idea to locate your heating unit a few feet from the smoking unit itself, especially if it's a small unit such as a 50-gallon barrel. This way you get more smoke than heat.

These are the instructions the USDA gives for using a 50-gallon barrel. Remove both ends, set the barrel over the upper end of a shallow, sloping, covered trench, and dig a pit at the lower end for the fire. Control the heat of the fire by covering the pit with a piece of sheet metal and mounding the earth around the edges so as to cut off most of the draft. Clean muslin or burlap hung over the top of the barrel will protect a 1-inch opening between the barrel and the cleated top, which rests on broomsticks supporting the meat.

We happened to have an old tool shed that was 4 feet square and 8 feet tall.

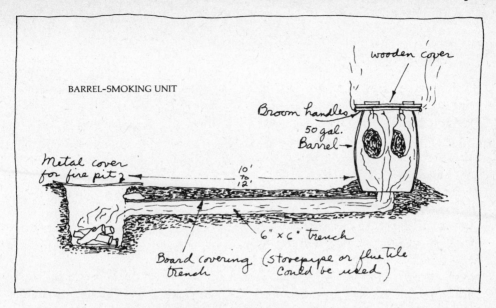

BARREL-SMOKING UNIT

We decided it would make a good smokehouse, so we scrubbed it out with stiff brushes and a strong premise disinfectant such as is used in barns. Then we drilled two ¾-inch holes on each side, 6 feet from the floor and equally spaced. Into these holes we ran two lengths of ¾-inch pipe. Next, just below these holes, we drilled three more ¾-inch holes, about 4 inches apart, on just one side. We covered these with tops from tin cans, nailed so that they could be opened by sliding them to one side. These made effective draft controls. Lastly, we cut a hole 6 inches in diameter in the side of the house about 6 inches from the floor to accommodate a 6-inch stovepipe. We had an old barrel-type wood stove, and we placed it about 3 feet from the shed. After adding an elbow and a length of pipe to fit into the 6-inch hole cut for this purpose, we had a very acceptable smokehouse.

Meat can be crowded into a smokehouse, but no piece should touch another piece of meat or a wall. The space required varies with the weight of the cut, but 12 inches in width both ways and 2 feet in height for each piece is a fair basis for estimating the capacity of your smokehouse. Two or more tiers of meat can be hung in the smokehouse. A really tall house such as ours can even accommodate three or four tiers and can be served by the same smoke source. You should locate any smokehouse that is going to be a permanent fixture at least 50 feet from the house or other wooden structures.

Smoking Cured Pork

Smoking colors, flavors, and dries cured pork and slows spoilage. It has a slight preservative action. Hang the cured, soaked, scrubbed meat to drip overnight in order to prevent streaking or smudging in the smoke. A wet surface will not take an even smoked color. Hang the meat so that no pieces are touching.

In the smokehouse build a fire of any hardwood: hickory, oak, apple, maple, pecan, or corncobs add the best flavor. Hardwood sawdust is excellent. Never use wood from trees that do not have leaves, such as fir or pine trees. They are too strong smelling. If it appears that our smokehouse is going to get too hot, we add some corncobs that we have soaked overnight; this gives added smoke while it reduces the heat. Hang the meat in the smokehouse and heat the smokehouse to between 110 and 120 degrees F, opening your ventilators to let the moisture out. On the second day close the ventilators and smoke for one or more days, or until the meat has the desired color. Be very careful not to overheat and scorch the meat. A good way to decide what type of hardwood chips you might want to use is to try a few chips of whatever you have on hand. If you like the smell of them, you'll most probably like the taste. We use hardwood maple chips under dry corncobs for our smoke.

Testing Smoked Meat

If you suspect that your meat has soured slightly or you're afraid it might have soured inside, there is a way to test it. Take a piece of clean wire that is not too large in diameter. Make a tiny hook on the end of it and slide it into the ham along the bone, toward the joint. When you pull it out, it will have a tiny piece of meat on it. If it smells sweet, it is all right to eat. If it has soured, you will be able to smell it immediately.

Unbagged smoked meat cannot be stored safely unless it is frozen. Frozen cured meats should be used within a short period of time—small pieces within three months and larger hams and shoulders within six months. Because of the salt in the cure, cured meats never freeze quite as solidly as fresh meats, and they can become rancid even in the freezer when stored for too long.

To wrap meats for cool storage in your root cellar or a cool room in your house, you should make sure that they are processed at a time of the year when bugs and small flies are not a problem. After the smoked meat has cooled, it is ready to be wrapped and stored. Wrapping protects meat from insects and partially excludes light and air, which speed the development of rancidity. Unbagged smoked meat cannot be stored safely, even in well-built, fly-tight smokehouses. Flies or fly eggs will get in, either on a piece of meat or when the door is opened. If each piece is properly cured and smoked, wrapped, bagged, and hung separately, it will keep in a cool, well-ventilated place for as long as a year.

Cover the meat with parchment paper and put it into muslin bags. Use a paper wrapping that is heavy enough to keep the grease from soaking through to the bottom of the bag. Fold over the tops of the bags and tie them securely. Make a loop in the outside tie string that passes through the meat, because insects may enter the package along the string. You can further protect each sack by painting it with yellow wash.

To make enough yellow wash for 100 pounds of hams or bacon, use 3 pounds of barium sulfate, 1¼ ounces of yellow ocher, 1 ounce of dry glue, and 6 ounces of flour. (Between the drugstore and the hardware store, you should be able to come up with everything you need.) Half-fill a pail with water and mix in the flour, breaking up all the lumps. Mix the ocher with 1 quart of water in a separate pan, then add the glue. Pour this mixture into the flour mixture. Bring it all to a boil and then add the barium sulfate slowly, stirring constantly. Make the wash the day before it is needed and cool overnight. Stir it frequently while using it and apply it with a brush. If you prefer, paint the bags with lime, clay, or flour mixed with water to a rather thick consistency.

Bacon is usually more tasty when freshly cured and smoked. It does not keep as well as hams and shoulders, and most farmers prefer to use it during the cool months.

If your meat should develop some mold, it does not mean that it is spoiled. Simply wipe off the mold with a damp cloth or cut off the part of the meat that has the mold and use the rest.

8

RAISING RABBITS

When it comes to meat production, there isn't a more efficient homestead animal than the rabbit. It takes a minimum of space and labor to raise, and the cost of its feed versus the amount of meat it produces is minimal. It can't even begin to be compared, pound for pound, with the cost of raising any other type of meat on a small homestead. The amount of protein in rabbit meat is exceeded only by roast chicken and certain cuts of lean beef. For every 100 grams of meat, rabbit has 29.3 grams of protein, roasted chicken has 32.3 grams of protein, and broiled lean beef sirloin has 32.2 grams of protein. And rabbits have another advantage that anyone considering small-scale homesteading should consider. If you live within the boundaries of some cities or towns, or even on the outskirts, you will frequently come up against zoning laws prohibiting such animals as pigs, goats, and chickens, but I have never heard of a community that banned a few rabbits. They make no noise, and when well cared for, they have no odor.

After the first year of our homesteading experience, my brother, who lives in a good-size, heavily populated community, decided to try his hand at raising rabbits. He had about an acre of land, and his two-car garage was actually built like a small barn with a loft. He built some sturdy cages, which he keeps in the loft in the winter and outside under the trees in the summer. He has found the experience to be extremely rewarding.

One good doe produces between thirty and forty fryer rabbits per year. In our first year we had three does and one buck, which produced ninety-six fryers that dressed off between 2 and 3 pounds each. If you like rabbit as well as my family does, three does and one buck, providing about ninety-six fryers per year, will not give you too much meat. When I fry rabbit for my family of five, I cook at least two. If your children are small and you are not big meat eaters, you could cut down to two does and one buck. Ninety-six fryers a year give us fried rabbit about once a week. This project alone netted us about 250 pounds of high-quality protein. We could have netted more, but we butchered our fryers at the weaning age of eight weeks. Their liveweight averaged 4½ pounds each. We weighed the cost of feed to raise them for four more weeks against the extra meat we would have and felt that it would not be practical from the point of view of cost to keep them any longer. Since then, for various reasons, we have had occasion to raise some to the twelve-week age and found our reasoning to be accurate.

Housing

Rabbits can be raised year-round in outside pens, as long as they are properly constructed to protect them from icy winds, rain, and snow in the winter and extreme heat and sun in the summer. As a matter of fact, they tolerate the extremes of cold far better than the extremes of heat. However, if you are intending to build housing for chickens and goats, you should consider making it large enough to house the rabbits, too. This isn't just for the sake of the rabbits. Remember, the raw cold winds of zero-and-below weather can make the job of tending your stock a pretty miserable experience, and you need to think of your own comfort.

Because I feel that you should get as much as you can out of homesteading right from the beginning, I shall give you instructions for constructing pens that can be used outside at first, until such time as a small shelter can be built to house all of your animals. If you already have a garage or other type of outbuilding, so much the better. These pens can be moved indoors whenever you're ready.

The area of our barn that houses our goats, chickens, and rabbits is not large, so to get the most out of it, we put our pens up double-decker style. Below you will find plans for constructing a single-decker pen. To double it up like we did, follow the same plans as shown here, but build the front side of the bottom tier higher; 30 inches is good. Leave the back side the same. Leave 6 inches between tiers at the front. This will give you an opening of 16 inches at the back, creating a steeper pitch for the roof of the bottom pen in order to allow the urine and manure to run off easily. A covering of roofing tin on the roof of the bottom pens prevents the urine from soaking into the wood. The 16-inch clearance at the back allows plenty of space to enable you to get in to do a thorough cleaning. Scraping it down every couple of days with a short-handled hoe keeps cleanup time to a minimum.

You can build the pens as large as you want, but don't build them any smaller than the specifications. Doors must be large enough to allow easy access for feeding and cleaning and to allow you to place your kindle boxes (nest boxes) in and take them out. Floors should be constructed of ½-inch hardware cloth or 12-gauge galvanized mesh wire. Anything less heavy than this will sag. We use 1-inch galvanized mesh for the sides. Don't use anything smaller than ½-inch mesh for the floors, because you need that much space for their droppings to come through. On the other hand, don't use anything larger either, or you are apt to lose a newborn bunny that is born outside the kindle box.

If the pens are built outside and must house your rabbits during the cold

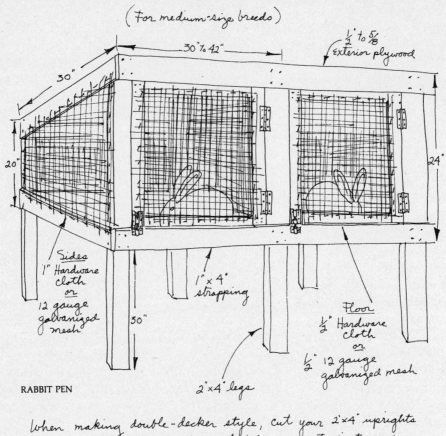

(For medium-size breeds)

30" to 42"

½" to ⅝"
Exterior plywood

30"

20"

24"

Sides
1" Hardware
cloth
or
12 gauge
galvanized
mesh

1" x 4"
strapping

30"

Floor
½" Hardware
cloth
or
½" 12 gauge
galvanized mesh

RABBIT PEN

2" x 4" legs

When making double-decker style, cut your 2"x4" uprights
7 ft. 6 in. The rest of the materials are cut just as you
would for your bottom pens.

weather, you must give extra thought to their construction. These are the things you will need to do in the early winter:

1 Try to place the cages where they will receive protection from westerly winds. A southern exposure is good, as long as you can move the pens in the summer to provide shade of some form.

2 Build pens in a single tier and make panels of ¾-inch plywood that can be screwed on the backs and sides from the top of the pen to the ground. Make sure that the panels meet well enough to stop icy winds.

3 Make hinged panels to open like doors across the open bottom of the cages; then you can open them for an occasional cleaning. Do not clean too often. The buildup of manure provides extra heat to keep your rabbits warm.

4 Tack burlap or grain bags to the top edge of the pens. When the weather is really bitter or your rabbits are going to kindle (give birth), you can pull these bags

down to hang loosely over the front of the pens when they have new bunnies.

5   In the summertime reverse all of these steps, and on extremely hot days wring out some burlap bags in cold water and place them on the floors of the pens to help keep the rabbits cool.

Follow these simple rules carefully, and with normal good care you can raise your rabbits outside year-round.

Nest Boxes

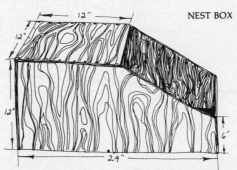

NEST BOX

A nest box is provided to a doe about five or six days before she kindles. Along with the nest box you should provide the hay or straw with which she will build a nest. She will pull hair from her body, mostly her neck, and line the nest to keep it warm. The box shown is very easy to construct. One sheet of 4-by-8-by-¾-inch plywood will build three nest boxes. Make sure to drill holes at least ¼ inch in diameter in the bottom for drainage. The first instructions we found for these boxes neglected to mention this, and I guess we weren't too swift, because we didn't think to do it. Our first two batches of bunnies made out all right, but it was bitterly cold when the third batch arrived, and they froze to the bottom of the wet box. This sad experience taught us a very important lesson.

It's a good idea to cover all the exposed edges of the boxes with metal strips (the kind you use for carpet edging works well). Rabbits love to chew wood, and they'll destroy their kindle boxes otherwise.

Keep kindle boxes clean. Between each use they should be scrubbed well with a stiff brush and some premises cleanser, available at farm supply stores. We keep an inexpensive propane torch on hand to singe out any hairs remaining in the boxes. This prevents the spread of disease. There is another way to singe them, though I don't recommend doing it unless you are in a pinch. Once in a while we run out of propane, and my husband takes the boxes out to an open area away from the buildings, loosely balls up a piece of newspaper, puts it in the box, and ignites it. The paper burns out before it has a chance to damage the box, and it does a pretty good job of cleaning up any remaining hairs. Then place the box out in the sun for a day to sanitize.

Feeding Equipment

The simplest type of feeder is made of coffee cans attached to the sides of the pens. If you use this type, make sure that you bend in an edge all around the top. The sharp edges of a top just cut off will injure your rabbits. Heavy crocks that can't be tipped make the best feeders, though they are not good for a rabbit with a litter. Little bunnies climb in and soil the food with manure and urine. For does with litters, the self-feeder type is best. Rabbit supply houses sell these.

There are some excellent watering devices on the market for rabbits, but most are so expensive that they just aren't practicable for the part-time farmer. Because a rabbit with a litter needs about a gallon of fresh, clean water a day, you can see that it's really important to work out something efficient. The "dew drop" nozzles that are sold to be set up with commercial watering equipment can be rigged up at the homestead by screwing them into a plastic bottle that has been turned upside down and attached to the outside of the pen. Punch holes in the end that's up so that the water can flow freely. We finally found a place that sells a plastic bottle with a ballpoint nozzle just for rabbits. It holds a quart of water and attaches with its own hook to the outside of the pen. If these bottles are not available in your area, you could write to Oasis Pet Products, Division of AtCo Manufacturing Co., Inc., 461 Walnut Street, Napa, California 94558. I'm sure they would be happy to send information and price lists on these bottles. Even little bunnies learn to drink quickly from these. The next best are the heavy crocks and, last of all, coffee cans.

Be sure to keep all feed and watering equipment clean. Wash it often in hot sudsy water and disinfect it with a chlorine solution. Liver coccidiosis is a common disease in rabbits and can cost you your stock if it gets out of hand. Cleanliness is the best preventative there is against this disease.

What to Look For When Buying Your Rabbits

Most people honestly believe that all rabbits are alike except for color. They are all furry and have ears, fluffy tails, and cute little noses, but when it comes to homestead stock for meat production, you've got to know the difference.

Small rabbits, such as the American Dutch, are really raised for show rabbits. They are not good meat producers. On the other hand, the Flemish Giant, which at maturity can weigh as much as 20 pounds, is not one of the best meat producers, either. The reason for this is that they are large-boned rabbits with heavy coats, and their dressed-out weight of actual meat usually falls below the net meat weight of a good medium-size breed with smaller bones and lighter coats. These rabbits also eat more in proportion to net meat production than a good meat-producing breed will.

For the homesteader, the two proven best breeds so far have been the Californian, which is a white rabbit with black markings on the nose, ears, feet, and tail. This rabbit was developed basically from crossing the New Zealand White with the Himalayan. The doe's mature weight runs about 8½ to 10½ pounds. These rabbits are very fine producers of offspring that become meaty fryers of a good size. The second breed best suited to meat production is the New Zealand White.

Commercial buyers consider this rabbit the ideal. The mature doe weighs an average of 10 to 12 pounds and the bucks 9 to 11 pounds. This breed also comes in a beautiful red color.

When selecting your breeding stock, try to buy from a reputable breeder. Breeding does from the breeds we've recommended should be six months old, bucks six to seven months old. It's hard for a novice to pick good breeding stock, but there are a few things you can avoid. Never buy stock that has a sore anywhere, a runny nose, a cough, diarrhea, a dirty, yellowed coat, or one that appears listless. Their eyes should be bright and their coat shiny. When moving around in their pens, they should act lively. A doe that appears curious and friendly when you approach her cage, one who comes to the front to look you over, will be a doe that is easy to handle. This type of doe is easier to breed and is less apt to kill her young if anyone is around when she kindles. Check the bucks for healthy, well-descended testicles. Make sure that the testicles are not withered or dry. These conditions indicate that the buck is either too old or that he's sterile.

A good doe will produce four to six litters of fryers a year until she is almost three years old. Then it's time to change your breeding stock. A doe from one of her litters would be a good replacement choice. Bucks are good for service for about the same length of time.

Feeding

While most pictures of rabbits show them happily munching on a carrot or a lettuce leaf, this is not an adequate diet for rabbits. Rabbits are vegetarians, but in order for them to grow well and produce high-quality protein, they need a good supply of protein in their own diet. For the small homesteader with limited time, equipment, and land, the easiest way to see to it that his stock is properly fed is to buy commercial pelleted ration that is especially prepared for rabbits and supplement this with a good-quality alfalfa hay.

Rabbits are mostly night-time eaters, so the majority of their feed is given at night. A mature doe that weighs about 10 pounds should receive about 6 ounces of feed a day. That should be broken down into 2½ to 3½ ounces of grain and the rest hay. If you are having problems getting hay for your stock, it's good to know that except for nest building, rabbits do not have to have hay. You could give them their entire ration in grain because much of their pelleted ration is made up of pressed alfalfa. For added roughage you could give them garden greens and grass. Bucks being raised for breeding require a little bit more, about 7 ounces, until they reach breeding age. A doe with a litter should have as much as she will eat. A pregnant doe should receive a ration that has at least 16 percent protein in it, and 20 percent is even better.

If you watch your stock closely, you can tell if they are being fed enough.

They will grow thin and their coat will lose its shine if they are underfed. In such a case, slowly increase the amount of feed given. Never overfeed your breeding stock, since fat tends to build up around the reproductive organs, and your does will have a hard time kindling. Don't make the mistake of thinking that your rabbits will require a lot more feed to keep warm in cold weather, or you will halt production completely.

Carrots and leafy vegetables are a good treat for your rabbits, but start easy when adding them to their diet. Too much can give them diarrhea. Root vegetables, such as carrots, potatoes, mangel beets, and artichokes, have more food value than leafy vegetables, but don't feed these before or with their grain ration. If you do, they will leave their grain ration and eat the tastier vegetables and not get enough protein.

Small salt blocks should be kept in the pens at all times, along with plenty of fresh water. Be sure to check a couple of times a day in cold weather to see if the water has frozen. It's a good idea to keep small twigs of fruit trees or alders in the rabbit pens. This gives them something to nibble on, and they are less apt to try to chew on their cages.

Breeding

Rabbits are supposed to be noted for their ability to multiply rapidly. This is not completely true, but their heat periods, which follow a twenty-one-day cycle, tend to overlap because egg cells are constantly developing and disintegrating, so it's not important to know when they actually are in heat.

Decide on a breeding schedule for each doe and breed her on schedule until she is bred. Always take the doe to the buck's pen for service. Mating should occur within a matter of minutes. When you see the buck fall over, it is a sign that mating has occurred. Put the doe back in her pen and repeat one more time several hours later. The reason for this is that many times if the doe is not in heat when you put her with the buck, the mating act will cause her to release one of her eggs. This takes a couple of hours, and in the meantime she might have urinated and washed off the semen. Breeding her again four to eight hours after the first time will ensure her getting pregnant. Never leave the doe in the pen with the buck, or he might injure her.

Keep accurate records of the names, ages, and breeding dates of all your stock for successful management. Our cards look like the one shown here. On the back of the card, we try to keep track of the does' parentage and their production records.

DOE	NAME BUCK	DATE BRED	DATE KINDLED	No. ALIVE	No. DEAD
Honey	Sam	3/4/78	4/7/78	8	0

Determining Pregnancy

We've been raising rabbits for several years, and we have had some does fool us completely. We've had does who developed large, hard bellies and heavy dewlaps, and we were sure they were bred, but it turned out to be false pregnancy. Others exhibited no changes at all and kindled six- and seven-bunny litters. You really should try, though, to determine pregnancy if you can, for successful meat production.

Around the twelfth to the fourteenth day, it is possible to palpate the doe. To do this, hold the ears and fold the skin over the shoulders in the right hand. Place the left hand between the hind legs, slightly in front of the pelvis. Place the thumb on the right side of the abdomen, and using light pressure, move the fingers and thumb gently forward and backward. (I always have someone help me hold the rabbit.) If the doe is pregnant, you should be able to feel little marble-size forms as they come between your thumb and fingers. Be careful not to use too much pressure.

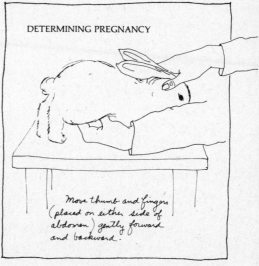

DETERMINING PREGNANCY

Move thumb and fingers (placed on either side of abdomen) gently forward and backward.

If you aren't sure, try again in a week. If it appears that the doe is not pregnant, you can try to put her in with the buck again, but sometimes that will cause her to abort if she has been bred. The best policy is to wait until it is thirty-four days since she has been bred and, if she does not kindle, breed her again right away. The gestation period for does is usually thirty-one days. Never use a buck for breeding more than two or three times a week. One buck is enough for ten does.

Good healthy stock can be bred when their bunnies are from four to eight weeks old, but even breeding when they are eight weeks old will give you four litters a year. A doe can't raise large litters in hot summer weather, so we follow a tight breeding schedule in the winter and breed six weeks after kindling.

Occasionally, especially in cold weather, a doe will lose her litter right after kindling, or she might kill them. Breed her right away again; do not wait. If she kills more than one batch, get rid of her; she will never make a good mother.

Kindling

Five or six days before the doe is due to kindle, place the kindle box in her pen and give her some clean hay or straw to form a nest. She will pull fur from her body to line the nest and keep her bunnies warm.

Rabbits usually kindle at night, but if you can see that they are getting ready to kindle during the day, try to keep noise and confusion to a minimum. It frequently happens that an excited doe kills her babies. This is a good reason for not placing your cages near a busy road or area of high activity.

If you can see that there isn't much fur in the nest after the doe has kindled, pull some fur from her neck and body and cover the nest. On occasion a doe will have her litter outside the nest or half of the bunnies in the nest and the other half outside. When this happens, the doe will not nurse both groups, so carefully try to place all the bunnies in the box.

A doe that has become accustomed to you and has been well cared for will allow you to check her nest and remove any malformed or dead bunnies. If the doe is an especially nervous one, you should wait a day or two and then rub Vaseline on the doe's nose so that she can't pick up the smell of your fingers on her bunnies, then check them out. We usually distract our does by giving them a treat to eat while we check on the babies.

In very cold weather, if the nests are not warm enough, the bunnies might appear to be cold and dead. Warming them between the palms of your hands or even putting them in a box near the warm stove for a while might save your litter. Put them back in the nest with extra fur. Keep extra fur in plastic bags for this purpose.

Leave only six to eight rabbits per litter if you want good-sized fryers. We have found that if two does kindle within thirty-six hours of each other, it's possible to take extras from the larger litter and give them to the doe with the smaller litter.

Young rabbits usually open their eyes by the time they are ten days old. They have all their fur by then, too, and are very cute miniatures of their mother. By the time they reach three weeks old they are scampering in and out of their box. At this age it's very hard to think of butchering them.

In order not to have any problems on this score, we made a rule at our homestead. All breeders can be made pets of, and the children may play with them. They may play with bunnies occasionally, too, as long as it is clearly understood that they are being raised for meat. We have never had any problems with the children accepting this rule.

Leave the young rabbits with the doe until they are about eight weeks old. By that time she has weaned them, and they are eating well. Fryer rabbits should be ready to butcher at this time.

Determining the Sex of Rabbits

If you want to raise any of your own rabbits for breeding stock, you will need to determine their sex. Male and female bunnies should be separated when they are weaned.

It is much easier to sex rabbits if you have someone to help you, but if you must do it alone, grasp the rabbit by the fold of skin on the back of its neck. Rest its rump on a box or shelf with its feet up in the air. This takes patience because they will squirm to get out of this unnatural position. With the right hand, press to either side of the sex organ. A doe's sex organ will look like a slit, and a buck's looks like a small round circle. A little gentle pressure will cause the buck's sex organ to protrude.

Butchering

Rabbits are much easier to butcher than any other animal on the homestead. They are even easier to butcher than chickens, because you don't have to pluck any feathers.

Start by stunning the rabbit. There are two ways to do this. Either hit it on the head with a good-size stick, striking it just ahead of the ears. Or cup its chin in your hand, with the thumb and small finger up by its ears, and with your left hand grasp the hind legs and quickly jerk them downward, snapping the neck. You have to have strong hands to do it this way, and it takes practice.

Cut the head off immediately and hang the body upside down to bleed by running a hook or piece of baling twine through the tendon in one hind leg. Cut off the other three feet. Then make an incision in the leg that is tied up; cut down to the groin; cut the other leg the same way; and then cut off the tail. Cut across between the two legs and peel the hide off, just the way you would peel off rubber gloves, inside out.

To eviscerate the rabbit, make a small cut in the stomach wall, just big enough to allow you to slip a finger in, then, with this finger to guide you, cut the stomach open, being careful not to cut into the intestines. Cut the liver, being careful not to cut into the gall bladder. Cut off the remaining hind foot and wash the carcass well, removing any loose tissue.

To cut the carcass for frying, cut the front legs off just behind the shoulders, cut this piece in half, then cut the hind legs off and cut that piece in half. Split the midsection into two pieces by cutting it lengthwise along the backbone. Cool quickly. Recipes for cooking rabbit are given in Chapter 11.

This is a good time to examine the livers. If you see any little white spots on them, do not eat them. It means that your rabbits have coccidiosis. It's perfectly all right to eat the rest of the rabbit. If your rabbits have coccidiosis, the chances are that all the rabbits in the adjoining pens have it too, so it's a good idea to treat them for it. Call a vet, explain what is wrong, and have him recommend a drug that is usually put in their water. He will also tell you where you can buy it.

Rabbit furs are no longer in demand now that so many fake furs are on the market, but if you'd like to try your hand at some project using rabbit furs, you must clean and dry the hides. Wash the hide well in cold water to remove all the blood. Cut away any fat or pieces of tissue and turn it inside out, as it came off the rabbit. Take an old coat hanger, shape it to fit inside the uncut hide and pull it to fit tightly on the inside. Hang it to dry in a cool, dry place. Do not dry hides in the sun.

Other Rabbit By-products

Offal from freshly butchered rabbit is very high-quality feed for your hogs, and rabbit manure is great for the garden. This manure has an advantage over the other manures in that it can be placed in the garden at any time. If it comes in contact with the plants, it will not burn them. The reason for this is that rabbits have a system of breaking down their excretions that makes them equal to manure that has been composted and aged.

When the addition to our homestead was made, some necessary dirt removal left my flower garden barren of good topsoil. For the next two years we plowed in compost and gave the flowers all kinds of tender loving care, but the flower garden still looked sick. I finally decided to put all the rabbit manure into the flower garden, and that year I had a beautiful garden again, with more flowers than ever before.

9

RAISING

A VEAL CALF

Small homesteads cannot provide enough hay, grain, and pasture to raise a beef or milk cow. It could be done if you were willing to purchase all feed commercially, but then you would be defeating your goals of self-sufficiency. However, it is very practicable to raise a calf or two for veal on the small homestead, since this project requires very little space, and only six to fourteen weeks of time. *Veal* is a term used to describe the meat of a very young calf, under fifteen weeks old.

Those of you who have tried to buy veal in the supermarket lately will find that it is one of the most costly meats available. Part of the reason for this is that it is high in protein and low in fat, making it very attractive to people who are diet-conscious. Veal is considered by most to be a delicacy because of the fine, even grain of the meat and its pale pink coloring; however, veal raised on the homestead might vary slightly in both coloring and flavor. It will depend on the type of feed and bedding used to raise the calf.

Housing

As with all animal projects on the homestead, you need to prepare in advance for the calf's arrival and care. Housing needs for the calf are very simple, and by raising it from May to August or June to September, you can keep you needs even simpler. Keep in mind that baby calves, like any baby animal, are more susceptible to illness than more mature animals, and veal calves are especially so because they are kept on a diet of just milk. The lack of iron in its diet makes it anemic. A calf needs to be housed in an area that is clean and draft-free. The building should be well ventilated. You do not need a large area for your calf; a tie stall (a stall in which the calf can be tied in place with a chain and collar) 2½ by 4 feet or a pen just slightly larger is plenty.

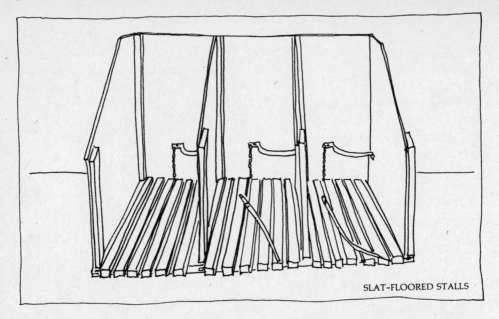

SLAT-FLOORED STALLS

Here at Sunnybrook we have found that one of the most important factors in keeping our calves healthy is keeping them dry, so the type of pen we use is based on this factor. There are many opinions on the best way to keep calves dry, so I will give you several to choose from. Method 1: Raise them on concrete floors with hay bedding, cleaned twice daily. Method 2: Keep them on concrete floors and allow manure and bedding to build up so that it will pack down; this will keep them warm and dry. Method 3: Keep them in stalls with slat floors to drain away excess urine. Method 4: Keep them on dirt floors with bedding. If you wanted to raise veal as close to commercial quality as possible, you would have to choose Method 3 because calves will nibble at their bedding, and this causes the meat to be a darker color.

We have tried each method, and our findings are as follows: Method 1: Calves wet so much that this method made it impossible to keep them dry. Method 2: Warmth is not really a major concern in warm weather, and because calves raised on milk have such an odor to their manure, we could not stand the smell in our barn. This method also attracted every fly in the neighborhood, a very undesirable aspect. Method 3: In spite of our best efforts to construct sturdy slat floors, the calves always managed to break at least one slat, which frequently resulted in hoof injuries. Method 4: We finally decided on dirt floors with plenty of bedding. Urine drains well, the bedding keeps them warm enough, and it is cleaned as often as it needs to be. Furthermore, we believe that the dirt floors keep our calves cooler in the summer, when it gets very hot in our little barn. For some reason that I can't explain, we have had fewer cases of scours since we switched to dirt floors. An outside pen can be used in nice weather, but it must have a roof and be built up on all sides to protect the young calf from the elements. I personally feel that very young calves do best in an area that is totally enclosed.

Children can become very attached to little calves. Our first Holstein-Angus calf could never have been used for veal (it would have been too tough) because the children would take him out and play with him like a puppy. He loved it, and even when he had grown into a two-year-old steer, he would get out of the pasture and go visit the neighbors to play. One Sunday morning a neighbor of ours, all dressed up in a long gown for a church program, came walking down the highway with Freddie in tow. She wasn't too happy, but Freddie thought it was great. Veal calves must be kept as confined as possible in order to keep the meat tender. If they develop firm muscle tissue from being active, it would make this meat that is low in fat content very tough.

What to Look For When Buying Your Veal Calf

Veal calves are usually sold at three days old and have been with their mother to be nursed for three days on colostrum, which contains the antibodies that protect them from infections in their early days. Because this is the biggest single factor in the future health of the calf, it is best to buy from a reputable farmer rather than at an auction. Some farmers sell their "bob" (one-day-old calves) to auctioneers without giving them any colostrum, and these young calves do not stand a chance against infection. We raise our own calves, so they receive only mother's milk, a factor in the darker color of our veal.

If at all possible, try to make arrangements with the farmer to keep the calf with its mother for at least six days. Offer to pay his costs for the loss of the extra milk from his dairy. Make sure that the calf you buy doesn't have scours (loose, watery stools) and that its navel is clean and dry. Don't buy a calf just because you fall in love with its beautiful large, soft eyes. Believe me, there isn't an animal as gentle looking and as winning as a tiny new calf. Do not buy calves that weigh under 90 pounds to raise; they do not gain quickly enough to make good veal.

Calves from any of the beef-type cows make good veal (Angus, Whiteface, Hereford, etc.), as do dairy-beef crosses from the heavier type of cow such as Holstein, Brown Swiss, and Ayrshire. Purebred dairy calves from these breeds also make good veal calves. We raise Holstein-Angus veal calves and beef cows, and we are very happy with their rate of growth.

Feeding

There are at least two practical ways to feed homegrown veal. If you want an end product that is as close to commercial veal as possible, then raise the calf on a high-energy commercial milk replacer only, using the following table as a guide.

MILK REPLACER FEEDING SCHEDULE, BASED ON TWICE-DAILY FEEDING

Age	Pounds of Dry Powder per Feeding
4 to 7 days	0.4
Second week	0.7
Third week	1.2
Fourth week	1.5
Fifth week	2.1
Sixth week	2.6
Seventh week +	upper limit is ability of calf to consume

SOURCE: Slack and Warner, 1965, U.S.D.A. Extension Service, University of Massachusetts Bulletin #106.
NOTE: Calves aged 1 to 3 days should be nursed by the cow or hand-fed colostrum.

The dry powder is usually mixed with water at the ratio of 1 pound of dry powder to 5 to 7 pounds of water, the higher water level being fed at earlier ages and the lower level at a later age to increase the quantity of the dry-matter intake. The rate of gain that you could expect from sturdy calves of 100 or more pounds at birth would be about 1 pound per day during the first two weeks, followed by 1½ to 2 pounds per day during the third and fourth weeks, and increasing to 2 to 2½ pounds per day or better during the fifth to eighth weeks. At the end of eight weeks, these animals should weigh 200 pounds and should have the desired fat cover to make them good veal. To raise them beyond eight weeks, feed as much of the seventh-week mixture as your calf will take. For example, 2 pounds of powder mixed with 11 pounds of water. This makes about 1½ gallons of mixture. If your calf will drink more than this, mix another batch.

The replacer you use should contain at least 20 percent protein and 20 percent fat. Since veal calves must be butchered before they reach fifteen weeks old (beyond that they will have to be kept until at least a year, since the meat in the interval of fifteen weeks to one year is tasteless, and it's tough and sinewy), it is not expensive to buy the commercial milk replacer. It takes about 200 pounds to raise the calf to thirteen to fifteen weeks.

Milk or milk replacer should always be fed warm, about 90 degrees F. In order to obtain the pale pink color of fine veal, you should not use bedding of any kind, as I mentioned before. Do not feed any grain or hay, and unless the weather is very hot, do not water veal calves; it tends to make them bloat, and they drink less milk.

We raise our veal calves on whole milk, either cow's or goat's. We start with about 8 pounds per day the first week and gradually increase until the calf drinks all it will take. We are careful not to overfeed our calves, and at the first sign of scours we go back to the previous level or lower until all signs of scours disappear.

Then we proceed slowly again to the next level. With whole milk we do not use any standard rate of increase. We find that each calf can drink only so much, and we let the calf tell us what it needs by watching to see if it develops scours or if it fails to gain fast enough. The first sign means that it is too much milk and the second means that it is not getting enough. It takes only two to five days on each level to know whether you are making a mistake or not. We do not feed grain or hay, nor do we give water, but we do use old hay or sawdust for bedding, and our veal does have a darker color to the meat than commercial veal, but it's tender and delicious.

Calves should be fed twice a day at regular times. They may be fed from a bottle, nipple pail, or regular pail. It's important that the feeding containers be clean. As I said earlier, veal calves tend to be anemic and get sick easily. We use a bottle to start our calves and switch to pail feeding at two months. We feel that we have fewer digestive problems with this method of feeding, because baby calves tend to gulp too fast and swallow too much air. To switch from bottle to pail feeding, use the same method I recommended for kids (see page 134).

Diseases

If you have taken care to buy a healthy calf from a reputable farmer, you have gone a long way toward preventing many diseases that veal calves are subject to. The most common problems you will have to deal with will be scours and pneumonia. Scours comes from overfeeding; infectious scours is a bacterial infection and is less common in a calf that has plenty of colostrum. Young calves are especially susceptible to pneumonia, so at the first signs of a cold, call a vet for antibiotics. He or she can teach you how to give the injections yourself. Again, though, prevention is better than cure, so make sure you have purchased a calf that has been with its dam (mother) for at least three days and keep your calves dry, warm, and free from drafts that will cause a chill.

If your calf is housed in a barn that contains other animals, it might catch lice (a common problem on the farm in the springtime). Lice reduce the calf's ability to gain weight, so it should be sprayed with a good commercial spray. You can buy several different brands at farm supply stores. Spray again a second time in two weeks to kill the lice that were hatched from nits (eggs) that had been laid just before the time of the first spraying.

Another problem that beginners are apt to experience is lead poisoning. This is usually caused by the calf's licking boards in its stall that have been painted with lead paint. It may have faded to the point where it is hard to tell that the board was ever painted, but it's enough to kill a calf. Don't risk losing your calf if you suspect that a board you are using may have been painted and you aren't sure what type of paint was used.

Keep your stalls as clean as possible to prevent attracting flies. Flies spread diseases in hot weather faster than anything. There are other types of funguses and bacterial diseases that affect calves, but on the small homestead where animals are well cared for they are not as apt to develop. A veterinarian can be called in if a problem arises that you are concerned about.

Butchering

We do not butcher our own veal because we are not set up to handle large carcasses, but we do have the slaughtering done at home by a local farmer to make sure that the calf does not suffer in any way. Then we bring it to our favorite butcher and have him cut and wrap it for us. I checked with the extension service to try to find a booklet on slaughtering and butchering that could be obtained for those of you who would like to try it at home, but there is very little printed information available on raising veal on a small scale, and nothing on slaughtering.

Veal calves can be butchered anytime after five weeks. However, for the homesteader who does not raise beef, it is more practical to wait until they are fourteen to fifteen weeks old. At that time they will dress out to approximately 225 pounds hanging weight. You could expect from this size carcass an approximate yield of the following:

12 to 14 pounds of ground meat
8 to 10 pounds of stew meat
10 pounds of organ meats (brains, liver, heart, tongue, and sweetbreads)
20 pounds of cutlets
20 pounds of chops
4 roasts, totaling 22 to 26 pounds
20 pounds or more of soup bones for soup stock

I feel that this is a conservative estimate. This amount of meat from one calf, or doubled if you raise two (and why not?), can add a considerable amount of nutrition and variety to your diet at a very reasonable cost.

10  RAISING POULTRY

CHICKENS

Even the smallest homestead can provide enough room for a few chickens, and when you take time to consider the many uses of the little egg, to say nothing of the high-quality protein that chicken itself provides, you will most probably want to include a flock of laying hens. Ten hens would be more than enough for the average family, and you could raise a few broilers and/or capons for meat. Eggs alone are a very high-quality source of complete protein besides being a wonderful addition to casseroles, sauces, fruit breads, and desserts.

What to Look For When Buying Your Chickens

There are several breeds of chickens that are especially suited to the noncommercial farmer. If egg production is your chief aim, good choices would include White Leghorn strains and crosses, California Whites, Rhode Island Reds, and Bantam strains. A more recent cross, sold by Sears, Roebuck and Company, called the Mini, is a small white bird that starts laying at twenty to twenty-two weeks and lays 75 percent or more large white eggs for a full year or more, with an average production period of fifteen to sixteen months. These birds only require about 74 percent as much feed per dozen eggs produced as the average layer.

When you are raising a small flock of hens for egg production, it is more practical to consider the virtues of the smaller breeds of hens. You should think in terms of feed costs, egg production, length of productivity, and space requirements. These factors are more important than the meat value of the bird. By the time you cull your laying flock (remove hens that are no longer laying), the hens will be too old to have any value as broilers, fryers, or roasters. They will make good stewing birds, but that's about all. It's far more practical to raise a separate flock of meat birds and to concentrate on good egg production from your laying flock at the lowest possible cost. You do not need a rooster for egg production. Unless you want fertile eggs for hatching your own chicks, you need not provide a rooster.

Once hens start laying, they usually average one egg per day throughout their laying period, so for a family of four, I would recommend a laying flock of between six and ten hens. This would give you plenty to eat and cook with, plus possibly a dozen or more a week to sell to help pay for their grain.

There are several possible ways to go about starting your laying flock. First of all, you can buy day-old chicks. These chicks will require more care and feed to raise to twenty to twenty-four weeks of age, at which time they will begin to produce. There is also a high risk of loss, because young chicks are susceptible to many diseases. Another way is to buy older, ready-to-lay pullets. These young hens will cost you more, but because you won't have such a high risk of loss, plus the expense of a heated brooder for the chicks, you might feel that this is more practical. The third possibility would be to buy seventeen- to eighteen-month-old hens from commercial egg producers. These hens no longer lay an egg every day, but the three or four a week that they will lay for another four to six months are usually much larger. If you can buy these hens at one-third or less the cost of a pullet just beginning to lay, it could be a very good alternative. We like to keep a pretty constant level of production, so we buy pullets just starting to lay in the fall and renew our flocks at the end of each twelve-month period. This way we maintain a steady ratio of feed to egg production, without any losses.

One other possible way to acquire a laying flock is to start your own chicks in an incubator. Fertile eggs can sometimes be purchased from a local farmer the first year. Some years we've raised our own this way. It's more work, but it's exciting and rewarding. Because we have needed to make the most of our time and equipment, we now buy our meat birds as day-old chicks and our laying hens as pullets. This frees our incubator for use in hatching extra duck eggs. There are many types of incubators on the market. For the small homestead the most practical type is the tabletop incubator. They come in two sizes, the fifty-egg size and the hundred-egg size. The fifty-egg incubator can also be used for quail and pheasant eggs. The hundred-egg incubator can be used for quail, pheasant, chicken, turkey, duck, or goose eggs. These are sold by Montgomery Ward and Sears, Roebuck and Company. The other type of incubator is the tray type. It holds more eggs, but it is four to five times more expensive and is usually used by commercial hatcheries only. The main advantage of the tray type, other than the fact that you can hatch many more eggs, is that most makes automatically turn the eggs for you, while the smaller, tabletop types require that you turn the eggs yourself two to three times a day. Each incubator comes with its own special instructions. The most important things to remember are that you must have eggs from a fertile flock (a flock with a

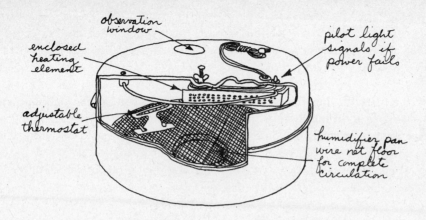

observation window

pilot light signals if power fails

enclosed heating element

adjustable thermostat

humidifier pan wire net floor for complete circulation

50-EGG CAPACITY INCUBATOR

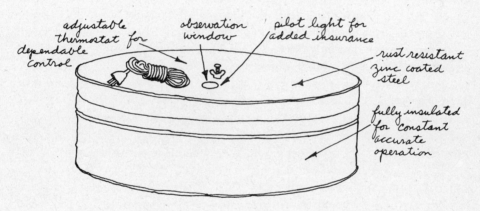

adjustable thermostat for dependable control

observation window

pilot light for added insurance

rust resistant zinc coated steel

fully insulated for constant accurate operation

100-EGG CAPACITY INCUBATOR

rooster) and that you must have twenty-one days at home in order to devote yourself to the project.

If you buy your birds, be sure to buy from reputable hatcheries. If there aren't any in your locality, Sears, Roebuck, which has mail-order houses all over the United States, has an excellent selection of stock. It is shipped quickly and carefully, with a guarantee of replacement for any immediate losses. It's a good idea to have your birds debeaked. A common problem with chickens, especially in the winter months when the days are short and they are more confined, is cannibalism. One chicken will start to pick at another, and as soon as blood is drawn, the rest of the flock will kill the injured bird. Having the chicks debeaked will prevent this, and it costs just pennies per bird. Chicks are shipped any time of the year except between November 15 to January 1, but if you live in colder climates, you should time their arrival for no earlier than April 1.

Housing and Equipment

When we first decided to start some day-old chicks, we consulted our how-to books for housing needs and were discouraged to find that they recommended approximately 1 square foot of floor space per chick. We didn't have any 25 square feet of floor space for the twenty-five chicks we wanted. Then they said that you had to have special brooders, or heating units, and so on. We were at the point of forgetting the whole idea when a wave of nostalgia hit me. I could remember my grandmother keeping her chicks in a cardboard box behind the wood stove in the kitchen. They remained there in the early spring for about four weeks until they feathered out, and they made out just fine. So we ordered our first twenty-five chicks and got a couple of good-size cardboard boxes, which we placed in a corner of the warmest room of the house. We covered the bottoms with sheets of heavy plastic and a layer of wood shavings. Over the top of the box we put a large-size window screen and threaded a light fixture with an extension cord through the center. We put a 150-watt bulb in the fixture. The temperature should be about 100 degrees F near the floor of the box. Most of the time it was warm enough for them just like this, but when it cooled down some nights, we put a blanket over part of the box, being careful not to let it come too near the light bulb. Every couple of days we would switch the chicks from one box to the other and clean out the dirty shavings and wash the plastic in the box that they had been in. When they were two weeks old, we divided them into two boxes and reduced the wattage of the bulbs to 75. We continued the same care until they were about four weeks old.

BROODER
BATTERY

By then they were well feathered out and could go into an outside movable wire coop. It was easy to tell when they were too warm because they would crowd into the outside corners of the box, and when they were too cool, they would huddle together under the light. We never lost a chick that year.

Commercial brooder batteries (stacked wire cages with a heated brooder unit at the top—see sketch) are available for raising chickens in small areas, but new ones are very expensive. We did have the good fortune to buy a secondhand one for a very reasonable cost, but they are scarce. We raise some broilers this way. Thirty birds can be raised to the fryer-broiler stage in these, and they require only about 3 by 4 feet of floor space.

Young chickens should never be placed in pens with older birds. The older birds will kill the younger ones. Another reason to separate them is that an infection that could be minor in an older flock of birds might very well become disastrous in a very young flock of birds.

Older birds can be raised in any shed or old building that is draft-free and that can be kept dry. They need protection from the cold and good ventilation in hot weather, but they don't need a heated building. You could use any old building that already exists if it meets these conditions, or you could construct a small unit such as the one shown here. We included our hen house in our small barn, which houses all our animals. Our meat birds—broilers, fryers, and capons—are raised mostly in outside pens that have one end enclosed to protect them from the elements. The other three-quarters of the pen is made of framing that is wire covered. These pens are reasonably lightweight and can be moved around to allow the chickens to have fresh grass and bugs to eat. Somehow these birds seem to taste better than those we have raised in the battery brooder.

HEN HOUSE

3 ft above floor

ROOST SPACE

It is recommended that you allow 3 to 4 square feet of floor space per bird. This can include roost space if you construct your roosts 3 feet off the floor instead of step fashion and clean out under the roosts daily to prevent diseases and parasites. We have found this to be an excellent way to house our laying flock in a small area. Incidentally, the only birds that need roosts are laying hens. Your roosts should allow about 12 inches of space per bird. The hen house should provide a nest for every four or five hens. Nest boxes 12 to 14 inches square are adequate. Feed and watering containers can be purchased in farm supply stores or made at home from simple materials. The important thing is to make sure that they are kept free from droppings at all times. Frequent washings with a good disinfectant are necessary. Clorox bleach will do as good a job as anything. A small night-light in the hen house during the short days of winter will help to keep egg production up, since hens require sixteen hours of light a day to lay.

Floors should be covered with 6 to 8 inches of good absorbent litter. Sawdust is good, and wood shavings or peanut hulls work well too. Clean the litter as soon as it gets damp and dirty. It's a good rule to clean and disinfect the hen

NEST BOXES

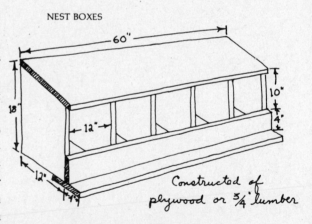

Constructed of plywood or 3/4" lumber

house in the early spring and again in the fall of each year. Sun is one of the best sanitizers there is, but it is not always possible to have enough sunlight in the hen house to do a good job. Premise cleansers, available from farm supply stores, are the best alternatives.

There is no need for hens to have an outside yard, but they do receive added benefits from fresh air, exercise, and sunshine. If we could, we would prefer to allow our birds to range freely, but we have two good reasons not to. Hawks, owls, and other predatory animals kill them, and when the tomatoes start to ripen in the

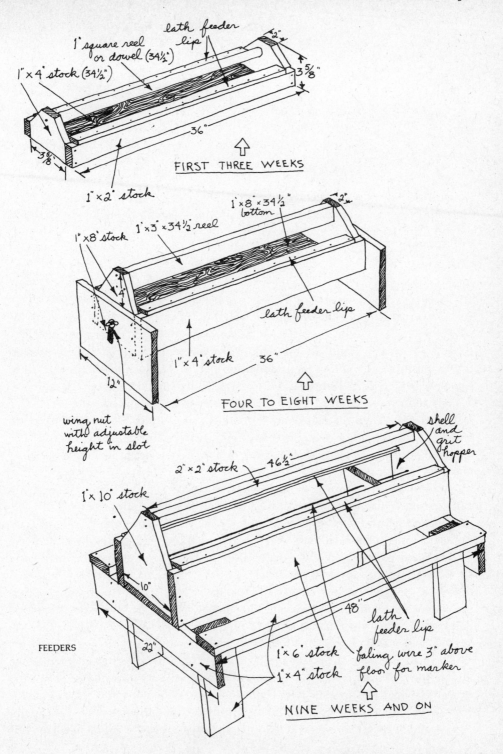

1" square reel
or dowel (34½")

lath feeder
lip

1" x 4" stock (34½")

2"

3⅝"

3⅝"

36"

1" x 2" stock

FIRST THREE WEEKS

1" x 8" x 34½"
bottom

2"

1" x 3" x 34½" reel

1" x 8" stock

lath feeder lip

4"

1" x 4" stock

36"

12"

wing nut
with adjustable
height in slot

FOUR TO EIGHT WEEKS

shell
and
grit
hopper

2" x 2" stock

46½"

1" x 10" stock

10"

48"

lath
feeder lip

FEEDERS

22"

1" x 6" stock

1" x 4" stock

baling wire 3" above
floor for marker

NINE WEEKS AND ON

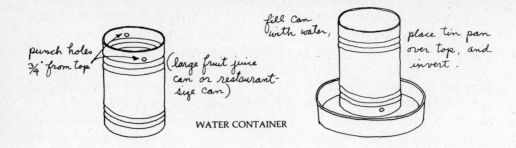

punch holes
¾" from top

(large fruit juice
can or restaurant-
size can)

fill can
with water,

place tin pan
over top, and
invert.

WATER CONTAINER

garden, the hens always seemed to find them before we did. To combat these problems, we built a good-size exercise yard that was totally enclosed, including the top, with 1-inch mesh chicken wire.

Feeding

If you are starting with baby chicks, you must feed them as soon as they arrive from the hatchery, so be sure to have starter mash on hand. When the chicks arrive, take each chick and dip its beak into some tepid water and then into the starter mash as you put it in the brooder (or box). Keep clean mash and water before them all the time. Temperatures in the brooder should be about 98 degrees F at first, and can be reduced by about 5 degrees every week until the chicks are feathered out. When the chicks are six to eight weeks old, it's time to switch to growing rations. Some growing rations supply grit, but if it isn't listed on the label and your supplier isn't sure that it's included, then you should include a feeder of fine grits in their pen.

Make sure that there is enough space at the feeder and waterer for all the chicks at one time, or some will not get enough to eat and others could be trampled on and killed. Our youngest daughter, Kim, who aspires to be a veterinarian, came upon one such chick soon after it had been trampled on. It had a broken leg, so Kim removed it from the brooder and set the leg in a splint made with Popsicle sticks and masking tape. She put the chick back with the others, and though it had to hobble, it survived. She changed the splint weekly as the chick grew, and in three weeks the splint was removed. The chick continued to thrive until "its time had come." If this chick had not been found immediately, it would have died, so keep a close watch on the chicks and cut down potential losses.

Laying hens are switched to laying mash two to four weeks before they start to lay, so if you have a breed that is supposed to lay in twenty-two weeks, you would start the laying mash anytime after eighteen weeks. Ground oyster shells or calcide crystals should be supplied at all times to provide calcium needed for firm shells. Feed is a big expense in egg production. Small breeds of hens eat an average of 85 to 90 pounds of feed per year per bird. Heavier breeds eat 95 to 115 pounds per year per bird. Laying hens should have feed before them all the time. We find that here in northern Vermont our flock eats more in the winter to keep warm, but egg production remains better than average even in the coldest of weather.

The small homesteader can cut the cost of feed for his or her laying flock considerably by supplementing the laying mash with table scraps, skim milk, cull (small, bruised, misshapen) potatoes, vegetables and peels, cabbage leaves, kale, and fresh grass clippings. If you have enough space to grow corn and a long-enough growing season to grow soybeans, you can provide almost all of your own feed. Corn should be an early variety that can dry on the stalk, and soybeans must have time to mature and dry, but they can be ground, shell and all, for feed. Small grinders are available from Montgomery Ward or Sears. Mixing one part ground beans to four parts ground corn and adding table scraps would supply nearly 100 percent of your flock's nutritional needs if they had an outside run to provide sunlight for vitamin D and dirt to scratch in for the balance of their vitamin and mineral needs. Even eggshells can be mixed with the oyster shell or calcide crystals. This would cut down on the amount of these feeds that you must purchase. Be sure to pulverize the eggshells very fine with a blender or hammer; otherwise the chickens will get the idea of eating their own eggs, and once they start, it's hard to stop them. Birds allowed to range freely require less commercial feed, but as I mentioned earlier, there are other disadvantages.

All chickens must have fresh clean water before them at all times. We use a

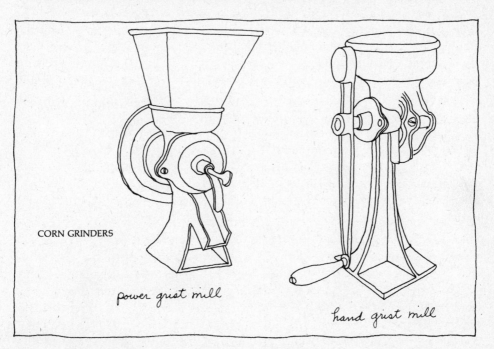

CORN GRINDERS

power grist mill

hand grist mill

heated watering unit during the winter months. It saves going out to the barn several times a day to crack the ice or to bring fresh water to the hens.

Meat chicks are fed the same as layer chicks the first few weeks. Broilers or fryers that are raised in a broiler battery brooder instead of in pens or on range must be fed a special battery brooder ration. Broilers are ready to butcher at about eight to ten weeks, and fryers are ready anytime from twelve to fourteen weeks on.

Capons

Capons are slow-moving castrated male chickens that are raised for large roasters. The meat is tender and very juicy. Their combs and wattles do not develop, so their heads seem out of proportion to the rest of their bodies. Their tail and saddle feathers grow very long, so they look very heavily feathered. You can start a capon flock two ways: Buy caponized chicks that are from any meat-type breed, or buy started capons that are sold by the commercial producers at four to six weeks of age. In most cases it's better to buy the started capons; then you don't have to worry about the risks of loss from the just-performed surgical operation. Capons grow well, fatten easily, and can be grown to as large as twelve to fourteen pounds.

Capons, chicks or starters (four-week-old chicks), are fed on high-quality chick starter until about nine weeks old. At that time they are switched to a high-energy growing ration until seventeen weeks. At seventeen weeks they should go on to a roaster ration (a mixture of grains that add fat for tenderness) or turkey finishing pellets until you are ready to butcher, at around twenty-four weeks.

It is recommended that the feed contain a coccidiostat to protect them from coccidiosis, a disease that is caused by a parasite common to most poultry farms. This is not as common a problem on the small homestead. If you decide to use a coccidiostat, make sure that it is the same one in each type of ration. For instance, you could lose your whole flock of capons by switching from one type to another as you change from starter ration to growing ration.

A flock of twenty-five average started capons will eat approximately 1,250 pounds of grain from four weeks to what is called market size, but supplements such as we've suggested for hens will cut the cost of this project considerably.

Moulting

Chickens go into moult (which means that they periodically cast off their outer layer of feathers) about every six months. If the novice homesteader is not prepared for this, it can scare him or her into believing that the chickens are dying for sure. Frequently they will lose all the feathers from one area of their body, usually the breast area. During this period of time, which can last for several weeks until they have grown new feathers, they do not lay well. Once the new feathers are grown, they resume laying. All forms of poultry go through this process. It is best not to butcher poultry at this time, because they are developing so many tiny new pinfeathers that it makes them difficult to clean.

Diseases

Breast blisters that appear on chickens confined to brooders or small coops are not really a disease. They form on the front part of the breastbone and are caused by the skin over the bone being irritated. These blisters will fill with a thick fluid and will often develop scabs. The best way to eliminate this is to give your birds enough space and to keep their litter dry and clean. Birds that roost will develop this problem too. Eliminating the roosts will help. Birds found to have this problem are perfectly safe to eat; simply cut off the blister when they are butchered.

Respiratory diseases are common in chickens and very hard to cure, so the best thing to do is keep your birds clean, dry, and free of cold drafts in the first place. Watch your flock for any signs of disease, and when you notice anything abnormal such as coughing, sneezing, difficulty in breathing, watery eyes, abnormal droppings, or poor appetite, remove this chicken from the flock immediately. Call a vet for a diagnosis and advice on treatment and start it right away. If the chicken doesn't respond quickly, kill the bird and bury it deeply to prevent the spread of the disease to the remaining flock. When this happens, you should always clean and disinfect the chicken house immediately.

Butchering

It takes very little equipment to process chickens on the homestead. The most important factor is cleanliness. Poultry that is contaminated with fecal droppings, dirty equipment, or people with transmittable diseases does not keep well. Bacteria will multiply very quickly. Try to keep the processing area as free from flies as possible, though in summertime it will be difficult.

Birds to be slaughtered should not be fed for twenty-four hours prior to slaughtering, but make sure they have plenty of fresh clean water.

All of the equipment shown here can be purchased in poultry or farm supply stores. Many items can be made at home. The first picture shows a killing cone, an instrument like a funnel with the spout removed. It should be the proper size to hold the bird snugly. These cones come in various sizes. A friend of ours made one with a spring-action blade attached to it. A small lever releases the spring-action blade, and the head is chopped off in one quick motion, just like a guillotine. Also shown here are the kinds of tools used in butchering: a knife sharpener, boning knife, tweezers, and scissors. Any small knife will remove pin feathers, so I do not bother with a pinning knife.

You will also need a pail for scalding, a plastic bag or some kind of container to put the feathers and offal in, and if you are going to feed the offal to the pigs or back to the remaining flock (this is an excellent source of protein for your stock), then you will need two containers, one for feathers and one for offal. You need another clean pan for giblets and some kind of table or bench to eviscerate the chickens on.

The nicest booklet I've ever read on butchering poultry at home is "Home Processing of Poultry." It's put out by the University of Pennsylvania for 4-H members. It's very well written and it has excellent pictures depicting every step in detail. It can be obtained either by writing to the Pennsylvania State University, College of Agriculture Extension Service, University Park, Pennsylvania 16802, or by contacting your local county extension service agent. As of this writing, the cost for this booklet is 50 cents.

DUCKS

The two most common breeds of meat ducks in the U.S. are the White Pekin and the Muscovy. The commercial industry relies solely on the White Pekin. They produce excellent-quality meat, and they reach butchering weight (7 pounds) in eight weeks. Large white-feathered birds, they have orange-yellow bills, shanks, and feet, and when dressed out their skin is a rich yellow. Adult drakes (males) weigh 9 pounds, and ducks (females) weigh 8 pounds. They are good egg producers but tend to leave their nests too much to make good setters. We usually hatch our White Pekin duck eggs in an incubator to ensure that we get enough ducklings. Our drakes are White Pekin–Mallard crosses, and they are white with beautiful green, blue, and black feathers around their necks and heads and a few on their wings.

Muscovies are peculiar in that they don't quack like other ducks. They make a hissing sound. Muscovies make excellent meat birds, though they tend to be tough if allowed to grow beyond four and one-half months old. Adult drakes weigh 10 pounds and ducks 7 pounds. They are not good egg producers but are excellent setters of the few that they do lay. Muscovies come in dark and white colors, with the white being most popular. Most hatcheries sell both adult ducks and ducklings. Sears, Roebuck and Company sells White Pekin ducklings.

Breeders or Ducklings

If you would like to raise ducks for egg production as well as meat, you should have your own breeders. Buy them as adults early in the spring. One drake is enough for every six ducks.

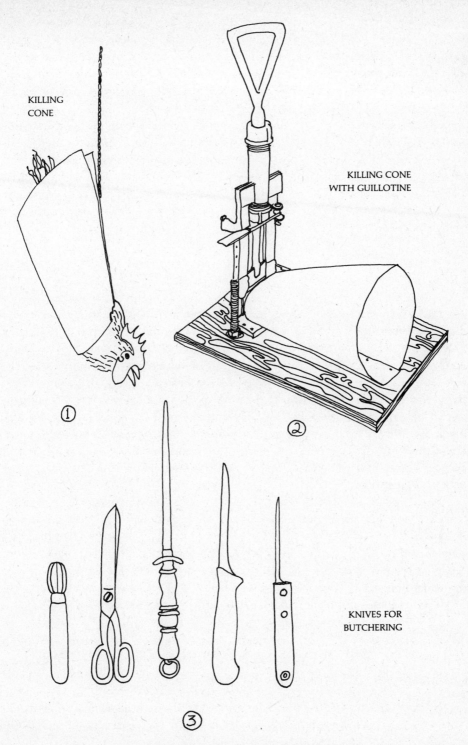

KILLING
CONE

①

KILLING CONE
WITH GUILLOTINE

②

KNIVES FOR
BUTCHERING

③

If you are buying ducklings to raise for meat only, you will need some type of brooder setup. I do not recommend the cardboard box arrangement that I suggested for chicks. Ducklings are terribly messy and could go through three boxes a day. A brooder battery or small confined area that can be heated should be used. Ducklings grow very fast, so be sure to use an area that is large enough. Ducklings need temperatures of 95 degrees F the first week; the temperature can be decreased after that by 5 degrees a week until they are completely feathered out, in about four weeks. In very warm summer weather, heated brooders are only needed for the first two to three weeks. If you're not sure if it's warm enough, play it safe and use heat. A duckling that gets chilled will die.

Housing

Housing for ducks five weeks old and older that must be confined should be similar to that of chickens. They require adequate space, light, and cleanliness. Do not allow their litter to remain wet or it will burn them. Ducks that are confined must have lots of water, and they make a terrible mess with it, so expect to do a great deal of cleaning. If ducks are allowed to range freely, as ours are, they need only a place to get in out of the bad weather. Our ducks spend their days down by the brook, both summer and winter, even in below-zero temperatures. At night they come up to be closed into the barn. Never let baby ducklings go out and get wet before they have feathered out; they will catch a chill, and you will lose them.

If ducklings are hatched by their mother, you need not concern yourself with them. She will see to it that they are properly fed and that they are dried off when they get wet. Ducklings that are raised by their mothers can swim in water before they have feathered out, because the mothers will dry them quickly so they won't chill.

Hatching Eggs in an Incubator

If you decide to gather the duck eggs and hatch them in an incubator, it's important to know that most duck eggs are laid at night, or before 7 A.M. We keep our ducks confined until 9 A.M. and then let them out and gather their eggs. Do not keep any to incubate that are cracked or very small. Wash the eggs in lukewarm water (110 degrees F), never in cold water, and store them, small end down, in a cool place. A root cellar that does not get over 55 degrees F would be a good place. Eggs can be saved for two weeks, but after the first week they should be turned daily. I store mine in egg cartons, and after the first week I simply turn the carton over each day. Warm the eggs to room temperature the day you are going to put them into the incubator. Follow the directions that come with your incubator. It takes twenty-six to twenty-eight days to complete a hatch.

Feeding

Ducklings from hatcheries or two-day-old ducklings fresh from the incubator must be fed as soon as they are put into the brooder. A special pelleted ration is made for ducklings. This can be supplemented with fresh chopped grass clippings, clover, or swiss chard when it is available. Do not feed ducklings chick starter ration because it contains medications that are fatal to ducklings. Water must be supplied at all times.

If you are raising your ducklings in a battery brooder that has feed and water trays hooked to the outside, you must remove them and place them on the inside. Ducklings will not reach through the wires for their feed. Ducklings are fed a starter ration for two weeks, at which point meat birds should be switched to a grower ration. Birds kept for breeders should be given a breeder developer ration. We do not take this information too seriously. We start our ducklings on the starter ration, but we keep them on this for four weeks. At four weeks our ducklings are set free to range. From then on they are fed cracked corn daily, but they seldom eat much of any kind of grain when they are on the range. They forage for most of their food from the brook and the yard, and they are not destructive like chickens in the garden. They might pick at a green leaf or two, but usually eat just the bugs.

At eight weeks those we are going to butcher are confined and fed cracked corn, and pelleted rations combined with garden greens. Most of our corn is raised right here on our homestead. Be sure that you never feed grain without water nearby. The grain gets stuck in their throats, and they choke.

Our layers continue the same diet as our drakes on the range until they are six months old. Ducks reach maturity at about seven months old, so at six months we add laying mash to their diet to stimulate egg production. Duck raising is one of the least expensive projects on our homestead.

Peculiarities

I'm sure that many of you live near a paved highway, as we do, so I'd like to tell you about a peculiar habit that our ducks have that could prove to be very dangerous if you allow them to range as we do ours. In the late spring and summer months if we should happen to get a heavy rainstorm or several days of continuous rainy weather, our ducks go out and walk the yellow line in the middle of the road. Our driveway is semicircular, and they go out the lower end, get onto the yellow line, and slowly make their way up the center of the road to the upper entrance. If it wasn't so dangerous, it would be a very funny sight to watch. However, it presents a very real danger not only to the ducks but to any poor unsuspecting drivers as they come around the bend, down the hill, and then suddenly come upon our "quackers on parade." This happened recently, and the lady driving the car did not dare to try to stop because she had three little children in the car with her, so we lost one of our ducks. We've checked with several authorities on poultry, and no one seems to know why they do this. The only solution we can offer to the problem is to pen the ducks up until the road dries out. They only go out onto the road if it is wet.

Butchering

Ducks are ready to butcher in ten to twelve weeks. Do not butcher between twelve and seventeen weeks because they go into moult, and when this happens, they lose weight and pinfeathers begin to grow. Picking ducks at this stage is very difficult. Ducks and geese are butchered and eviscerated just like chickens with the following exceptions:

1   They must be scalded in much hotter water (190–200 degrees F). Move the bird up and down and back and forth to get hot water up under all of its feathers. Ducks and geese have an oily coating that protects them from water, and it's important to get the hot water down to the tips of the feathers near the skin. Take the bird out of the water and pluck as many feathers as quickly as you can. If necessary, dunk the bird again.

2   Proceed as with chickens up to the point of eviscerating. Ducks and geese are chilled quickly by putting them in cold water to cool until they become very firm. Then they are refrigerated for two days before they are drawn to improve the flavor. When they are ready to be drawn, eviscerate as you would chickens and cook them immediately or freeze for later use. The feathers can be washed and dried for use in stuffing pillows.

GEESE

When we first started homesteading, we wanted to include in our plans as many small animals and poultry variations as possible in order to keep our diet from becoming dull and boring, so we read all the information we could find on each variety. Among the praises that were sung of geese were statements such as that geese are easy and cheap to raise, fun to have around, friendly, good watchdogs, and finally that "geese are great garden weeders." With fanciful dreams of beautiful white birds strutting around the yard majestically greeting visitors, a weed-free garden, and a golden-brown roast goose gracing my Thanksgiving table, I traveled all the way over to the other side of the state for two pair of year-old Embden geese. Geese mate for life, so I felt it was important to have two pair.

As it turned out in the year that followed, we had three geese (females) and one gander (male) because geese are very difficult to sex, and the breeder had neglected to tell us that he wasn't sure. That wasn't the only thing we found out about geese that year. They happen to be one of the few animals that will bite the hand that feeds them, and while they make good watchdogs because they make so much noise whenever a stranger is around, they will chase anyone, including their owners, especially during the breeding season, when the gander is very protective of the goose. Their huge wings make them dangerous foes to deal with. They can injure man or beast quite badly.

"Oh, well," I thought to myself, "at least they'll keep the garden cleaned up." And they certainly did. They cleaned up the strawberries, the asparagus, as well as the early lettuce, onions, and Swiss chard. In fact, they cleaned out everything but the weeds. With feelings somewhat akin to despair, I finally decided to pen them up until fall and butcher them for Thanksgiving and Christmas. At least that golden-brown roast goose would grace my Thanksgiving table, and all would not be lost. When fall came, lo and behold! We finally found something good about them. They were delicious to eat. Now we keep them penned from early spring until we're through with our garden; then we let them out to help clean up.

There are three popular breeds of geese available almost everywhere in the United States: the White Embden, the grey Toulouse, and the White Chinese. The Embden and the Toulouse are large geese averaging 12 to 14 pounds liveweight at maturity. The Chinese are slightly smaller, but popular nonetheless. Both the Embden and Chinese are available through Sears, Roebuck and Company if they are not available in your area. Day-old goslings are much more expensive than chickens or ducklings, but they are still much cheaper than mature birds. Geese do not mature until they are two years old, so if you want to raise your own breeders, it would be more practical to start with birds that are at least one year old. Geese tend to be monogamous, mating for life, though occasionally a gander will mate with two geese, and they must be together for a while before they will mate and produce fertile eggs. Because of this, it's best to start them in the fall; then they will be ready to mate and hatch goslings in the early spring.

If you decide to buy mature geese for breeding, plan to confine them for at least a few days when you bring them to your homestead, so they will get used to their new home. Since I had read that geese could range freely, we neglected to give any thought to this; we just turned them loose. Within twenty-four hours they had wandered off. Our investment in these geese had been considerable, and not wanting to lose it, Ray decided to follow the brook up through the woods a way in an attempt to find them.

About a mile from our homestead he spotted them eating grass in a neighbor's meadow, but as soon as they saw Ray approach, the geese jumped into the brook. Not one to be daunted by a little water, Ray jumped in after them, and he managed to catch all four. However, when he got out of the water with four huge geese in his hands (he had two by the feet in each hand), he found that the weight of the water was pulling his pants down. He decided that it would be faster and easier to return home by way of the main highway, so he hurriedly made his way to the road.

He stopped frequently in an effort to hitch up his pants with the use of his wrists and forearms, but he has such narrow hips that it was really an exercise in futility. His pants slowly inched lower and lower, until the situation was near disaster. Brushing tears of laughter from my cheeks, I ran to his aid, and it was none too soon either, because rather than lose his precious geese, Ray was ready to throw propriety to the winds.

Feeding

If you decide to start with goslings for meat production only, raise them as you would ducklings, using a commercial geese ration. I caution you not to use chick ration, since certain types of medications in chick starter can be fatal to goslings. A good inexpensive starter ration for the homesteader is chopped bread soaked in warm milk. Add grass and garden greens as soon as they are available. Goslings should not be allowed to be exposed to the elements before they are completely feathered out, or they will catch a chill and die. Goslings raised by their mother do not need special rations; she will feed them herself. Except in the coldest weather, geese that are not penned will forage for all of their food. Their favorite food is grass. During the cold weather we supplement their diet with corn that we grow ourselves. Most homesteads, even the smaller ones, have enough garden space to plant a few extra rows of corn for ducks and geese. Montgomery Ward and Garden Way Centers both sell a small cast-iron corn sheller that is inexpensive and works well. It can shell up to 14 bushels of corn in an hour. During the breeding season, we add some laying mash to their diet (this is the only commercially grown food we must buy for them).

Geese do not require water to swim in as ducks do, though they do mate more easily in water. However, they must have water to drink. They drink by immersing their head in water, so make sure that you use a deep container to water them with.

Housing

Geese do not need elaborate housing. Any type of three-sided enclosure that will protect them from wind and storms will do. Some people take large wooden barrels, lay them on their sides, and provide hay or straw for the geese to build their nests with. Early in March ours are confined in a pen that has a small three-sided building for their nests and a large exercise yard. All our geese have the wing-tip feathers on one wing cut off to prevent them from flying out over the top

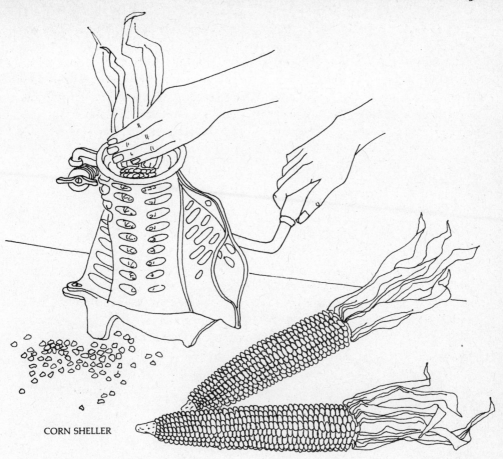

CORN SHELLER

of the fence. We could allow them to range freely a little longer, since it is too cold here in Vermont for any gardening in March, but this is when geese start to lay, and we want to have complete control over the number of eggs they lay and the goslings when they are hatched. They remain penned in until early October.

In the winter they are allowed to range freely during the day and are put in the barn at night. Like ducks, they seem to tolerate even the sub-zero cold very well. During this time of the year our current gander, Toulouse the Goose, still chases everyone in sight.

Nesting

Geese will make their own nests, and they are very protective of them. Geese are very good setters. Our first year, before we penned ours up, our goose would

OUR GOOSE HOUSE

steal hen and duck eggs and even tried to hatch a pint-size canning jar. We would fish it out and throw it away, but she would just come right back and get it.

The average goose will hatch from eight to twelve goslings. She will lay many more eggs than this, but she can't cover them all, so we take away the first few and use the eggs for cooking and the eggshells for homemade Christmas ornaments. Be very careful when you remove any eggs from the nest, for the goose and her gander will attack you if they see you taking them. It's best to distract them with something to eat and then take all the eggs but one out of the nest every three days. Mark the one that you leave and always leave the same one, then you will not be taking any stale eggs. We usually take the first dozen that are laid over a period of ten to twenty days and leave the rest. It takes twenty-eight to thirty days to complete the hatch. Occasionally, when a goose has nested very early in the spring, she will lay a second clutch again in August, but this is not common. A goose will set on a clutch of eggs that are not fertile. Remove her after she has been nesting more than 40 days without results and throw away the eggs.

Butchering

Geese are butchered and processed the same way that ducks are (see page 190). They are ready to butcher late in the fall and are at their best at that age. Give them extra corn during the last month before butchering, or sooner if the grass dries up very early in the fall. Goose meat is all dark meat and very moist. When roasting goose, be sure to prick the skin all over to allow the extra fat to drain off.

Goose feathers are very much in demand today, and they bring a high price from clothing manufacturers. It might be very well worth your while to look into a market for down feathers if you decide to raise geese.

TURKEYS

Turkeys can be raised on small homesteads, but they do require much more care and equipment than other types of poultry. For this reason, we have not attempted to raise them ourselves. Turkeys should not be raised in the same area as chickens, and young turkeys cannot be kept in the same building as older turkeys. Buildings that have housed chickens within the past three months cannot be used, and land used for chickens or other turkeys that have ranged should not be used as range for new turkeys until at least three years have gone by.

Turkeys are subject to so many diseases and require such elaborate housing, including enclosed sundecks and wire runs to protect them from the elements and predatory animals, that we feel that they take too much time and care for the small homesteader who would like to attempt raising a variety of small animals and poultry. Furthermore, they're so dumb that you really have to have a great deal of patience to raise them.

If, in spite of our dire warnings (after all, we're not authorities on turkeys since we don't raise them), you would like to learn more about raising turkeys, I suggest that you get in touch with your state extension service agent for more information on their needs and a source of supply in your area.

11

COOKING FOR
THE HOMESTEAD

The hours you spend in your kitchen preparing the foods that you have grown yourself to nourish your family and warm the hearts of your friends should be happy hours filled with pride and a feeling of accomplishment.

Your memories should be for you and your children, a storybook of memories for the future. The Christmas cookies, the sugaring-off party, the family reunions. My cherished memories of childhood holiday celebrations will be with me all the days of my life. New Year's Day at *Mémé* Guay's was a never-to-be-forgotten occasion. My grandmother would take the dining room table from the room and set up sawhorses covered with plywood all around the room. She covered these with her finest snow-white linens; there were no paper napkins on these tables. We would gather as many as forty-five for dinner. She would serve a turkey weighing at least 35 pounds and a large roast beef or whole ham, with tourtières à la viande (pork pies), mashed sweet and white potatoes, boiled onions and mashed turnip, and an assortment of homemade rolls, pickles, and relishes, topping off the meal with her richest fruitcakes and pies. I was always seated next to my youngest uncle. I could feel my eyes grow wide as he heaped his plate, and it filled me so full just to watch him that I could barely nibble a little at my own plateful.

After dinner my *Pépé* Guay would gather the family in the double parlors, and with glasses filled with rich port wine and brandy, he would lead us in singing the traditional French-Canadian songs. Since I was a frail child, everyone thought a sip of port wine would do me good, and by the time I was bundled up for home, rosy-cheeked and heavy-lidded, little did anyone suspect that the reason might be other than that "she's had a busy day for one so young." These are the kind of warm, happy memories I want to create for my own children.

The summer days when someone runs as quickly as he can to get the corn from the garden and into the pot, not wanting to lose a fraction of its tender sweetness, and the canning and butchering days. These are all precious times that will grow into memories and knowledge for your children. These memories will give them something to share with their children someday.

When I have a chance to talk about food and cooking, I'm at my happiest, because my experiences with food have always been times of sharing with others. Some of these occasions are especially memorable, but all of them have been good. One of the most memorable occasions was also one of the most recent. My son Gary was being transferred from Kansas to Germany, so he brought his wife, Gail, and our grandson home for a visit before he left. No one in the family had met Gail yet, and we had never seen our grandson, so we planned a large family reunion. Everyone came, and we represented five generations: my paternal grandmother, my father, myself, Gary, and Gary junior. It was just wonderful, and I was so proud. Everyone brought fresh salads and baked beans, and my mom just had to spoil all of us with delicious desserts. It was another page in our memory scrapbook.

This is not meant to be a complete cookbook. Instead, it's a group of recipes that will help you to get more out of your homesteading efforts than the average cookbook does. Meat-roasting charts are available in any good cookbook, and I feel that this chapter coupled with one of the better cookbooks on the market, such as *Joy of Cooking*, by Irma S. Rombauer and Marion Rombauer Becker (published by Bobbs-Merrill, 1961), will help you to some very happy hours in your homestead kitchen. Along with one good general cookbook, you might also want to obtain one good book on the latest methods of canning, freezing, and dehydrating foods. My favorite is *Putting Food By*, by Ruth Hertzberg, Beatrice Vaughan, and Janet Greene (published by Stephen Greene Press, 1973). The instructions are clear and easy to follow.

My mother is a fantastic cook, and so was her mother before her. Unfortunately, however, though my grandmother was a very fine woman in every respect, she guarded her recipes jealously, and she never felt honor-bound to include every ingredient in her recipes when she passed them on to us. This often resulted in our efforts lacking the special taste or texture that we found exciting in her food. Searching for the missing ingredients helped me to learn a lot about basic food composition, and many of the recipes in this chapter are the results of experiences I had in learning to cope with Grandma's somewhat immoral attitude toward recipe giving.

Homegrown Versus Store-Bought

I'd like to make a few comments on food in general. Homegrown food is so far superior in freshness, taste, and quality that even if it weren't so inexpensive to grow or raise, it would still have just about every advantage possible over store-bought foods.

Quality food supplies are very hard to find in the markets. There are still some foods sold to consumers that are not filled with food additives and preservatives, but even these are usually a long way from being fresh, and you have no way of knowing, when you buy canned or frozen food, how fresh it was when it was processed or how many times the frozen food was defrosted and refrozen before it got to you, robbing it of all its nutrients.

What about convenience foods? There isn't a packaged convenience food on the market that can't be duplicated at home for a fraction of the cost, and without all the fillers and additives. I'm going to include many in this chapter, and with a little imagination, you can surely come up with more, based on your favorites.

Equipment for Homestead Cooking

You need to prepare yourself for homestead cooking in the same way you would prepare yourself for any other task on the farm, by getting together all the items you will need to make it as easy as possible. I'm going to give you a basic list of all the items you will need and the uses you will have for them.

BLENDER: All-purpose; an absolute necessity for the homestead.

BOXES, BARRELS, AND CROCKS: Root cellar storage, making pickles and wine, brining meat and vegetables.

BUTTER CHURN: A blender can be used for this, but there are other types. My favorite is a little motorized churn that consists of a 1-gallon jar with paddles connected to a small motor that sits on the top.

CANNING JARS, FREEZER CONTAINERS, WRAPPING MATERIALS: Food preservation.

CHEESECLOTH AND MUSLIN: Straining juices; making jelly, butter, cheese, and wine.

CHEESE PRESS: Making cheese; some can be used for pressing lard.

CORKS: Making wine.

CREAM SEPARATOR: A necessity for separating the cream in goat's milk, since it is naturally homogenized. (There are other ways, but they are less effective. See page 213.)

CUTTING BOARDS: Everything.

DAIRY, CANDY, AND MEAT THERMOMETERS: Pasteurizing milk, making cheese, making candy, roasting meat, making soap.

FERMENTATION LOCKS: Making wine. These can be made at home by taking a piece of plastic hose, inserting one end through a cork in the wine jug and the other end into a glass jar filled with water. The purpose of this is to keep air from getting into the wine while at the same time allowing the fermenting gasses to escape.

FREEZER: The most indispensable item on the homestead.

FUNNELS: Two or three sizes. Canning, freezing, wine making.

GALLON JUGS: Glass vinegar jugs for making wine. Wide-mouth jars for storage of dry mixes, milk, dried beans, and dehydrated foods.

LARGE BOWLS: Everything.

LARGE ENAMEL CANNERS: At least two. Canning, blanching, making cheese, and making soap.

LARGE ENAMEL OR STAINLESS STEEL DISHPAN: Use to make large amounts of bread. Makes a very good bottom for canners when large double boilers are needed in cheese making. (Just put a couple of bricks in the dishpan, fill with water to the top of the bricks, and put the canner in as a top pan.)

LARGE PLASTIC BUCKETS, PAILS, OR CROCKS: Brining meat in preparation for smoking, brining pickles, making salt pork, making wine. Metal containers *cannot* be used for these items.

LONG-HANDLED WOODEN SPOONS: Everything.

MEASURING CUPS AND SPOONS: Everything.

MEAT MALLET, GRINDER, AND SAUSAGE STUFFER: Meat preparation.

PARING KNIVES, BUTCHER KNIVES, MEAT CLEAVER, BONING KNIFE, KNIFE SHARPENER: Canning, cooking of all kinds, butchering, and meat preparation.

PLASTIC ½-INCH HOSE: Syphoning wine.

PRESSURE CANNER: Canning, soup stocks, and all large-quantity cooking.

PUMPING NEEDLE: Smoking meat.

STRAINERS: Large and small. Making butter, steaming, blanching, freezing, making wine, making cheese.

WOODEN BOXES: Making soap; make a good homemade dehydrator

Here are some additional things you will need for general all-purpose cooking that have not already been listed:

Bread tins	Large- and small-size pots	Rolling pin
Food grinder and slicer	and pans with covers	Small electric mixer
Kitchen scales	Large roaster	

The following is a list of items that are not necessary but that do make homesteading more fun:

Apple peeler	Green-bean frencher	Small grain grinder
Bread maker	Ice-cream maker	Sprouter
Cherry pitter	Noodle maker	Yogurt maker
Corn sheller	Pea and bean sheller	

If members of your family ask for suggestions for Christmas or birthday gifts, you might give them this list.

Homemade Equipment

Some of the equipment that you will need can easily be made at home, such as the bean sprouter, dehydrator, yogurt maker, and cheese press. I'll give you instructions for these before I go on with the recipe section.

BEAN SPROUTER

A quart jar with cheesecloth over the top makes a good bean sprouter. In the recipe section I will give instructions for using it.

YOGURT MAKER

Yogurt, too, can be made in a glass jar, either placed at the back of a wood stove, in a gas oven with a pilot light, or in jars simply set in warm water. Anything that can maintain a temperature of 100 to 110 degrees F for several hours can be used.

DEHYDRATOR

We made a very successful little dehydrator one summer by taking a wooden box into which a large jelly roll or cookie tin would fit and lining it with tinfoil. We put in a small light fixture hooked to an extension cord, and a 100-watt bulb. Then we sprayed the underside of the jelly roll or cookie tin with black paint to draw the heat. On warm, sunny days we just sliced our vegetables, blanched them according to instructions, placed them on the tray, covered it with an old piece of clean nylon curtain (cheesecloth will work too) to protect the food from bugs, and set it out in the sun. On days that were cloudy, or overnight, we brought the dryer into the house and turned on the light in the box. It was very successful.

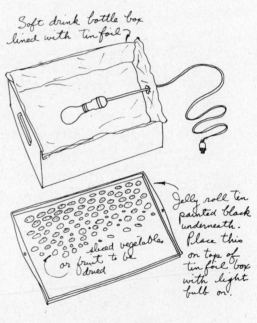

Soft drink bottle box lined with tin foil?

Jelly roll tin painted black underneath. Place this on top of tin foil box with light bulb on.

sliced vegetables or fruit to be dried

DEHYDRATOR

A gas or electric oven can be used if it can be set low enough. The temperature should be maintained at 140 degrees F for at least two-thirds of the drying time.

CHEESE PRESS

There are two general types of cheese presses. The one that I have was made for me by a friend and my brother. It consists of a stainless steel cylinder 5 inches in diameter and 6 inches tall. The bottom is a circular piece of stainless steel welded onto the cylinder, with drainage holes drilled in the bottom. This cylinder sits on a steel platform that has had a hole cut out of it slightly smaller than the diameter of the cylinder. The cylinder sits over this hole. The platform has two upright, threaded bolts. A stainless steel bar, with holes drilled to accommodate the bolts, slides down over them. In the center of this bar is another hole, drilled only halfway through the bar on the *underside*. The shank of the follower fits into this, and the follower, too, is made of stainless steel. Wing nuts are used to tighten down this bar, which pushes the follower down into the cylinder over the cheese, to create the amount of pressure required to press the cheese curd. The bottom platform has four small footed pieces welded on to raise it about an inch off the table. This allows the whey to drain out.

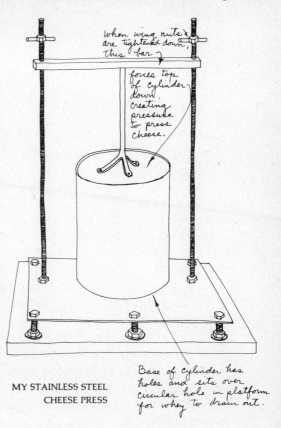

when wing nuts are tightened down, this bar forces top of cylinder down, creating pressure to press cheese.

MY STAINLESS STEEL CHEESE PRESS

Base of cylinder has holes and sits over circular hole in platform for whey to drain out.

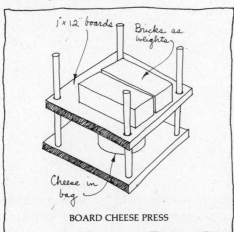

1˝ x 12˝ boards

Bricks as weights

Cheese in bag

BOARD CHEESE PRESS

Using wood and a 2-pound coffee can, you could come up with the same type of press.

Another, simpler type of press is made by just cutting two pieces of ¾-inch-thick smooth pine board to a size that is 12 inches square. Drill ½-inch holes in the four corners and buy a piece of dowel that is ½ inch in diameter and 48 inches long. Cut the dowel into four equal pieces. To use this type of press, you would put your cheese curd in a cheese bag and tie the bag securely. Place the bag in the center of the bottom board and cover with the top board. Thread the dowels into the four corners and place bricks on the top until you achieve the desired weight. I'll say more about this when I get to the cheese recipes.

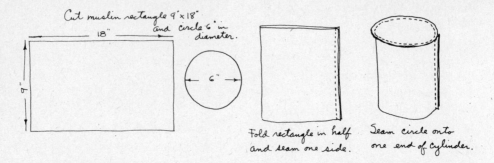

Cut muslin rectangle 9" x 18" and circle 6" in diameter.

18"

9"

6"

Fold rectangle in half and seam one side.

Seam circle onto one end of cylinder.

CHEESE BAG

I have never had good luck dressing cheese the way most instructions tell you to. Either the bandage would slip and make my cheese misshapen or I would not be able to get the cheese back into the cheese press for further pressing. So in order to have a nice smooth finished product, I decided to make cheese bags. The results are nice smooth cheeses, perfectly shaped, with no lumps and bumps.

To make a cheese bag, you need to cut a piece of muslin that is either the circumference of your can and 3 inches higher, if that's what you are using, or a piece that is 18 inches wide by 9 inches in length. Cut a circular piece of material that measures 6 inches in diameter, or the diameter of your can. Stitch a seam up the side (on the length) and then fit the circle to one end and stitch in place. To use, turn with the seam side *out*, making a smooth bag for your cheese.

In a can-type cheese press, fold the top over the cheese curd as smoothly as you can. If you are using the board-style of press, it's a good idea to draw the bag snugly together over the cheese curd and then tie it securely. Place the *top* of the bag down on the center of your board. The reason for this is that your top board will fit down more smoothly on the top of your cheese and your bricks will not topple to one side.

Pork

Of all the meats grown on a small homestead, I think that pork adapts itself to the greatest number of different tastes. Starting with just plain pork chops and roasts, you go on to bacon, ham, salt pork, sausage, scrapple, pickled pigs' feet, headcheese, and many other combinations. I will start you off with the easier variations. In years to come you may want to investigate the other possibilities, such as salami, frankfurters, bologna, pepperoni, and many others, most of which are a combination of pork and beef.

Before starting to work with any products, make sure that your meats are clean and well chilled and that all the items used for preparation, including the shelf or table you will be working on, have been thoroughly cleaned.

These recipes are not the last word in flavors or methods of preparation, but they are my favorites, and I hope that you will enjoy them.

🌸 *Sausage with Sage*

20 pounds fresh pork   ¼ cup black pepper
  (⅓ fat and ⅔ lean)   ¾ cup salt
1 cup ground sage   1 cup white sugar

Grind pork and fat, using first the large blade and then the fine blade of a meat grinder. (If you have an especially sharp grinder, you may omit grinding it twice.) Combine the spices and the sugar and mix this into the ground pork well, using your hands to make sure it is well distributed. Chill overnight and mix well again. Package for the freezer by either stuffing into muslin bags or simply dividing it into meal-size portions and wrapping it in freezer wrap. Use within six months. *Makes about 21 pounds*

🌸 *Sausage with Ginger and Cloves*

20 pounds fresh pork   8 teaspoons black pepper
  (⅓ fat and ⅔ lean)   1½ teaspoons powdered cloves
¾ cup salt   3 tablespoons sage
8 teaspoons powdered ginger

Follow instructions for Sausage with Sage (see above). *Makes about 21 pounds*

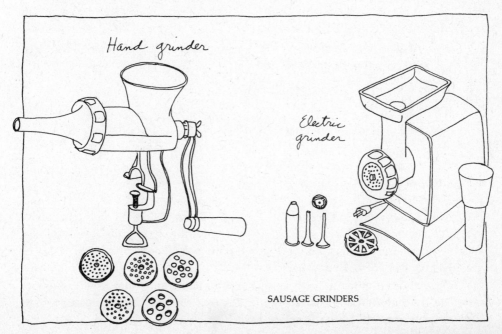

Hand grinder

Electric grinder

SAUSAGE GRINDERS

❀ Sausage with Onions and Garlic

6 pounds fresh pork
  (⅓ fat and ⅔ lean)
2 onions
1 clove garlic
1 teaspoon cayenne

1 tablespoon salt
2 teaspoons black pepper
1 sprig dried thyme
½ teaspoon ground sage
½ teaspoon allspice

Put pork, onions, and garlic through a meat grinder. Combine the spices together and mix them in well with your hands; then put the mixture through the grinder again. Package and freeze or use as needed. If packed in crocks and covered with a thin layer of fat, it will keep a long time in the refrigerator. *Makes about 6½ pounds*

❀ Sausage with Brown Sugar and Herbs

2 pounds fresh pork
  (⅓ fat and ⅔ lean)
2 teaspoons salt
½ teaspoon black pepper
2 teaspoons brown sugar

½ teaspoon ground sage
1 teaspoon dried marjoram
¼ teaspoon dried thyme
1 teaspoon dried parsley

Mix according to instructions for Sausage with Onions and Garlic (see above). May be stored in the same way. This is an exceptionally good sausage. *Makes about 2 pounds*

❀ My Favorite Sausage

This sausage is by far the easiest to prepare, and all the guesswork has been taken out of it for you. It's really delicious.

24 pounds fresh pork (⅓ fat and ⅔ lean)
8 ounces Morton's Meat, Poultry, and Sausage Seasoning

Follow instructions for Sausage with Sage (see page 203). *Makes about 24½ pounds*

❀ Salt Pork

2 pounds coarse salt
5 quarts boiling water
25 pounds trimmings, jowls, or back fat

Combine the salt and water to make a brine, bring to a boil, allow to cool, then chill it to 36 to 40 degrees F. Place cold trimmed cuts of pork into a clean crock or barrel. Cover with the cold brine. Weight the meat to keep it from floating above the brine. Use enough brine to submerge the meat.

Seven days later rearrange the pork so that the pieces that were on the bottom are now on the top. Again make sure that the brine covers the meat. Salt pork may be left in solution until used. Place the crocks in a cool place or in a root cellar. If the brine should turn ropy, remove the meat and scrub well with a stiff brush, then return to a clean crock and cover with a weakened solution made of the same amount of salt and 6½ qts. boiling water. (Make sure to chill the brine before adding it to the crock.) *This is enough brine for 25 pounds of pork.*

❀ Headcheese

4 pounds pork (lean and fat)	⅛ teaspoon ground cloves
1 onion chopped	1⅓ teaspoons allspice
1 teaspoon cinnamon	1 clove garlic, minced

If you are using the head for this, you must clean it well.* Remove snout, eyes, and ears. Scrub the rest well with a stiff-bristled brush. Place the head in a large pot and fill with water. Bring to a boil and boil hard for 5 minutes; drain. Rinse off the head and the pot and return the head to the pot. Repeat the above procedure. Drain again and refill the pot.

Add ¼ cup of cider vinegar, 1 clove of garlic, 4 or 5 dried red peppers or 1 teaspoon of crushed red pepper, 2 tablespoons of salt, and 1 teaspoon of black pepper. Bring to a boil and simmer, covered, until the meat falls off the bones (approximately 3 to 4 hours). Drain and reserve the broth.

For each 4 pounds of meat and fat (grind the grizzle and include it) add the above ingredients and mix well.

Pack into loaf tins and cover with strained stock. Weight down the meat until it has been chilled. Store in refrigerator for up to 2 weeks. Freeze for longer storage. *Makes about 4½ to 6 pounds*

❀ Scrapple

Scrapple, an especially favored breakfast dish in many sections of the country, is made of cooked pork and broth that has been thickened with cornmeal, flour, and sometimes shorts. Cook the head, heart, and trimmings until they are tender and the bones can be removed. Remove the bones. Grind all remaining meat through a meat grinder using a fine plate. Return all ground meat to the strained broth and bring to a boil. The cereal mixture to be added may vary widely. Either 7 parts cornmeal and 3 parts white or buckwheat flour, or 7 parts cornmeal, 2 parts shorts, and 1 part buckwheat flour. These measurements are all by weight; for example, 7 pounds cornmeal and 3 pounds white flour.

A preparation that is 4 parts (by weight) ground meat, 3 parts broth, and 1 part

---

* It is not necessary to use the head for this recipe. You may use pork butt or any part of the pork that is a combination of lean and fat; however, this is a good way to get the most out of your hog. It leaves you with almost no waste.

dry cereal mixture will produce a richly flavored scrapple. Use more cereal and broth as desired.

When you add the cereal mixture, moisten it with some of the cooled broth so that it may be added to the hot broth without forming lumps. Boil for about 30 minutes, stirring constantly to prevent sticking. Add the seasoning just before cooking is finished and stir it in well. Use the following seasoning for 25 pounds of scrapple, including broth and cereal (you may omit any seasoning that you are not particularly fond of):

¼ pound salt	¼ ounce nutmeg
1 ounce black pepper	¾ teaspoon mace
½ to 1 ounce dried marjoram	½ pound ground onions
½ to 1 ounce ground sage	1½ teaspoons crushed red pepper

Pour the hot scrapple into small, shallow pans and chill promptly. If carefully made, it can be sliced and fried quickly without much crumbling. The slices may be dipped in egg before they are fried. Refrigerate up to 1 week. Freeze for longer storage. *Makes 25 pounds*

❀ Pickled Pigs' Feet

In preparing pickled pigs' feet, take special care to clean them thoroughly first. The toes and dewclaws should have been removed when the carcass was dressed. Trim out glandular tissue between the toes and remove all hair and dirt. Unless you care for them properly, feet begin to spoil about as quickly as any part of the carcass; therefore, put them into the cure immediately after thorough chilling. Cure clean, chilled feet in brine for 2 to 3 weeks.

Make the brine by dissolving 1 pound of salt, ¼ pound of sugar, and ¼ ounce of saltpeter in 9 cups of water that has been boiled. Weight the feet to keep them from floating to the top of the solution. Use enough solution to submerge the meat. Keep the pork cold throughout the curing period (36 to 40 degrees F).

Slowly cook or simmer the cured feet until they are tender (2 to 4 hours, depending on the age of the pig). Cook them slowly to keep the skin from parting excessively and the feet from pulling out of shape. Thoroughly chill the cured, cooked feet and pack them in cold, moderately strong white vinegar, to which you can add spices such as 2 to 3 bay leaves or 5 to 6 whole allspice. You can use the feet at once or keep them in the vinegar for about 3 weeks.

❀ Liver Sausage

5 livers	⅔ to 1 ounce sage
20 heads, tongues, skins, and hearts	1½ teaspoons crushed red pepper
½ pound salt	½ ounce allspice
½ ounce black pepper	

To make liver sausage, 10 to 20 percent of liver by weight is usually added to other cooked products. Cook heads, tongues, skins, hearts, and other pieces until tender. Remove from the broth when the cuts can be boned. Then scald the livers. If you cut them deeply with a knife, they will be sufficiently seared in about 10 minutes. Grind all cooked materials moderately fine and add about one-fifth as much broth by weight, using enough broth to make the mixture soft but not sloppy. Season to taste and mix thoroughly. The seasonings listed are standard quantities, given by the U.S. Department of Agriculture, for 25 pounds of the mixture.

Stuff seasoned, well-mixed sausage into beef casings and simmer in water until it floats; the time required is usually 10 to 30 minutes. After cooking, plunge the sausage into cold water, chill for at least 30 minutes, and hang up to drain. If the meat is cooked too much in the first cooking, the second cooking, after the sausage has been stuffed, will destroy the tight texture of the finished sausage. A good place to buy casings of any kind is a local meat-processing plant. *Makes 25 pounds*

🏵 Lard

I started rendering lard before I had read very many how-to books, so it came as quite a surprise to me, when I finally came around to instructions on how to render lard, to find that their methods were somewhat different than mine, and more complicated. The following recipe for rendering lard is not only easy, it leaves you free to go about your business without having to watch the pot. We even let it go overnight without getting up to check.

Cut the leaf fat and fatback into small cubes. Take a large roaster and place a rack in the bottom. Add ½ cup of water and pile the pieces of fat on top of the rack. Place in the oven at 225 degrees F. As the rendered fat accumulates, pour it off into a strainer lined with cheesecloth or through a dairy strainer with a milk pad in place. Make sure that the bowl you are pouring into is ovenproof, or use a tinned pail. You can go several hours without pouring it off. As the pieces in the roaster reduce in size, add more pieces to the pot. With the exception of the very last of the last batch of rendered lard, your lard will be pure white and of very fine quality. If you would like to make fried bacon rinds, you can either take out the pieces of fat before they are completely rendered (leave on only a thin layer of fat) or trim the rind off before you render the lard. Cool the rendered lard slightly before packing it into plastic buckets or tinned pails for storing. Lard must be kept refrigerated, and if you have a great deal of it, you can freeze some to keep it fresh.

🏵 Fried Bacon Rinds

To fry bacon rinds, you should use vegetable oil because you need very hot fat, and lard tends to smoke at lower temperatures than oil. Heat 3 inches of oil to

375 degrees F and carefully drop the pieces of rind into it. Do not try to fry too many at once. Fry until the rinds are puffed and bubbly. Remove from the pan and drain. These may be salted with plain salt or any type of seasoned salt that you enjoy.

✿ Tourtière à la Viande (French-Canadian Pork Pie)

There are almost as many variations to this recipe as there are French people. The following is my favorite. It's not overly spicy and is good served either warm or cold. We keep it on hand throughout the Christmas season to serve to guests who come to make a holiday visit. Ordinarily, the custom was to serve it on Christmas Eve after everyone came home from midnight mass, and again on New Year's Day.

2 pounds ground beef
4 pounds ground pork
   (lean mixed, but not too fat)
2 cups water
4 teaspoons salt
1½ large spanish onions, diced
   very fine

½ teaspoon nutmeg
½ teaspoon allspice
½ teaspoon black pepper
3½ to 4 cups fluffy bread crumbs

Combine all the ingredients except the bread crumbs and bring to the simmering point. Simmer for 30 minutes. Remove from the heat and add the bread crumbs. Cool thoroughly. If, after it has cooked, you feel that it is still too moist, add more bread crumbs, but go easy; it does not need to be a stiff mixture. Make piecrusts for three 9-inch pies. Fill each crust-lined pie plate with one third of the cooled mixture. Top with crusts and seal the edges. Cut vents in the top crust and bake in a preheated oven set at 400 degrees F for aluminum pie plates and 375 degrees for glass. Bake until the crusts are browned, about 30 minutes. These are delicious served with ketchup and/or pickled beets. *Makes three 9-inch pies*

Chevon

Chevon can be used in any recipe that lamb or veal is used in because it is close in flavor to both. To roast chevon, follow lamb-roasting charts; however, the top should be covered with some sort of fat. I use a covering of bacon, and it lends a very nice flavor.

Chevon is also very good in any dish calling for ground meat. I'd like to give you my recipe for making meatballs in large quantities, and though the recipe calls for beef, you may use ground chevon with equally good results. The great thing about these meatballs is that they are frozen individually and then packaged for the freezer in bags. When unexpected company arrives or when you are short on the time needed to prepare a good meal for your family, you just have to take out the number of meatballs you want and pop them into your own canned or frozen spaghetti sauce, and dinner is done in just a short time. This dish, served with a large salad and homemade bread, is a good-enough company meal for anyone.

Meatballs for Spaghetti

8 eggs	1 teaspoon black pepper
1 tablespoon crushed red pepper	4 tablespoons grated Parmesan cheese
3 tablespoons Italian seasoning	2 large onions, diced fine
3⅓ tablespoons garlic salt	4 slices bread, crumbled
2 tablespoons salt	8 pounds ground beef or chevon

Put everything except the meat into the blender in the order given and blend well. Pour this mixture over the ground meat and mix thoroughly with your hands. Form into 1-inch balls and place these just slightly apart on a lightly greased cookie sheet. Bake in an oven preheated to 400 degrees F for about 15 to 20 minutes. Cool. Freeze on clean cookie sheets covered with waxed paper. When the meatballs are frozen solid, remove them from the cookie sheets and pack in freezer bags. Whenever you need to, take out the number you want and simmer them for about 30 minutes, or until the meatballs are heated through. *Makes about 10 pounds or approximately 200 meatballs*

I have another quick and easy dish using ground chevon. It's my version of Hamburger Helper.

Macaroni and Chevon

1½ pounds ground chevon	½ teaspoon black pepper
2 large onions, diced	1 rounded teaspoon salt
4 tablespoons bacon drippings	3 cups uncooked elbow macaroni
2 quarts canned tomatoes	½ pound grated cheese (homemade,
6 ounces tomato paste	Velveeta, or whatever you like)

Fry the ground meat and onions in the bacon drippings until the meat is browned. Add the remaining ingredients except the cheese. Stir well to combine. Cover and cook over medium heat until the macaroni is cooked, about 30 minutes. Stir occasionally. Stir in the cheese and heat for 1 or 2 minutes longer to melt it. *This serves 6 to 8 people and may be cut in half, unless you are serving 4 very hungry people.*

Chicken and Rabbit

The following recipes can be used for either chicken or rabbit, so I will not list them separately.

✿ Fried Chicken Coating Mix

4 cups all-purpose flour
4 tablespoons oregano
4 teaspoons garlic powder
4 teaspoons salt

1 teaspoon black pepper
1 tablespoon paprika
3 tablespoons dried parsley flakes

Stir all ingredients together well and keep the mixture in an airtight container on the shelf. Fry up a batch of chicken or rabbit with this delicious coating mix (see instructions below) and take it on a picnic along with a potato salad, fresh vegetables, and corn on the cob. When we take it to a family gathering, we find a lot of people sitting at our table, so I've learned to cook plenty of extras. This also makes a very good coating for fried summer squash, green tomatoes, or any other vegetables you like fried. Just slice your fresh vegetables and coat the pieces according to instructions for Fried Chicken or Rabbit. Fry only till tender-crisp and browned. *Makes about 5 cups of mix*

✿ Fried Chicken or Rabbit

If you are using rabbit or very large pieces of chicken for this recipe, you should parboil them for about 15 minutes first and let them cool in the broth. The reason for this is that rabbit does not have skin or very much fat and tends to dry out faster, and large pieces of chicken take too long to fry this way unless they are parboiled. Allowing them to cool in the broth gives them a nice sweet flavor and keeps them moist. It is not necessary to parboil small broilers. Pat pieces of chicken or rabbit dry with paper towels. Coat the pieces well with plain flour. Shake off the excess. Dip in a mixture of 1 egg and ½ cup of milk that has 1 teaspoon of onion powder added to it for each chicken or rabbit (make sure that this mixture is well blended). Again shake off the excess, and dip into Fried Chicken Coating Mix (see recipe above). Fry in hot fat (375 degrees F) for about 20 minutes, or until done, turning once halfway through the cooking time. *One small chicken or rabbit serves 3 to 4.*

✿ Fried Chicken Wing Appetizers

Simmer chicken wings for about 15 minutes. Cool them in the broth and drain well. Coat with Fried Chicken Coating Mix (see above) and freeze in a single layer on a cookie sheet. Then package in plastic bags for the freezer. To make a quick appetizer, fry them, still frozen, in hot oil until browned and heated through, about 8 to 10 minutes. Serve a large platter of these with barbecue sauce for a snack or the main part of a meal. *Plan on 4 to 5 wings per person for a main course.*

✿ Chicken or Rabbit Stew

Even though young chickens or rabbits can be used for this recipe, it is best to use the older and tougher pieces of meat. This is a good recipe to make in large quantities and freeze at butchering time when you are culling your stock.

Wash the chicken or rabbit well and put it in a pot, covered with water. If you are going to separate the meat from the bones to serve it, you don't even need to cut it up into individual pieces. For each chicken or rabbit add 2 carrots, 1 large onion, and 1 stalk celery, 1 teaspoon poultry seasoning, and salt and pepper. Simmer until tender, about 3 to 4 hours, depending on the toughness of the meat. Strain the stock, discard vegetables, then return the stock to the pot and reduce until nicely flavored. Add 8 to 12 carrots, 4 to 6 onions, 4 celery stalks cut in pieces, 4 to 6 potatoes (if you are going to freeze this, do not add potatoes until you use it), or any other vegetables that you like in stews. Cook until the vegetables are almost done, and return the meat to the pot. If you are going to freeze this mixture, stop at this point and cool. Divide and package it for the freezer. Whether you freeze it or not, to serve, cook the meat and vegetable combination until the vegetables finish cooking. Thicken with flour and water and adjust seasoning.

When using rabbit for this recipe, we like to use homemade chicken stock to cook the rabbit in right from the beginning. Rabbit is very mild in taste, and the chicken stock gives this dish a much richer taste. If you don't have chicken stock on hand, you could use chicken bouillon; just make sure to adjust the amount of salt in the recipe accordingly. *Serves 4 to 6*

✿ Chicken or Rabbit Liver Pâté

Liver pâtés have always been served as company fare, either as an appetizer or as party hors d'oeuvres. The reason for this is that chicken livers are considered a delicacy and are very expensive in the supermarket. While they certainly do qualify for honors in this category, homesteaders, with their abundance of chicken and rabbit livers (these taste just like chicken), can afford to use them to make this pâté to be eaten as a high-protein snack, served on crackers, toast, or celery sticks at any time of the day.

1 pound chicken or rabbit livers	2 dashes of Tabasco sauce
1 medium onion	1 generous dash of garlic powder
2 tablespoons butter	1 egg, hard-boiled
Homemade chicken broth to cover (use bouillon if you haven't any broth)	½ teaspoon brandy extract (optional)

Sauté livers and chopped onion in butter till livers are lightly browned. Barely cover with bouillon or broth and add Tabasco sauce and garlic powder. Simmer, uncovered, gently about 15 minutes. Place in a blender with hard-boiled egg and brandy extract. Blend until smooth. Chill. *Makes about 3 cups*

🌸 Soup Stock

We never throw away chicken or turkey carcasses or beef or ham bones around our homestead. Homemade soup stocks are used in many ways in our everyday cooking, and this is the cheapest way to make them. Put plastic bags in the freezer for each individual type of bone and when you have enough bones and scraps of meat, use the following recipe. If you like browned beef stock, put all of the bones in the oven in a roaster that has 1 cup of water in the bottom. Roast the bones for 2 hours at 350 degrees F before putting them into the soup kettle with the drippings in the bottom of the roaster. Make sure to scrape up all the little bits of brown in the bottom of the roaster.

To make soup stock:

10 pounds meat trimmings and bones	1 tablespoon salt
3 carrots	1 teaspoon black pepper
2 large onions	Saved juices from cooking vegetables
1 cup celery leaves	Water to fill large canner or soup pot
2 tablespoons dried parsley flakes	

Simmer ingredients for about 8 hours. Strain and cool. Make sure that you save any small pieces of meat. Put them in a container, cover them with stock, and save for a hearty soup. Save the clear stock for more soups, gravy, and casseroles. If space is a problem, boil the stock until it reduces to a couple of quarts and store it in the refrigerator. It will keep indefinitely if it has a little layer of fat on the top. Every couple of weeks, if you have not used it all, bring it to a boil again with a little water and simmer for 5 minutes. Cool and return it to the refrigerator. *Makes about 3 gallons*

It's important today to save as much energy as possible, and cooking large batches of soup stocks and sauces overnight can help you to do this. In the summer cook at night when it's cool and you won't have to use a fan to cool the house. In the winter you should also cook at night because the moisture released in this kind of cooking makes the air in the house more humid, and humid air takes less energy to heat than dry air. You can set your furnace at least 5 degrees lower at night.

Dairy Products

🌸 Homemade Butter

One of the biggest treats on the homestead is homemade butter. Butter made from goat's cream is just as delicious as butter from cow's cream, but collecting the cream to make it is a little more difficult.

Goat's milk, being naturally homogenized, does not separate easily, and should be separated with a cream separator. The Garden Way Living Center in Vermont carries a separator now, but it's still quite costly. We bought ours from a farmer for just a fraction of the cost of a new one, and I would advise you to do some looking around, even advertising in the want ads, before investing in a new one. Make sure that the parts are all there and that it works, or you won't have saved any money.

As a last resort, you can skim goat's milk if you have a little patience. Chill the milk quickly after milking. When

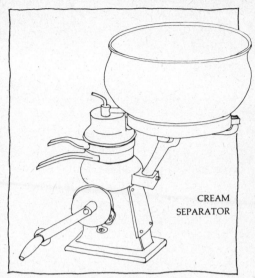

CREAM
SEPARATOR

you have 1 or 2 gallons collected, place the milk in a large shallow bowl or enamel pan. Cover lightly with cheesecloth to prevent dirt from falling in and allow it to sit at room temperature until the cream has formed a "skin" on the top. This skin is a thick layer of cream that looks almost rubbery. The process takes at least twenty-four hours and sometimes longer. It helps to speed it up if you heat the milk to the scalding point, then put it back to cool in the bowl or pan for another few hours (which is why I recommend using an enamel dishpan for setting your cream). Handle it carefully, though, or the cream will not remain suspended.

Now lift this "skin" off carefully, trying not to get any of the milk. Use this to make butter and ice cream. Cow's milk is easy to separate because the cream rises to the top within a matter of hours.

If you can't get enough cream from your milk and you'd like to make homemade butter, you might be able to buy some raw milk from a nearby farmer. It's well worth the investment of the small amount it would cost you.

BUTTER
CHURNS

There are several types of butter churns on the market. Again, Garden Way Living Center carries a large selection. They are beginning to appear in shopping catalogs and specialty stores now, too. They all come with instructions for their use. Because of this, I'm going to confine my instructions to making butter in your blender. It's the least expensive and quickest way to make up small amounts.

Leave the cream at room temperature until it reaches 60 degrees F. Put 2 to 3 cups of cream in your blender and blend on the highest speed until it becomes very thick and the curds of butter separate from the milk. This takes just 3 to 4 minutes. Cream that has been kept refrigerated for 2 or 3 days will churn faster than fresh cream. You may have to help it along with a rubber spatula as it becomes thicker. When the milk looks bluish and the curd separates and comes to the top of the blender when it is stopped, pour the contents of the blender into a strainer that has been lined with cheesecloth. Strain into a bowl if you are going to be saving the buttermilk to cook with or for the animals.

Rinse the curd well under cold water, working it through thoroughly with your hands, to get all the buttermilk out of it. Place it in a bowl and salt to taste, working the salt in well again with your hands or the back of a wooden spoon. Make sure that you keep butter made from raw milk chilled, for it tends to sour more quickly. *One quart of heavy cream makes about 1 pound of butter.*

🏵 Buttermilk

Buttermilk may be used for drinking, sweet as it is right after making butter, or clabbered for cooking. If you want to drink it sweet, refrigerate it right away. If you want it clabbered, leave it at room temperature until it has reached the stage you desire. Mixing in a little cultured buttermilk will give your buttermilk a more uniform consistency, but it isn't necessary.

🏵 Homemade Yogurt

1 quart skim milk
⅓ cup nonfat dry milk solids

¼ cup plain yogurt or yogurt culture
(follow package instructions)

First blend the skim milk with the dry milk; this makes a thicker yogurt. Heat until it's lukewarm. Take a small amount of the warmed milk and blend it with the yogurt. Now mix this with the rest of the warmed milk. Keep in jars at a temperature of 100 to 110 degrees F for about 10 hours. This can be done by putting it in a gas oven that has a pilot light, by using an electric yogurt maker, or by putting the jars in hot water that you change frequently. Yogurt sets even more as it chills.

Homemade yogurt can be used in any recipe that uses sour cream. It can also be combined with fresh fruit and honey or jam, and it's far better than the commercial yogurt. Make sure to save enough from each batch to start another one. After a while you will have to use some commercial starter to get your own going again. *Makes about 4½ cups*

🏵 Yogurt Cream Cheese

This tangy cream cheese also makes a delightful dessert (see recipe for Yogurt Cheese Pudding on the next page).

Take a large square of muslin and line a strainer with it. Pour the yogurt into it carefully, trying not to break up the curd any more than you have to. Fold the edges of the muslin over the curd, or bring it together and tie it and allow the curd to drain until it has formed a stiff cream-cheese-type of texture, about 24 hours. Use this to make dips or in cooking. Refrigerate immediately. This tastes better chilled. *One gallon of yogurt makes almost 1 pound of cheese.*

❀ Yogurt Cheese Pudding

Put 2 cups of Homemade Condensed Milk (see recipe below) into a blender. Add 1 pound of Yogurt Cream Cheese (see recipe above). Blend until smooth. Pour into pudding dishes and top with fruit preserves. Chill. Commercial condensed milk works just as well. *Makes about 4 cups*

❀ Homemade Condensed Milk

Place milk in clean quart jars in these proportions: 2 cups of skim or whole milk to 2 cups of granulated sugar. Cover the jar tops with cheesecloth and place the jars on a rack in an open kettle. Fill the kettle with water to the level of the milk in the jars. Heat to just below the boiling point and maintain that temperature until the milk mixture in the jars has reduced by half. This takes a long time, about 48 hours, and it's not practical to do unless you have a wood stove that would be going anyway to furnish heat. *Each jar yields about 2 cups.*

❀ Ice Cream

The following recipe makes the best ice cream that I have ever eaten: Scald 2 quarts of cream. If it's very thick, add 2 cups of milk. Melt 2 cups of sugar in it and cool. After it's cool, add vanilla extract or whatever flavorings you like, to taste.

Put this mixture in an ice-cream maker and freeze according to the manufacturer's instructions. When adding fruits and nuts, wait until the ice cream is partially frozen, and add up to 2 cups of any fruit that is not too runny. Finish freezing. Do not use fresh or frozen pineapple.

To make a lighter kind of ice cream, beat the whites of 4 eggs till fluffy but not dry, and fold into the ice-cream mixture halfway through the freezing process.

This ice cream may be made in trays in your freezer. Pour the ice-cream mixture into the trays and allow to freeze until ice crystals form around the edges of the trays. Remove and beat well, return to the trays, and repeat the process again when the ice cream is partially frozen. You may add fruit or nuts at this point. *Makes about ½ gallon*

🌸 Cheese

Cheeses are not hard to make, but don't make them on a day that you're in a hurry or not in a good mood. It takes time and tender loving care to produce a really nice-quality cheese. Make cheese often, because the more you make it, the better it will be. The biggest secret to good cheese is in learning to tell just the right moment when it is cooked enough. Only by making it often can you become an expert at this. I love to make mine on my Franklin fireplace. The temperatures rise slowly and are easier to control than either gas or electric heat, though I've made some excellent cheese that way, too, because I have to use my gas stove in the summer.

When making cheese the first few times, always follow the recipes exactly until you have acquired some experience. Trying to include tips from each writer's recipes is very confusing to the inexperienced cheese maker. A good example of this is what happened to my aunt. Over a period of a couple years, I had given this dear lady several little booklets on cheese and butter making. When she decided she would like to try her hand at making some cheese, I gave her a gallon of milk to take home and anxiously awaited the results. The first inkling that I had that something had gone amiss was a letter I received from her stating that she had started getting ready to make the cheese that morning and at five o'clock in the afternoon, when she was writing this letter, she was still waiting for the milk to "taste right" before starting her cheese. I couldn't imagine what she was waiting for it to taste like. A week later when I went for a visit, she told me that she had stayed up until four-thirty in the morning to finish her cheese, and she said, "Boy, am I ever going to appreciate every bite of cheese that I eat from now on."

I couldn't believe my ears, so we sat down to discuss what went wrong. She had combined the recipes from each of the booklets that I had given her, and the poor thing had let the milk stand at room temperature for several hours, as one recipe suggested, and then had put in the buttermilk and let it stand for several hours more until it developed an acid taste, as another suggested. Being unsure of just how acid the "acid taste" should be, she didn't start making her cheese until eleven o'clock that night. The result was a very sour cheese and a very tired aunt. Once you have made cheese a few times, you can experiment with one new variation at a time until you come up with what will be the best method for you.

GENERAL RULES FOR MAKING CHEESE

Cheese can be made from either cow's or goat's milk, raw or pasteurized. This book is based on my own experiences, so I'm going to give you instructions for making cheese with raw milk. I'm certain that if you have pasteurized milk, you will have the same results. I always take the milk I'm going to use for cheese out of the refrigerator 12 to 18 hours before starting, to ripen it. (The longer time is for cooler weather.) Allow the milk to come to room temperature. I make all my cheese with Junket rennet tablets. If you use any other type of rennet, such as Hanson's, be sure to read the instructions carefully, as the amount needed varies with each product.

To make cheese, you will need the following items: 1 large enamel pan, 1 large pan such as a dishpan to serve as a double boiler, a rack or a couple of bricks to set in the bottom pan, a dairy thermometer (this has lower temperature readings than a meat or candy thermometer), wooden spoons, a long-handled wide-blade knife or spatula, a strainer, cheesecloth or muslin, and a cheese press. As you can see, most of these items are things you would have around anyway. Directions for making a cheese press can be found on page 201. Be sure that everything is spotlessly clean and free of odors before you start. Cheese will pick up the faintest of smells.

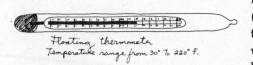

Floating thermometer
Temperature range from 30° to 220° F.

For a double boiler I like to use a dishpan that is quite a bit larger than my cheese kettle, with two bricks in it on which to place my kettle. That way if the temperatures are rising too quickly, it's easy to ladle out a little hot water and replace it with cold water. This slows the cooking process very effectively.

Most recipes call for a starter. The most common type is cultured buttermilk, but I have used both homemade clabbered buttermilk and yogurt with good results. You can also buy cheese coloring if you want very yellow cheese. I prefer to keep mine a natural color.

There are two words that I consider important in successful cheese making: patience and gentleness. Cheese curds in the early stages of processing are fragile; stirring should be done carefully or you will break the curd down too much and lose a lot of your cheese. Attempting to raise the temperatures too fast will result in cheese that is dry and rubbery.

Most of the recipes in this group embody the same principles:

Step 1—Heating the milk to 86 degrees F.
Step 2—Adding the starter.
Step 3—Ripening the milk for 2 to 4 hours.
Step 4—Adding the rennet (cheese color is also added at this point).
Step 5—Setting the curd.
Step 6—Cutting the curd.
Step 7—Cooking the curd.
Step 8—Draining and salting the curd.
Step 9—Pressing the cheese.

Each recipe is handled a little differently, some omitting one or two steps, others, such as the one for Cheddar cheese, adding one more process. Though the instructions sound long and complicated, cheese making is not hard and does not require hours of tedious work, but you have to have a full day around the house to devote to it.

CUTTING CURDS

I will explain how to cut the curd now, because it's the same for all recipes. Take a long-handled knife or spatula and cut across in rows. Then cut across the opposite way, making squares whatever size the recipe calls for. Holding your knife at an angle, cut the curd diagonally, turning the pan four quarter-turns to make sure you have cut all the curd into small pieces. When stirring the curds, I always use my hands. It's easier to tell if you've left any large pieces uncut. If you find any, cut them with a knife, don't squash them with your hands. The curd is ready to cut when you can stick your finger in at an angle and bring it up and the curd breaks clean over your finger.

AGING THE CHEESE

Once the cheese has formed a crust, you can either eat some of the curds right away or you can age them. The longer they are aged, the more distinctive a taste they have. Cheddar cheese should always be aged at least 60 days, and is best when aged 90 days or longer.

To age my cheese, I coat the cheeses with melted paraffin, first dipping one end quickly into melted paraffin and allowing it to cool and form a hard coating, then dipping the other end. Aging cheese should be kept in a cool place. A refrigerator is really too cool. They age best at temperatures of 50 degrees F. I age mine in a special little screened box that my dad built for me, in the root cellar. It's just an open wooden frame containing two shelves and covered with screen to protect the cheese from flying insects or rodents that might work their way into the root cellar.

Soft cheeses are the easiest to make, so we will start with these.

COTTAGE CHEESE

Dissolve ¼ Junket rennet tablet in ½ cup cold water. Add this solution to 1 gallon room-temperature skim milk, along with ¼ cup buttermilk. Stir well. Cover with a towel and let stand at room temperature for 12 to 18 hours, or until a firm curd forms. Cut the curd into ½-inch pieces, using a large spatula or butcher knife, turning the pan as you cut again diagonally, so as to cut all the curd into small pieces. Heat the curd slowly over hot water, uncovered double-boiler fashion, until the temperature is 110 degrees F. Hold the curd at this temperature for 20 to 30 minutes. Stir at 5-minute intervals in order to heat the curd uniformly. When the curd has cooked sufficiently, pour it into a colander lined with cheesecloth and allow the whey to drain off. Move the curd back and forth by lifting the corners of the cheesecloth to allow it to drain more quickly. After the whey has drained for 2 or 3 minutes, lift the cheesecloth filled with curd and immerse it in cold water for 1 to 2 minutes. Drain the curd until it is free from whey and put the cheese into a bowl. Add salt to taste and enough cream or milk to give it a nice consistency.

Chill. This cheese must be used within 1 week. *Makes 1 pound*

RICOTTA CHEESE

This mild-tasting cheese is often used in cooking. It makes a delicious dessert by just adding fruit or flavoring. Ricotta made of goat's milk has a different taste than that made of cow's milk. It's firmer and not quite as creamy as the cheese made of cow's milk, but it is much tastier, and it's very easy to make. For each quart of milk you will need the juice of 1 lemon or 1½ tablespoons of bottled lemon juice. Mix the juice with the milk in an enamel pan. Slowly bring it almost to the boiling point—the milk will then start to coagulate. Just before it boils, remove the pan from the heat and put it into another pan of warm water, double-boiler fashion, cover the pan, so that the milk stays warm and doesn't cool below 80 degrees F. In about 12 hours the ricotta should be done and ready to drain. Pour into a cheesecloth- or muslin-lined colander, bring the cheesecloth up over the cheese curds, and allow to drain for 7 to 8 hours in a fairly warm room. You can then salt or flavor it as you wish. Refrigerate it immediately, because ricotta does not keep well for more than a few days. *Each gallon of whole milk makes about ¾ pound of cheese.*

CREAM CHEESE

Next to ricotta, this is the easiest cheese to make. Cream cheese is made with whole milk and needs no rennet, just a buttermilk starter. For ½ gallon of milk, you'll need ½ cup of cultured buttermilk. (In this recipe, I found that it was important to use buttermilk that had been made with a culture; regular homemade buttermilk did not make as nice a cheese.) Mix the starter in gently, trying not to make bubbles. Then let it rest, covered, for about 9 hours, or until it reaches the point of coagulation. When the milk has coagulated, pour it carefully into a muslin bag or double layer of cheesecloth, and hang it with a bowl underneath to allow the whey to drip out. Let it drain in a cool part of the house if possible, as close to 50 degrees F as you can get. The refrigerator is a little too cool, but in the summertime it works all right if you've no other place; just let it drain a little longer. At this point it's very creamy. If you want it a little drier, like commercial cream cheese, cut the curd into large chunks and allow it to drain a little longer. Salt it lightly and refrigerate immediately, as soon as it's done draining, or it will turn sour. *One half gallon of milk yields about 6 ounces of cheese.*

Instructions for the following three hard cheeses will be given for making cheese with 3 gallons of milk. To make it with lesser amounts of milk (never use less than 1 gallon), just cut down the ingredients in proportion, but remember to follow the same instructions exactly. It's just as important for 1 gallon of milk to take a long time to reach a certain temperature as it is for a large amount of milk. You will have to watch it more closely, because the smaller amount of milk will tend to heat up much more quickly.

COLBY CHEESE

3 gallons whole milk
2 cups homemade buttermilk (see page 214) or 1½ cups cultured buttermilk
3 Junket rennet tablets, dissolved in 1 cup cold water

Place the milk in a cheese kettle, set up double-boiler fashion. Raise the temperature to 86 degrees F. Add the starter and stir well. Let stand, covered, for 2 to 3 hours, maintaining a constant temperature of 86 degrees F. Add the rennet mixed with cold water and stir well for at least 1 full minute. Cover and let stand until curd has formed, about 30 minutes.

Cut the curd in 1-inch cubes and slowly raise the temperature to 100 degrees F, stirring every 15 minutes. You must take a *minimum* of 30 minutes to heat the curd. When you stop heating it, the temperature will continue to rise to about 104 degrees. Break up any large pieces that tend to mat together.

If it has taken 1½ to 2 hours (I like to do it very slowly) to raise the temperature, the curd is usually ready by then and doesn't need to cook any further. Decide whether or not to let it set for another hour at 104 degrees by testing the curd for doneness. To test the curd for doneness, bite into a piece of curd. If it squeaks against your teeth, it is ready to drain. Here is where it takes practice. (The worst that can happen if you are wrong is that it will be either a softer cheese if it isn't done enough or a drier cheese if it's done too much; after a while you will be able to tell exactly when it's ready.)

If it's not done, hold it at 104 degrees F until it's ready. Drain the curd by ladling off as much whey as you can and then pouring the rest into a cheesecloth- or muslin-lined strainer. (Save the whey for the animals.) Stop the curd from cooking by dipping it into water that is *slightly* cooler than the curd (90 to 95 degrees F). Drain.

When most of the whey has drained from the curd, sprinkle the cheese with salt, using about 1 tablespoon of salt per gallon of milk used in the recipe. With your hands work the salt well into the cheese curd. Keep track of the amount of salt you use, because you might want to add more or less in future batches.

If you are using a container-type cheese press, place your muslin cheese bag in the press and fit it smoothly. Add your cheese curd, smoothing and pressing it down with your fingers, so that it will fill the total area of the can. Occasionally pull up on the bag along the sides of the can as you press down on your cheese. This will prevent the bag from wrinkling. When all of the cheese curd is in the press, fold the top of the bag down as smoothly as possible over the top of the curd. Put the follower in place and apply pressure equal to about 5 pounds. After 15 minutes increase the pressure by 5 pounds and continue to increase the pressure over the next 1½ hours until you have 30 to 40 pounds of pressure. Allow the cheese to remain like this overnight. Next day check the cheese to see if the bag needs smoothing down, then return it to the press under the same amount of pressure for another 24 hours.

If you are using the double-board method, follow the same directions for filling the bag, using a 1-pound coffee can to hold the bag while you are filling it. Gather the top of the bag together, and tie it as securely and tightly as possible over the curd. Take the bag from the can and place it between the boards, with the top of the bag pointing downward. Thread the dowels into the four corners and use bricks for weights. An average brick weighs 3 to 4 pounds, so calculate the weight of your bricks and proceed with the instructions for pressing the cheese as you would for a container-type press. When using bricks it's all right to increase the weight just one brick at a time as long as you reach the required total weight.

When the cheese is ready to come from the press, remove it and put the bag into a bowl of cold water for 1 minute to make it easier to remove the bag without tearing the cheese. Leaving the cheese in the water, carefully work the bag off, holding the cheese with one hand and working the bag off with the other. If there are any rough edges, trim them smooth. To seal any cracks, dip the cheese in warm water and smooth the cracks over with your finger. Place the cheese in a cool, dry spot for 1 week to form a crust. Turn the cheese daily. Sometimes in the summer when the weather is hot and humid, I have found that little bits of mold form on the cheese while I am drying the crust. These are not harmful and can be wiped off with a damp cloth. A good way to prevent this mold from forming is to rub the cheese liberally on the outside with salt.

Once the cheese has formed a crust, you can either eat it right away if you like a very mild cheese or age it for 30 days or longer. The longer you age it, the stronger the taste becomes. To age cheese, follow the instructions at the beginning of this group of recipes. *Three gallons of milk yield about 3 pounds of cheese.*

ITALIAN CHEESE

3 gallons whole milk
3 Junket rennet tablets, dissolved in 1 cup cold water
1½ cups buttermilk, either cultured or homemade

Place the milk in a large enameled pot. Add the buttermilk as soon as the temperature reaches 86 degrees F, stirring it well. Let stand at room temperature, covered, for 2 hours. Place the pot on the stove, double-boiler fashion. Slowly raise the temperature of the milk to 88 degrees F. Stir in the rennet tablets dissolved in cold water. Stir for 1 full minute. Cover the pan and remove it from the heat until a curd has formed, usually about 30 minutes. When the curd has developed sufficiently, break it up with your hands, reaching down deep into the pot so that you don't leave any curds unbroken. Heat the curd slowly to about 120 degrees F. This will be just about as hot as your hands can stand. Stir the curd every

15 minutes. Be sure to take at least 1 hour to heat the curd—2 hours is even better. When the curd is ready, it will mat easily into a rather firm ball in the whey.

Remove the curd mass from the whey and place in the cheese bag, drain, and put the bag in the press. Press the cheese firmly, for about 2 hours. Take the bag of cheese from the press and put it back into the whey, which has been reheated to just below the boiling point and removed from the heat. Italian cheese is not usually salted, but if you would like a little tastier cheese, as we do, add to the whey 3 tablespoons of salt per gallon of milk used in the recipe and stir it in well. Allow the cheese to remain in the whey until the whey is cold. Remove the cheese from the whey and then from the cheese bag. If you want to age it, proceed according to instructions for aging cheese, but Italian cheese can be eaten right away. This type of cheese also lends itself well to smoking. I feel that this cheese tastes just like provolone. *Three gallons of milk yield 3 pounds of cheese.*

CHEDDAR CHEESE

I recommend that you make Colby and Italian cheese several times before you try to make Cheddar cheese. It takes knowing when the curd is cooked sufficiently to make this cheese successfully. Cheddar cheese *must* age to be good, so if you haven't made it right, you might go on to make several cheeses of this type before you find out your mistake.

Use the same instructions that I gave for Colby cheese, but add the rennet 3 hours after the temperature reaches 86 degrees F. These curds will be softer and should be cut into slightly smaller pieces than Colby cheese, about ½-inch cubes. Follow the instructions for Colby cheese up to and including testing for doneness. At this point, the curd should be tiny (it will look like scrambled eggs) and spring back when you squeeze it with your fingers.

This is where the process changes. Do not rinse. Strain the whey out of the curd as you would for Colby cheese, but then take a cookie sheet and set a cake-cooling rack in it. Top this rack with cheesecloth to fit the size of the rack. Put the curd into a bowl and sprinkle it with 1 tablespoon of salt for each gallon of milk used in the recipe. Mix it in well, but be careful not to break down the curd. Pile the curd on top of the cheesecloth-covered cake rack. Put the cookie sheet containing the rack of cheese over a pan of hot water. Heat the curd to 100 degrees F and maintain that temperature for about 1 hour. The cheese will mat into a solid mass; when it does, cut it into 1-inch strips. This will release more whey. Turn the strips over every 15 minutes to cook the curd evenly.

The curd is done when the strips are slightly firm, and if you pull on one, you will notice that it's quite stringy. Remove the curd from the heat and cut it into small chunks. Rinse it with warm water. Salt it again after it has drained off most of the water. It's hard to tell you how much salt to use. You shouldn't use too much, but keep in mind that Cheddar cheese is supposed to be saltier than other cheeses, and when you put it in the press, some of the salty flavor will be pressed out. Finish draining as you would Colby cheese, and follow the same instructions for pressing and aging. Age this cheese for at least 60 days; after 3 months the taste really improves. *Three gallons of milk yield about 3 pounds of cheese.*

Convenience Mixes and Their Variations

There are a lot of convenience mixes that you can make at home. These mixes are free of preservatives and food additives, and the end product is far superior to anything you can find in the supermarket. For people who purchase basics in large quantities through food cooperatives, this is an ideal solution to the quick-mix problem. I use King Arthur all-purpose unbleached white flour in all my recipes. I've used all the popular brands at one time or another over the years, and I feel that they can't begin to compare with the quality of this flour in terms of the finished product. If you are unable to buy this flour in your area or prefer to use one of the less expensive brands, you will have to use more of whatever flour you do use. They all vary slightly, but a good rule of thumb to follow would be to start with an extra tablespoon of flour for each cup of flour called for in the recipe.

Biscuits and Breads

BASIC BISCUIT MIX

10 cups all-purpose flour
7 tablespoons baking powder
2½ teaspoons salt

2½ teaspoons cream of tartar
3½ tablespoons sugar

Sift everything together several times to mix evenly. Store in an airtight container. *Makes about 11 cups of mix*

BAKING POWDER BISCUITS

2 cups Basic Biscuit Mix
1 cup milk

½ cup shortening

Blend everything together well, then drop by large spoonfuls on an ungreased cookie sheet. Bake in a preheated oven, at 450 degrees F for 10 to 12 minutes, or until golden brown. If you use these for creamed chicken, you might want to add ½ teaspoon poultry seasoning to your batter. It gives them a nice taste. If you want to make rolled biscuits instead of drop biscuits, cut the milk down to ⅔ cup. *Makes 8 to 12 biscuits, depending on their size*

PANCAKES

1¼ cups Basic Biscuit Mix
1 egg

1 cup buttermilk
2½ tablespoons vegetable oil

Put everything in a blender and blend until smooth. Cook on a hot, lightly greased griddle. Turn the pancakes as soon as they have puffed and are full of bubbles but before all the bubbles break. Turn and bake on the other side until golden brown. *Makes about 8 to 10 pancakes, each 5 inches in diameter*

PUMPKIN BREAD

This also may be made with cooked, mashed, and drained-dry types of winter squash or with carrots.

Sift together:

3 cups Basic Biscuit Mix   1 teaspoon allspice
3 teaspoons cinnamon

In large bowl, beat together:

2 cups sugar   2 cups mashed pumpkin,
½ cup melted lard   winter squash, or carrots

Add the dry ingredients and beat in 4 eggs, one at a time. Blend thoroughly and add:

2 teaspoons vanilla extract   1 cup chopped nuts
1 cup raisins

Pour the batter into two greased and floured 9-by-5-by-3-inch loaf pans. Bake in a preheated oven at 350 degrees F for 1 hour, or until a toothpick inserted into the center comes out clean. You'll never find a nicer fruit bread than this one. Remove from pans and cool thoroughly before slicing. *Makes 2 loaves*

ZUCCHINI BREAD

Sift together:

2 cups Basic Biscuit Mix   3 teaspoons cinnamon

In a large bowl, beat together:

3 eggs   1 cup vegetable oil
2 cups sugar

Add the dry ingredients and mix in:

2 cups grated zucchini (with peel)   1 cup chopped nuts
1 teaspoon vanilla extract

Pour the batter into two greased and floured 8½-by-4-by-2½-inch loaf pans. Bake in a preheated oven at 350 degrees F for 45 minutes to 1 hour, or until a toothpick inserted into the center comes out clean. Remove from pans and cool thoroughly before slicing. *Makes 2 loaves*

BANANA BREAD

2 cups mashed ripe bananas	1½ cups granulated sugar
(4 to 6 whole bananas)	¾ cup milk
2 tablespoons lemon juice	1½ cups Basic Biscuit Mix
¾ cup lard or shortening	½ cup chopped nuts
3 eggs	

Put the bananas and lemon juice in a blender and blend well. Add the shortening, eggs, and milk and blend again until smooth. Pour into a large bowl and add the sugar. Beat well for at least 1 full minute. Add the Basic Biscuit Mix in three parts, beating well after each addition. Add the nuts. Pour the batter into two greased and floured 9-by-5-by-3-inch loaf pans. Bake in a preheated oven at 350 degrees F for 1 hour, or until a toothpick inserted into the center comes out clean. Remove from pans and cool thoroughly before slicing. *Makes 2 loaves*

DATE-NUT BREAD

Place 1 cup of chopped dates and ½ cup of chopped nuts in a small bowl. Cover with ½ cup boiling water. Set aside to cool.

2½ cups Basic Biscuit Mix	¾ cup milk
1 cup sugar	1 egg
½ teaspoon salt	Cooled date-nut mixture
3 tablespoons vegetable oil	
or melted lard	

Place all ingredients in a large bowl, in the order given, and beat with an electric mixer at medium speed for 30 seconds, scraping the sides and bottom of the bowl constantly. Pour into two greased and floured 8½-by-4-by-2½-inch loaf pans. Bake in a preheated oven at 350 degrees F for 50 to 60 minutes, or until a toothpick inserted into the center comes out clean. Remove from pans and cool thoroughly before slicing. *Makes 2 loaves*

APRICOT-NUT BREAD

Make as you would the Date-Nut Bread, substituting 1 cup of chopped soaked apricots for the dates, except allow the apricots to sit in the boiling water that has been poured over them until they are puffed and moist, at least 2 hours or even overnight.

✿ Cookies

Children love cookies, and there is no reason why they can't be a treat and a nutritional addition to their diet at the same time. Variations of the following basic cookie mix let you add different combinations of nuts, seeds, and fruits. They are all valuable foods and important to the healthy growth of children. (P.S. I bet when you bake these, you'll catch some grown-ups with their fingers in the cookie jar, too.)

BASIC COOKIE MIX

6 cups unbleached
  all-purpose flour
3 cups whole wheat flour
  (preferably home-ground)
4 tablespoons double-acting baking
  powder

1 tablespoon baking soda
4 teaspoons salt
3⅓ cups butter or lard
3¾ cups sugar

Mix everything together well until the texture is like cornmeal. Store in airtight containers in the refrigerator. *Makes about 18 cups*

PEANUT BUTTER COOKIES

2½ cups Basic Cookie Mix
¼ cup honey
1 egg

½ cup peanut butter
½ cup chopped salted peanuts
  (optional)

Blend all ingredients together well. Form into 1-inch balls. Place each ball 3 inches apart on a lightly greased cookie sheet. Dip the bottom of a medium-size lightly greased glass into granulated sugar, using it to flatten each ball. Bake in a preheated oven at 350 degrees F until cookies are set but not hard, about 8 to 10 minutes. Remove from cookie sheet. Cool on a cake rack. Store in covered container. *Makes 3 dozen*

OATMEAL-RAISIN COOKIES
In a large bowl, mix together:

¾ cup tightly packed brown sugar
2 eggs

¼ cup water
1 teaspoon vanilla extract

Add and blend in:

2½ cups Basic Cookie Mix
1 teaspoon cinnamon
½ teaspoon ground cloves

2 cups quick-cooking oatmeal
1 cup raisins
1 cup chopped nuts

Drop by rounded teaspoonfuls onto a lightly greased cookie sheet. Bake in a preheated oven at 350 degrees F for 12 to 15 minutes, or until you no longer leave an imprint when you touch the cookies with your finger. Remove from cookie sheet immediately and cool on a wire rack. Store in a covered container. *Makes 3 dozen*

CRISPY DATE COOKIES

1 large egg	1 teaspoon lemon extract
¼ cup honey	½ cup chopped nuts
¼ cup melted butter	1 cup chopped dates
2½ cups Basic Cookie Mix	

Blend the first three ingredients together thoroughly. Add the Basic Cookie Mix and the lemon extract and blend together well. Stir in the nuts and dates. Drop by rounded teaspoonfuls onto an ungreased cookie sheet. Flatten each mound with the bottom of a glass dipped in granulated sugar. Bake in a preheated oven at 400 degrees F for 10 to 14 minutes, or until the cookies are very lightly browned. Remove from cookie sheet and cool on wire racks. Store in covered container. *Makes 3 dozen*

CARROT COOKIES

⅓ cup honey	1 cup grated raw carrot
1 egg	1 cup quick-cooking oatmeal
½ teaspoon nutmeg	½ cup raisins
1 teaspoon cinnamon	½ cup sunflower seeds
2½ cups Basic Cookie Mix	

Blend the first four ingredients together thoroughly. Add the Basic Cookie Mix and mix together well. Stir in the carrots, oatmeal, raisins, and sunflower seeds. Drop by tablespoonfuls on a lightly greased cookie sheet and bake in a preheated oven at 400 degrees F for 14 minutes until the cookies are still soft to the touch but spring back when pressed with a finger. Remove from cookie sheet and cool on wire racks. Store in covered container. *Makes 3 dozen*

CHOCOLATE CHIP COOKIES

2½ cups Basic Cookie Mix	1 teaspoon vanilla extract
½ cup tightly packed brown sugar	½ cup chocolate chips
2 eggs	½ cup chopped nuts

Blend the first three ingredients together well, then stir in the vanilla, chips, and nuts. Drop by teaspoonfuls onto a lightly greased cookie sheet. Bake in a preheated oven at 375 degrees F for 10 to 12 minutes, until lightly browned. Remove from cookie sheet and cool on wire racks. Store in covered container. *Makes 3 dozen*

❀ Doughnuts

BASIC DOUGHNUT MIX

16 cups sifted flour
2 teaspoons nutmeg
2 teaspoons mace

1½ teaspoons cinnamon
4 teaspoons baking soda
4 teaspoons salt

Sift all ingredients together until thoroughly blended. Store in an airtight container. *Makes about 16 cups*

To make doughnuts, mix:

1 cup sugar
¼ cup melted lard

2 eggs

Add alternately:

3½ cups Basic Doughnut Mix

1 cup buttermilk or sour milk

Stir until smooth. Chill for 2 hours or overnight. Roll out on a board or shelf floured with additional doughnut mix. Cut and fry in hot fat at 375 degrees F till golden brown on each side. Drain well. *Makes about 2½ dozen*

❀ Piecrust Mix

12 cups flour
4 cups lard or vegetable shortening
   (lard works better)

6 teaspoons salt

Place all ingredients in a large flat-bottom pan. Using an electric mixer or a pastry cutter, cut the fat in until it is evenly coarse, the size of small peas. If this mix is made with lard, it must be refrigerated. If it is made with vegetable shortening, such as Crisco, it can be stored in an airtight container on the shelf.

To make a two-crust pie, use about 2¼ cups of mix with 5 to 7 tablespoons of ice water. Mix well, and roll out on a floured board. *Makes about 6 double- or 12 single-crust pies*

❀ White Cake Mix

Sift together several times to mix evenly and thoroughly:

8 cups all-purpose flour
3 tablespoons double-acting
   baking powder

1¼ teaspoons salt
4 cups sugar

Store the mix in an airtight container. *Makes four 8-inch layer cakes*

To make a cake, stir the mix well and lightly spoon out:

2¾ cups White Cake Mix

In a separate bowl, cream together:

½ cup lard or shortening   2 small eggs
1 teaspoon vanilla extract   ¼ cup of the measured-out mix

Add the rest of the mix alternately with:

¾ cup milk

Stir the batter until smooth after each addition. Pour into greased and floured 8-inch layer-cake pans. Bake in a preheated oven at 375 degrees F for 25 minutes until a toothpick inserted in the center comes out clean. This cake is very good filled with preserves.

The texture of this cake is rich, heavy, and moist, like old-fashioned cakes. If you would like a lighter-textured cake, you can decrease the amount of mix you use in the recipe until it's as light as you want.

❀ Chocolate Cake Mix

Sift together several times to mix thoroughly:

2 cups unsweetened cocoa   3 tablespoons baking powder
6 cups sugar   3 tablespoons baking soda
9 cups flour

Store the mix in an airtight container. *Makes enough for 6 cakes*
To make a cake, stir the mix well and lightly spoon out:

3 cups Chocolate Cake Mix

Place mix in bowl with the following all at once:

6 tablespoons shortening   2 tablespoons water
1 egg   ½ cup milk
1 teaspoon vanilla extract

Mix thoroughly. When well mixed, add ½ cup of boiling water and mix well again. Pour into either two greased and floured 8-inch layer cake pans or one greased and floured 9-inch-square cake pan. Bake in a preheated oven at 400 degrees F for 20 to 25 minutes, until toothpick inserted in center comes out clean. This cake is very moist and much like a devil's food cake.

❀ Brownie Mix

Sift together:

1¼ cups nonfat dry milk solids   4 cups sugar
4 cups all-purpose flour   1¾ cups Hershey's unsweetened dry
4 teaspoons baking powder   cocoa (carob powder may be used
2 teaspoons salt   too)

This makes 10 cups of mix.

To make brownies, combine:

2½ cups Brownie Mix	½ cup chopped nuts

Mix separately:

2 eggs	1½ teaspoons vanilla extract
3 tablespoons water	½ cup plus 1 tablespoon vegetable oil

Gradually stir this into the dry mix and blend well. Spread in a greased and floured 9-inch-square cake pan. Bake in a preheated oven at 350 degrees F for 35 to 40 minutes, until a toothpick inserted in the center of the pan comes out clean. Cool. *Makes about 16 brownies*

Many of the people I know seem to feel that corn bread was meant to be served with pea soup or baked beans and that's all. Big hot chunks of this slightly sweet corn bread with fresh sweet butter makes a delicious addition to everything from soups and chowders to fried chicken or chili. After you've made it once, you'll never want to be without this mix on hand. Make it in special little tins for corn sticks, and serve them warm with a large fresh green salad for a summer treat.

❀ Corn Bread Mix

4 teaspoons salt	3 cups cornmeal
9 cups all-purpose flour	4 tablespoons baking powder

Mix thoroughly to blend. *Makes about 12 cups*
To make corn bread, blend together:

¾ cup granulated sugar	2 eggs

Beat this mixture well, then add:

3 cups Corn Bread Mix

Blend in:

1 tablespoon melted shortening or butter	1½ cups milk

Blend only until the ingredients are moistened. Pour into a greased 9-by-13-inch pan. Bake in a preheated oven at 400 degrees F for about 30 minutes, or until a toothpick inserted into the center comes out clean. This is the best corn bread I have ever eaten. *Makes 12 servings*

Specialty Breads

🌸 Bran Muffins

It would be hard to find a nicer way to let someone know that you are happy to have them drop in for a visit at any time of the day than to offer them some of these warm bran muffins. The mix makes up a large batch of batter that can be refrigerated for up to 6 weeks. They bake in less than 30 minutes, and served with homemade butter and honey and a big steaming mug of coffee or tea, they are absolutely delicious.

2 cups boiling water	½ cup honey
2 cups all-bran cereal	1 cup lard
5 cups sifted flour	4 eggs, well beaten
5 teaspoons baking soda	1 quart buttermilk
2 teaspoons salt	4 cups Grapenuts cereal
1 cup sugar	

Pour the boiling water over the all-bran cereal and let it stand to cool. Sift together the flour, baking soda, and salt. In a large bowl, cream together the sugar, honey, and lard until it is light. Add the eggs and beat well. Blend in the buttermilk, Grapenuts cereal, and all-bran mixture. Stir in the dry ingredients. You can store this batter in a gallon jar in the refrigerator for up to 6 weeks.

To make muffins, fill greased muffin tins two-thirds full and bake in a preheated oven at 400 degrees F for 20 to 30 minutes, or until browned. *This recipe makes about 5 dozen muffins.*

🌸 Breakfast Bars

These have everything in the supermarket beat for both taste and nutrition. It's a recipe I developed for my own children.

Place in a 2-quart saucepan:

1½ cups honey	2 squares (2 ounces)
4 tablespoons butter	unsweetened chocolate

Bring to a boil and boil hard for 1 minute. Mix in:

1 cup roasted sunflower	½ cup toasted wheat germ
seeds or nuts of any kind	dash salt
⅔ cup peanut butter	1 teaspoon vanilla extract
1 cup unsweetened coconut flakes	5 cups quick-cooking oatmeal

Blend all ingredients together well. It will make a stiff batter. Roll into balls 2 inches in diameter. Place on waxed paper and flatten with the bottom of a glass.

May be coated with chopped nuts if desired. Allow to dry slightly until firm before storing. *Makes approximately 40 bars*

🌸 Pizza Crusts

Just about everyone loves pizza, and with all your homemade sauces, cheeses, and sausages, it would be a shame not to have some pizza crusts tucked away in the freezer for some of these nourishing treats. Make these crusts up and freeze them on cookie sheets until solidly frozen. Then cut a piece of cardboard the size of your crusts and stack them on it. Wrap tightly and return to the freezer. This way of freezing the crusts allows you to take them out one at a time as you want them.

3 cups warm water (105 to 115 degrees F)	1½ tablespoons salt
3 tablespoons (3 packets) dry yeast	6 tablespoons olive oil or vegetable oil
2 tablespoons sugar	8 cups all-purpose flour

Place the first five ingredients in a large bowl in the order given. Add 2 cups of flour and blend with an electric mixer. Continue to add flour with a spoon or your hands until you have a stiff dough. Knead until smooth and elastic. Cover and let rise until doubled in bulk, about 45 minutes. Punch down and divide into 6 equal parts. Let sit for 5 minutes on a floured board. With greased hands, spread the dough on ungreased 9-by-13-inch cookie sheets. Bake in a preheated oven at 350 degrees F for 10 minutes, or until set but not brown. Remove from oven and cool. Place cooled cookie sheets of crusts in freezer until frozen solid, and wrap and freeze according to directions given above.

To make your pizza, remove the desired number of crusts from the freezer. Preheat oven to 425 degrees F and brush the crusts lightly with oil (it is not necessary to defrost them). Then top with pizza sauce and your favorite toppings. Bake until the cheese is bubbling and the other toppings are cooked, about 20 minutes. *Bon appétit! Makes six 9-by-13-inch crusts*

🌸 Bread Dressing

This is a good bread dressing to make with leftover stale bread or crumbs that you have been saving in the freezer. To stuff a turkey 8 to 11 pounds or two roasting chickens, heat:

½ cup butter

In this sauté:

3 medium onions, diced	¾ cup diced celery

Add this to:

2½ quarts day-old bread crumbs (not finely crushed crumbs)	¾ teaspoon black pepper
1 tablespoon poultry seasoning	1 tablespoon dried parsley flakes or 2 sprigs fresh parsley, diced
1½ teaspoon salt	

Moisten this with homemade chicken or turkey stock until it holds together. Do not get it too wet unless you like a very moist dressing. Let it sit for 5 minutes, then stuff your turkey or chicken. This is also very good for baked stuffed pork chops. To make this dressing even more delicious, add ½ pound of sausage to the onion and celery when sautéing, and cook until well done (about 20 minutes). *Makes approximately 8 cups of dressing*

🏵 Croutons

butter or oleo   seasonings   day-old bread

Melt the butter and add whatever seasonings and herbs you like, such as minced garlic, minced onion, dried parsley flakes, salt, and so forth. Spread this on both sides of the bread. Cube the bread and place the cubes on a cookie sheet in a preheated 225-degree F oven. Stir every 10 minutes until the croutons are slightly browned and dry. This takes about 30 minutes. Cool, and store in an airtight container.

🏵 Homemade Bread

Though the ingredients for making the two breads that follow are different, the methods of preparing them are the same, so I will give you the ingredients for each and then the instructions for making them.

WHITE BREAD

5 cups warm water (105 to 110 degrees F)	⅓ cup lard or shortening
2½ tablespoons (or 3 packets) dry yeast	½ cup wheat germ
1 tablespoon salt	11 to 12 cups all-purpose unbleached white flour
⅓ cup honey or sugar	

Makes four 2-pound loaves

MY SPECIAL WHOLE WHEAT BREAD

7 cups warm water (105 to 110 degrees F)	⅔ cup lard
3 tablespoons (4 packets) dry yeast	3 cups stone-ground whole wheat flour, ground fresh if possible *
1½ tablespoons salt	12 to 14 cups all-purpose unbleached flour
⅔ cup honey	

Makes six 28- to 30-ounce loaves of whole wheat bread

*If you don't grind your own, you should add ½ cup of bran to compensate for the loss of bran in commercially milled flour.

To make either bread, place the first six ingredients in a very large bowl in the order given. Add 2 cups of flour. Blend this mixture until smooth with an electric mixer at high speed. Continue to add flour until you can no longer use the mixer. Add additional flour with a large spoon until the dough is too stiff to add any more.

Turn the dough out onto a well-floured board. Knead in additional flour until the dough feels tacky but no longer sticks to your hands. The dough

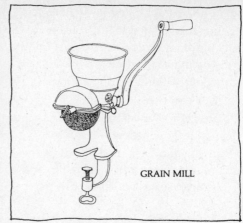

GRAIN MILL

should form a fairly firm mass that springs back when you push into it. It should resemble a fat baby's dimpled bottom.

Lightly grease the top of the dough and cover the bowl first with waxed paper or plastic wrap and then with a large turkish towel. When the dough has doubled in bulk, in about 1 to 1½ hours, punch it down. If you are not ready to finish making the bread then, let it rise another time.

After the bread dough has been punched down, knead it five or six times. Divide the white bread dough into four equal parts and the whole wheat dough into six equal parts (these loaves should average 28 to 30 ounces each).

On the floured board, pat the dough into rectangles, and, starting on the long side, roll them up. With the side of your hand, seal the ends, then tuck them under. Place, seam side down, in greased 9-by-5-by-3-inch bread pans.

Lightly grease the tops of the loaves and cover them again. Let them rise until doubled in bulk. These loaves are very large and should rise about ¾ inch over the top rim of the pans before you turn the oven on.

Place in a *cold* oven* and set the oven temperature to 375 degrees F. Bake for 35 to 40 minutes, or until the loaves are browned on the top and they sound hollow when tapped on the top. Remove them from the oven and then from the bread pans. Cool on cake racks. If you want soft, tasty crusts, brush the tops with melted butter.

STICKY BUNS

When you get to the part of your bread making where you shape your loaves (see above), after patting the dough into rectangles, butter one of the rectangles and sprinkle with brown sugar, cinnamon, and raisins. Roll the rectangle and seal as for bread. Slice the roll into ½-inch slices and place it, cut side down, into greased muffin tins or on a greased cookie sheet. Let rise, covered, until doubled in

*If you are using a wood stove, I recommend that you preheat your oven first, because wood stoves vary in the length of time they take to heat up.

bulk and bake in a preheated oven at 375 degrees F for about 15 to 20 minutes, or until done. Tops will be nicely browned. Remove from tins by immediately turning upside down on a cake rack to cool. (If you don't take them out of the muffin tins right away, the sticky brown sugar will harden, and it will be difficult to get them out without tearing them.) *Makes 14 to 16 buns*

NO-KNEAD HOMEMADE ROLLS

½ cup sugar
1 tablespoon salt
¼ cup lard or shortening

3 cups boiling water
(very hot tap water will do)

Stir everything together and allow to cool to 110 degrees F. Add:

2 scant tablespoons (2 packets) dry yeast

Blend well and add:

2 eggs, slightly beaten

Blend again and add in four parts, blending well after each addition:

7 to 8 cups all-purpose unbleached white flour

The dough will be softer than bread dough. Refrigerate for at least 2 hours before shaping, but it can be kept up to 72 hours. Stir the mixture down before using.

To make rolls: Grease muffin tins, and with floured hands, shape the dough into cloverleaf rolls the size it takes to fill your tins two-thirds full. Shape 3 balls, each about 1 inch in diameter, and place in the greased and floured muffin tins. If 1-inch balls are either too large or too small to fill the muffin tins two-thirds full, adjust the size of the balls. Let rise, covered, until doubled in bulk. Bake in a preheated oven at 400 degrees F until brown, about 15 to 20 minutes. These rolls freeze well, so you can make them all up at the same time. To reheat, take them from the freezer 1 hour before dinner. Fifteen minutes before dinner, place the rolls in a brown paper bag and moisten the bag with cold water (don't drench it). Bake in a preheated oven at 425 degrees F for 15 minutes. The rolls will be crisp on the outside and light and fluffy on the inside. *This recipe makes about 4½ dozen rolls.*

Soups and Chowders

My husband has a full-time job in the city. Being a part-time farmer during the late spring, summer, and early fall months takes just about all of his extra time, so we try to make Sundays in the late fall, winter, and early spring something special around our homestead.

We have open house for all who'd like to come. Anyone and everyone is welcome, and it's not unusual to have as many as fifteen to twenty people drop in during the course of the day on some Sundays. To make it as hospitable as possible, we make up two large kettles of soup or chowder and serve them with plenty of homemade bread and butter. People can eat anytime they are hungry, and it's a very happy custom.

We usually serve one light vegetable-type soup as well as a heartier chowder, such as the following Turkey Chowder. This chowder is rich and delicious and a favorite with all who come. Children coming in cold from playing in the snow are warmed quickly by a bowl of this hearty soup.

✿ Turkey Chowder

Take off all the small bits and pieces of meat that you can easily get to on the carcass and put them in the refrigerator. Put the carcass in a large soup kettle. Leave any bits of dressing that cling to the carcass; they just add to the flavor. Cover with cold water, and add 2 large scraped carrots, 1 large onion, a fistful of celery tops, and 2 sprigs of fresh parsley. Bring to a boil and simmer, covered, for 4 hours or even overnight. Strain the broth and reduce it if you need to, until it has a nice, rich taste. Save all the little pieces of turkey that fall off the bones and add them to those that you took off earlier. Refrigerate or freeze the meat along with the strained broth until you want to make chowder. If you won't be using it within 4 days, it should be frozen.

To make the chowder, in a large kettle, sauté in 6 tablespoons of bacon drippings or butter:

3 large onions, diced	2 quarts turkey broth
2 cups diced carrots	2 teaspoons salt
2 cups diced celery	½ teaspoon black pepper
turkey bits	

Cook only until the vegetables are limp; do not brown. (This is really just sweating the sweetness from the vegetables, but it makes the broth much tastier than it would be if you omitted this step.) Add the turkey bits and broth (if you have less than 2 quarts, don't worry; just make sure the vegetables are covered with stock, adding water if necessary). Add the salt and pepper. Simmer until the vegetables are cooked. Add:

2 cups whole-kernel corn	2 cups cream-style corn

Add enough rich milk to make the chowder reasonably thick. Reheat to just below boiling. Remove from heat and adjust the seasonings. *Makes about 5 quarts*

✿ Fish Chowder

1 pound any type of freshwater fish	water to cover

Simmer until the fish flakes. Drain the fish, reserving the stock. Sauté for about 5 minutes in 2 tablespoons of bacon fat in the soup kettle:

1 large onion, diced   2 stalks celery, diced   2 large carrots, diced

Add the following and simmer until the vegetables are tender, about 8 minutes:

4 medium potatoes, diced	1 tablespoon dried parsley flakes
½ teaspoon salt	¼ teaspoon mace
¼ teaspoon black pepper	fish stock and/or water to cover
dash garlic powder	

When the vegetables are tender, return the fish to the pot, add 1 quart of rich milk or more, and heat to just below the boiling point. For a company chowder, you can add a can of minced clams at this point. *Makes 8 large servings*

🌸 Cream of Potato Soup

When it comes to homestead cooking, I'm a firm believer in cooking plenty. Food is usually in abundance on a homestead, and having extras makes it enjoyable to ask friends or neighbors who happen to come by around mealtime to join you. Leftovers often taste better than the original dish, especially soups, stews, and sauces, because the flavors have had more time to blend. As a last resort, you can always feed the leftovers to the animals if they aren't used up, so you don't lose a thing.

I seem to have a special talent for always having leftover mashed potatoes on hand. The following soup is one of the nicest ways I've found for using them up, and as an added bonus, it makes a very quick nourishing lunch on a busy day.

For each cup of mashed potatoes, you will need 1 large onion, 1 tablespoon of butter, ½ cup each of chicken stock and light cream or rich milk. Slice the onions and sauté them in butter until barely limp but not brown. Add the chicken stock, cover, and simmer for about 15 minutes, or until the onions are very soft. Place the onion mixture in the blender with the mashed potatoes and cream or milk. If you are making a large amount, you will have to process a little at a time. Blend until smooth, adding extra cream or milk to get the desired consistency. Return to the pan and reheat. Adjust the seasonings. Serve garnished with chopped fresh chives. *Each cup of mashed potatoes makes 2 servings of soup.*

🌸 Corn Chowder

2 large onions, diced	4 cups fresh corn kernels (canned
2 tablespoons bacon fat	whole-kernel corn may be used)
2 tablespoons butter	2 cups cream-style corn
4 large potatoes, diced	about 6 cups rich milk
salt and pepper	

Sauté the diced onions in the bacon fat and butter in a soup kettle until they are lightly browned. Add the potatoes and enough water to cover. Add 1 teaspoon of salt and ¼ teaspoon of black pepper. Simmer until the potatoes are tender, about 8 minutes. Add the fresh corn and simmer, covered, for another 5 minutes. (If you are using canned corn, do not simmer any longer.) Add cream-style corn and milk to get the desired consistency and adjust seasonings. Reheat. *Makes about 12 large servings*

Macaroni-Beef Soup

1½ pounds ground beef
2 cups diced onion
2 cups diced celery
2 quarts beef stock or water

2 quarts canned tomatoes
1 tablespoon salt
½ teaspoon black pepper

Put everything into a soup kettle all at once. Bring to a boil, then simmer for 1 hour. Add 1 cup of uncooked macaroni. Return to a boil, and cook, uncovered, over medium heat for another 30 minutes. Let stand for 30 minutes more before serving in order to blend flavors. This makes a very large batch; the ingredients can be cut in half. *Makes 10 large servings*

Fresh Vegetable Soup

Combine 2 cups each of any combination of the following fresh vegetables. Make sure you include at least seven or eight vegetables. Make in a large soup kettle.

onions
celery
green beans
yellow beans
cabbage

cauliflower
carrots
fresh corn
peas
broccoli

lima beans
peeled tomatoes
green peppers
white turnip

Dice the vegetables and add beef stock to cover (this stock is a must). Add ¼ cup of rendered beef or bacon drippings, 1 tablespoon salt, and 1 teaspoon black pepper. If you did not include fresh tomatoes, add 1 quart of canned tomatoes and one 6-ounce can of tomato paste. If you did add tomatoes, just use the tomato paste. Cover, and bring to a boil. Simmer until vegetables are tender-crisp. Let stand for 1 hour to blend flavors. Freeze some of this soup for a taste of summer when the snow is two feet on the ground.

Green Pea and Ham Soup

Stock for this nourishing soup can be made ahead according to the instructions I gave for soup stocks (see page 212). If you have just one ham bone, use the instructions I gave for turkey chowder on page 236.

3 quarts ham stock
⅛ teaspoon powdered cloves
1 pound dried green split peas
bits and pieces of ham

2 carrots, diced
1 large onion, diced
½ cup diced celery

Put everything into a soup kettle and simmer, covered, until the peas are mushy, about 1½ to 2 hours. Adjust the seasonings. If you like a smoother pea soup, leave the ham out when you are cooking the vegetables. When the peas are done, puree the soup in a blender. Return the soup to the pot and put pieces of ham in. Reheat. *Makes 8 large servings*

✿ *French Onion Soup au Gratin*

6 large onions, sliced
3 tablespoons beef drippings or butter
1½ quarts beef stock
salt and pepper
3 tablespoons dry sherry or 1 teaspoon
  sherry extract (optional)

6 tablespoons grated Parmesan cheese
6 ounces grated Swiss or Gruyère
  cheese (or 3 ounces Swiss, 3 ounces
  Gruyère)
4 slices french bread,
  toasted and buttered

Preheat oven to 425 degrees F. Sauté the sliced onions in the drippings until limp. Add the beef stock and season to taste with salt and pepper. Cover and simmer until the onions are tender, about 20 minutes. Add the sherry at the last minute of cooking. Ladle the soup into warmed crockery bowls. Top with whole slices of french bread. Sprinkle each bowl with 1½ tablespoons grated Parmesan cheese and top with 1½ ounces grated Swiss or Gruyère cheese. Bake until the cheese bubbles, about 20 minutes. *Makes 4 servings*

Homemade Dressings and Sauces

✿ *Homemade Mayonnaise*

This is exceptionally good mayonnaise, and it's much thicker than commercial mayonnaise.

1 large egg
¼ teaspoon dry mustard
½ teaspoon salt
1 tablespoon lemon juice

1½ teaspoons honey
1 cup good vegetable oil (you can use
  part olive oil)

Break the egg into a blender. Cover and blend at high speed for 30 seconds. Add the dry mustard, salt, lemon juice, and honey and blend again at high speed for 15 to 20 seconds. While the blender is still running, add the oil in a very slow, steady stream. As the mayonnaise thickens, you will have to stop the blender and stir some of the oil in, then turn the blender back on high. With a spatula, scrape the emulsion toward the blades. *This makes about 1½ cups of very thick mayonnaise.*

THOUSAND ISLAND DRESSING

1 egg, hard-boiled   ½ cup mayonnaise   ½ cup chili sauce (sweet type)

Chop or grate the egg very fine, and add it to the other two ingredients. Blend well. *Makes 1¼ cups*

RUSSIAN DRESSING

½ cup mayonnaise   ½ cup ketchup

Blend until smooth. *Makes 1 cup*

BLUE CHEESE DRESSING

1 cup mayonnaise   ½ cup light cream
3½ ounces blue cheese   2 teaspoons honey

Blend until smooth. *Makes about 2 cups*

HOMEMADE RANCH-STYLE DRESSING

1 cup mayonnaise   1 teaspoon dried chives
6 tablespoons milk   ⅛ teaspoon dry mustard
⅓ teaspoon onion powder   1 tablespoon lemon juice
⅓ teaspoon garlic powder   dash salt
1 teaspoon dried parsley flakes

Blend everything together thoroughly in a blender. This dressing is much better if it's made a day ahead. *Makes about 1½ cups of dressing*

TARTAR SAUCE

½ cup mayonnaise   drained sweet relish to taste   drained horseradish to taste

Blend with a fork until well mixed. *Makes about ¾ cup*

❀ Oil and Vinegar Dressing

3 cups vegetable oil   ½ teaspoon salt
1 cup cider vinegar   ¼ teaspoon black pepper
4 small cloves garlic   1 teaspoon paprika
2 teaspoons granulated white sugar or   2 teaspoons dry mustard
  honey

Blend well in a blender or shake in a jar. *Makes 1 quart*

✿ Tomato-Soup French Dressing

2 tablespoons dry mustard
2 teaspoons salt
6 tablespoons honey
2 cups vegetable oil

2 tablespoons chopped onion
1 cup cider vinegar
1 can tomato soup

Blend this very well in a blender. This is especially good on fresh garden greens. *Makes about 4½ cups*

✿ Basic Spaghetti Sauce

¼ cup fat or vegetable oil
6 pounds ground beef (you may omit this and add it later just before you serve)
6 large onions
6 quarts canned tomatoes
six 6-ounce cans tomato paste

6 cloves garlic
3 tablespoons Italian seasoning
1 tablespoon crushed red pepper
¼ cup granulated white sugar
2 teaspoons salt
½ teaspoon black pepper

If you are using beef, brown it in the fat. Blend the remaining ingredients in a blender, a little at a time. Put everything into a large kettle with the beef, if used; otherwise just add the fat, and simmer, uncovered, for about 4 hours, or until thick. *With meat, this makes about 7 quarts of sauce.*

✿ Pizza Sauce

Take 1 quart of Basic Spaghetti Sauce and add 1 teaspoon dried sweet basil to it.

✿ Barbecue Sauce

1½ large onions, diced
¼ cup vegetable oil
1 quart ketchup
¾ cup water
4 teaspoons honey
3 tablespoons prepared mustard

4 teaspoons salt
6 tablespoons cider vinegar
2 teaspoons Worcestershire sauce (optional)
1¼ teaspoons Tabasco sauce

Sauté the onion in vegetable oil for 5 minutes. Add the remaining ingredients and simmer, uncovered, until thick. It takes about 20 minutes. This is delicious served with fried chicken or rabbit. *Makes about 5 cups*

✿ *Many-Cheese Sauce*

½ cup cottage cheese
½ cup water
¼ pound Cheddar or processed
    cheese (such as Velveeta),
    chopped

¼ cup grated Parmesan cheese
¼ teaspoon dry mustard
1 tablespoon flour

Put everything into a blender and blend until smooth. Cook in a double boiler over hot water until thickened, about 10 minutes, stirring constantly. *Makes about 1½ cups*

✿ *Brown Sugar Syrup*

2 cups tightly packed brown sugar
1 cup white sugar

1¼ cups water
2 tablespoons maple flavoring

Place first three ingredients in a saucepan and bring to a boil. Boil, uncovered, for 3 minutes. Remove from the heat and add maple flavoring. Keep refrigerated. This tastes just like maple syrup. *Makes about 3 cups*

Miscellaneous

The following recipes didn't fall into any special category, but I thought you might like them, so I've collected them for you in this small group.

✿ *Sprouts*

Homegrown bean sprouts are easy and fun to grow, and they can be grown year-round, giving you some fresh salad material as well as a nutritious addition to many other dishes. Any dried bean or seed can be sprouted as long as it hasn't been treated with any chemicals. My favorites are alfalfa sprouts and mung bean sprouts, but you can use any type that you like. You can find many kinds of seeds and beans for sprouting in health food or specialty stores.

Take ½ cup of dry beans and soak them overnight in four times their volume of water. Don't use less, as they will swell to nearly double in size. In the morning drain and rinse the beans or seeds and place ¼ cup in a glass quart jar. If you use a lot of sprouts you will have to use several jars; this recipe is for about four jars, depending on the size of the bean or seed used.

Cover the top of the jar with two layers of cheesecloth and hold this in place with the band of a canning lid or rubber bands. Place the jars on their sides so that the beans form a single, even layer. Store in a warm, dark place. Once or twice a day rinse the sprouts by pouring warm water into the jars through the cheesecloth, swirling it around, and draining it. Sprouts are ready to use in about 3 to 5 days. Don't let them grow beyond 1½ to 2½ inches. You can remove the hulls by placing them in a bowl of cold water and letting the hulls rise to the top, where you can scoop them off.

❀ Homemade Soybean Meat Extender

1½ cups soybeans that have been cooked 30 minutes	⅛ teaspoon black pepper
1 large carrot	1 teaspoon dry mustard or
1 medium onion	1 tablespoon prepared mustard
½ teaspoon salt	(I prefer the latter)

Put everything into a blender, a little at a time. You will have to keep pushing the mixture toward the blades in the center, since it gets very thick. Do just a small amount at a time. Mix this half and half with ground beef or chevon to make hamburgers.

To make a delicious meatloaf, mix ¾ pound of the extender with ¾ pound ground beef and add 1 egg; crumbs from 1 slice of bread; 1 small onion, chopped; and ½ cup of milk. Mix well and place in a greased loaf pan. Bake in a preheated oven at 375 degrees F for 1½ hours. *Makes about 2 pounds of meat loaf*

❀ Baked Beans

1 pound any kind of dried beans	salt and pepper
¼ teaspoon baking soda	5 small whole onions
8 tablespoons brown sugar	¼ pound lean mixed salt pork
1 teaspoon dry mustard	

Put the beans into a large bowl and fill with water twice to three times the volume of the beans. Soak overnight. In the morning, drain and rinse the beans. Put them into a large kettle (8 quarts) and cover with fresh cold water and add the baking soda. Bring the beans to a boil, uncovered, and simmer for about 20 minutes, or until they can be pierced with a fork. Watch them carefully or they will boil over. Skim them frequently while they are boiling to remove any scum that collects on top. Drain and put them into an ovenproof dish or bean pot. Add the brown sugar, dry mustard, salt, and pepper. Cover with hot water. Arrange the onions on top with small chunks of salt pork. Bake, uncovered, in a preheated oven at 325 degrees F for 5 hours, adding more water when necessary. *Makes 5 to 6 servings*

❀ Homemade Noodles

6 eggs plus 3 egg yolks	4½ cups flour
5 tablespoons water	1 tablespoon vegetable oil
⅛ teaspoon salt	

Combine the first three ingredients in a blender. Blend for 1½ to 2½ minutes. Put this mixture into a large bowl and beat in 3 cups of the flour to a smooth paste. Allow to sit, uncovered, for 10 to 15 minutes. Work in the rest of the flour with your hands until the dough is smooth and elastic. Sprinkle on the oil a little at a time, kneading it in. If you have a noodle maker, take parts of the dough and put them through, at whatever size widths you would like. If you haven't a noodle maker, roll out the dough on a floured board as thinly as possible. If the dough is too elastic and springs back, let it rest on the floured board for about 5 minutes and try again. Cut into desired widths. Dry on cotton towels until brittle. Store in an airtight container.

To cook, place in a large pot of boiling salted water and boil for 7 to 10 minutes. *Makes about 2½ pounds of noodles or ten 2-ounce servings*

✿ Pickled Eggs

Never pickle eggs that are fresher than two days old, because they are hard to peel without tearing. Place the eggs in a pan of cold water with water to cover. Bring to a boil, uncovered, and simmer for 8 minutes. Cool immediately under cold running water until just cool enough to peel. Peel and pack into jars. Pour over them enough white vinegar to cover, then cap the jars and refrigerate. These are ready to eat in 24 hours. With all the extra eggs we have on the homestead, we usually make up a gallon of these at a time to serve as snacks. These eggs keep indefinitely.

✿ Potato Chips

The best potatoes for making chips with are winter potatoes. New potatoes do not fry up as nicely, though they can be used. To make your chips, either peel the potatoes or, if the skins are still nice, leave them on and scrub the potatoes well with a stiff brush. Slice as thinly as possible into a large bowl of salted ice water. Heat 4 inches of oil to 375 degrees F in a deep kettle. Before frying, drain only a handful of raw chips at a time until they are very well drained; leaving on too much water will make the grease foam up and you could get burned. Drop the chips one at a time into the deep hot fat and fry until lightly browned. Drain on paper towels, and salt.

Beverages

I will only include a couple of beverages here. Any good recipe book has many more, but these two are different.

🌺 Solar Tea

The cheapest type of iced tea that I know of is called solar tea. Take a glass gallon jar. Put 6 to 8 tea bags in it and fill with hot tap water. Place the jar outdoors in the sun for several hours, or until the tea is as strong as you like it. Remove the tea bags and refrigerate.

🌺 Instant Cocoa Mix

10 cups nonfat dry milk solids	8 ounces nondairy creamer
2 pounds Nestlés Quik or equivalent	¼ teaspoon salt

Combine all ingredients and store at room temperature in an airtight container. The original recipe that I received from my sister called for 2 cups of powdered sugar, but I found it to be too sweet; however, you can add it if you like very sweet cocoa. *Makes about 18 cups of mix*

To make a single cup of cocoa combine:

2 tablespoons Instant Cocoa Mix	1 cup boiling water

Wines and Liqueurs

You don't have to drink alcoholic beverages yourself to enjoy serving nice-quality homemade wines and liqueurs to your guests. We like to use ours for Christmas presents too.

The following recipes are all very good, very easy to make, and, compared with market prices, exceptionally inexpensive. You do not need any special equipment for making these wines. The ordinary, everyday items that I listed at the beginning of this chapter will do fine. Don't let anyone tell you that if you were to buy any or all of the special equipment that has flooded the market for making wine in recent years, it would make better wine. It just isn't so. One thing you must do if you plan on making more than a gallon is to register with the Federal Tobacco, Alcohol and Firearms Division of the IRS. You are allowed to make up to 200 gallons for home consumption each year, but you must register. There is no fee involved; just obtain two copies of Form No. 1541 from your local IRS office and send both to your local assistant regional commissioner.

🌺 Grape Wine

This wine is the easiest kind of wine you could ever hope to make, and you don't even need your own grapes. To make it you will need:

2½ quarts (80 ounces) sweetened grape juice (homemade, canned, or reconstituted frozen)

1 gallon vinegar jug
1 large cork that will fit the neck of the vinegar jug

4½ cups white sugar for sweet wine, or 2½ cups for dry
1 tablespoon (1 packet) dry yeast

2 feet of ½-inch plastic hose
1 quart Mason jar filled with water

Combine the grape juice with the sugar and stir well to dissolve. Take a small amount of the juice and warm to lukewarm. Add the yeast and dissolve. Pour this and the rest of the juice into the gallon jug. Fill to the bottom of the neck of the jug with water. Punch a hole in the cork large enough to accommodate the plastic hose. Put the hose through the cork and down into the jug. Put the other end of the hose into the quart jar of water (if you are making several gallons of wine, you can use the same jar of water for as many plastic hoses as will fit into it; it isn't necessary to have a different quart of water for each

Cork with tubing to let gasses escape without letting air back into wine jug

GRAPE WINE MAKING

Jug of wine

water

gallon of wine). This allows fermenting gasses to escape without allowing any air into the wine bottle to ruin the wine. If the hose isn't tight enough to seal the jug from the air, pour some melted wax around the top of the cork where the hose is inserted. Let this wine ferment for 30 to 40 days. It is then ready to drink, but it is even better if it is bottled and aged.

To bottle the wine, syphon it off into wine bottles that have been thoroughly cleaned and sterilized. A good way to sterilize them is to use one of the iodine-compound sanitizers that you use for your milking machine or milk pails. After you have bottled the wine, place plugs of cotton batten in the tops of the bottles for 1 week to 10 days, until you are sure that the wine is through working. It is through fermenting when there are no more bubbles rising. Cork and store the bottles in a cool place on their sides to prevent evaporation.

The room that you use to ferment your wines in should maintain a temperature of 70 to 75 degrees F most of the time. *Makes 4 quarts or 5 fifths*

✿ Beet Wine

This wine is delicious and is my favorite. I make it in a large plastic (30-gallon) garbage can that has been scrubbed and sanitized with a chlorine- or iodine-compound sanitizer. This recipe makes about 17 gallons, but you can reduce it to one quarter; just follow the same instructions. To make it, you will need from 5 to 17 gallon vinegar jugs, depending on how much you make. You don't need that many corks or plastic hoses, because the method of making this wine is different. For approximately 17 gallons you will need:

Plastic container with beet liquid   Cover container loosely with towel and board

    20 pounds beets (tops cut off
        close to the beet)
    9 gallons water

Scrub the beets thoroughly but do not peel. Chop the beets small or, better still, cut them into small pieces and put through a blender with the 9 gallons of water. Divide this among three large canners. (You will have to plan on a full afternoon to get this ready.) Simmer the ground beets, covered, in the water for 3 hours. Strain the juice through muslin into large pails or pans. Discard the pulp or give it to the animals. Measure the amount of juice you have and pour the strained juice into the plastic barrel, adding water in an amount equivalent to the amount of juice that you have. You should have approximately 17 to 19 gallons of liquid. Add:

    40 pounds white sugar* for dry wine,   250 mg vitamin C (ascorbic acid),
        50 pounds for medium wine,   in tablet form, per gallon
        or 60 pounds for sweet wine   1 tablespoon (1 packet) dry yeast
        (this is much like port)   for each gallon of total liquid,
    1 pound raisins   added when juice has cooled down
    3 unpeeled oranges, chopped (optional)   to 105 degrees F
    3 unpeeled lemons, chopped (optional)

Stir well. Cover the barrel with a light towel. To keep the towel from falling into the barrel, it's a good idea to put a small board on top of it, but be careful not to cover it completely with the board; it's important that fermenting gasses be allowed to escape. Stir with a wooden spoon or long clean stick daily for 10 days. Syphon the wine into clean, sterilized gallon vinegar jugs or large wine bottles.

Mix 2 envelopes of unflavored gelatin in 2 cups of cold water to soften. Remember to use less if you make a smaller batch. Divide this mixture among the gallon jugs and stir well. This will help to clarify the wine. Plug the tops of the jugs with cotton batten and allow the jugs to sit undisturbed for another 10 to 14 days. When the wine has completely stopped working and has clarified, taste it. If it isn't

*Wines made with root vegetables are subject to variation in the amount of sugar used, because some years the vegetables are sweeter than others, depending on how much rain you get and on the condition of the soil.

sweet enough, add more sugar. Add only ½ to 1 cup at a time (otherwise you might add too much) and wait 1 week after each addition before tasting again. Be sure to keep the cotton plugs in place all this time. When you feel that you have the taste to your liking and it's no longer working (it will start to work again each time you add sugar), syphon it off carefully into clean sterilized wine bottles, and seal and store as for Grape Wine. *Makes about 17 gallons*

🏵 Carrot Wine

For each gallon of water, you will need:

20 carrots, ground as for Beet Wine (do not peel)	3 unpeeled lemons, chopped (optional)
3 unpeeled oranges, chopped (optional)	5 pounds white sugar
	1 tablespoon (1 packet) dry yeast

Simmer the ground carrots in about 1 gallon of the water, covered, for 2 hours. Pour this mixture, *pulp and all*, into a clean, sanitized 3- to 5-gallon crock or plastic bucket. Add all other ingredients except the yeast. When cooled to 105 degrees F, add the yeast and mix well. Cover lightly with a towel and let sit undisturbed until the carrots sink to the bottom. This takes 10 to 14 days. Syphon off the wine into sterilized gallon vinegar jugs or large wine bottles. Clarify as for Beet Wine but use only 1 tablespoon of unflavored gelatin. Plug the tops of the bottles with cotton batten. When the wine has stopped working and is clear (after 5 to 21 days), syphon it off carefully into wine bottles so as not to disturb any sediment. Cork and store as for Grape Wine and Beet Wine.

This wine tastes much like sherry after it has been aged. *Makes about 1½ gallons*

🏵 Grandma's Chokecherry Wine

10 quarts chokecherries	1 tablespoon (1 packet) dry yeast
15 pounds white sugar	5 gallons water

Pick over the chokecherries but do not wash them. Run them through a food chopper twice with a fine blade. Combine the fruit and the remaining ingredients in a 20-gallon crock or plastic pail. Cover lightly with a towel and let sit for 3 weeks. Stir daily and remove any scum that forms on the top. Drain the juice from the pulp, discard the pulp, and return the juice to the cleaned crock. Add 1 pound more of sugar for each gallon of juice that you have. Let sit for another week. Do not stir. Follow instructions for syphoning, clarifying, and storing in the recipes for Grape Wine and Beet Wine, using 1 tablespoon of unflavored gelatin for this amount of wine. This is an exceptionally fine-quality wine with a beautiful clear deep-rose color. *Makes about 5 gallons*

✿ *Homemade Coffee Liqueur*

2 cups (4 ounces by weight)
  instant coffee
4 cups boiling water
4 pounds white sugar

2 vanilla beans, diced,
  or 2 tablespoons *pure* vanilla extract
½ gallon cheap vodka or brandy

Stir the instant coffee into the boiling water. Add the sugar, stirring until dissolved; cool. Place the diced vanilla beans in a clean, sterile gallon jug. Pour the cooled coffee mixture into the jug and add the brandy or vodka. Add extra brandy or vodka if necessary to fill jug. Cap and store for at least 30 days before using. *Makes 1 gallon*

These recipes that I have given you in this chapter were just meant to get you started, to stir your imagination. Once you have learned how to cook from scratch, you will be able to adapt your own favorite foods to this way of cooking. I hope you will have as many happy hours in your homestead kitchen as I have had in mine.

12 POTPOURRI

Before I bring to a close this discussion of ways to have a better life for less money, I would like to go into just one more area that takes a large slice of our budget each year. That area is gift giving and holiday expenses. The following is a list of some of the items that can be used as gifts. Many of these items cost little more than the time and effort it takes to put them together. We start our Christmas gifts at canning time, making sure that we put up extra jams and jellies, pickles and relishes, and wines and liqueurs in pretty little dishes or bottles. Frequently I will stop at roadside flea markets or garage sales and pick up several cheap little glass dishes or bottles of different shapes and sizes. These can also be filled with fudge, dried fruits, and homemade cookies. Wrapped in clear plastic wrapping from the kitchen and topped with a pretty bow or tiny decorated pine cones, they make welcome gifts. Year-round there are many items in the freezer or the root cellar, on the shelves, in the cheese-aging box, or in the garden that make nice gifts. Recipes for some of the items can be found in Chapter 11. I will include instructions for making some of these items at the end of this chapter. Recipes for all other items can be found in any good cookbook or book on the home preservation of food.

Gifts from the Kitchen

Homemade cheeses and cheese spreads	Maple syrup
Homemade hard sausages	Maple butter
Dried herbs	Honey
Herb breads	Honey butter
Herb vinegars	Homemade candies
Herb butters	Jars of shelled homegrown nuts
Herb teas	Toasted sunflower seeds

Small pots of fresh herbs
Baskets of homegrown fruits
Fruit breads
Fruitcakes
Dried fruits
Fruit leathers
Jams, jellies, and preserves
Pickles and relishes
Wines
Liqueurs
Apple cider

Toasted pumpkin seeds
Smoked hams
Pickled eggs in jars or crocks
Buckets of homemade cocktail meat-
    balls and sauce
Crocks of liver pâté
Homegrown popcorn in a pretty jar
Homemade soap
Homemade candles
Bone candlestick holders
    and napkin rings

Other Gifts from the Homestead

Bouquets of dried flowers and grasses
Terrariums
Potted plants, such as cherry tomatoes,
    green peppers, pot cucumbers, flow-
    ers, ivy, or other trailing vines

Pressed flowers
Paintings and etchings
Macrame
Needlework of every description

I'm sure that all of you can come up with more to add to this list, such as items from the workshop including birdhouses, planters, bookcases, and so on ad infinitum. In making and giving these gifts, you will be giving yourself the finest gift of all—the wonderful feeling that comes from sharing a part of yourself. For an extra wonderful Christmas, fix a basket of food with little extras for a needy family. Let the children help to prepare this gift and they will grow up knowing the true meaning of Christmas.

We have another holiday custom in our home that I'd like to share with you. We make all of our own Christmas tree decorations, and instead of sending Christmas cards, we bring our friends a decoration for their tree. Throughout the year we gather materials for our project from the fields and forests. Pine cones; acorns and other nutshells; dried corn; dried milkweed pods, burdock, cattails, bittersweet, and holly. Just before Christmas we gather evergreen boughs and creeping types of evergreens. Each area of the country has its own wild plants that can be turned into beautiful decorations. We also use eggshells from our chickens, ducks, and geese to make lovely decorations and gifts. Even milk-strainer pads can be used; they make beautiful snowflake decorations.

woodshaving

Formed woodshaving

Crocheted star

Embroidered stuffed dove

Felt applique and yarn embroidery

MISCELLANEOUS CHRISTMAS TREE DECORATIONS

Decoration made from egg carton section

We get started the first Sunday after Thanksgiving. With the soup kettle on the wood stove and plenty of homemade bread and butter, we invite everyone to come and create with us. We load the center of the table with spray paints of several colors, always including gold and silver; poster paints; glitter; pieces of ribbon and thread; old buttons and beads from long-ago-discarded gowns; old earrings and other jewelry; and tiny figurines that we buy from time to time. We cover a separate table with newspaper and load it with our bounty from the fields and forests. Each person chooses what he or she would like to work with and creates something unique, from wreaths to tiny new decorations for the Nativity set. Whenever people are hungry, they enjoy a bowl of soup with bread and butter. Not only do we end up with beautiful decorations for our home and friends, but we prolong our holiday season in a meaningful way. There are no commercial banners flying in our lives saying, "Shop early and avoid the Christmas rush." We have no Christmas rush, just wonderful weeks of sharing with those we love.

Decorations

Milkweed-Pod Tree

You will need:

newspapers
masking tape
Elmer's glue
straight pins
dried milkweed pods
green and gold spray paint

white poster paint
spray glue
silver glitter
waxed paper
burdock burs

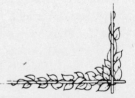

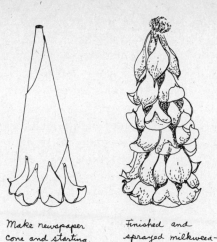

Make newspaper
cone and starting
at base glue and
pin pods to cone.

Finished and
sprayed milkweed-
pod tree.

MILKWEED-POD TREE

Take 14 to 16 sheets of newspaper (7 to 8 sheets folded at the crease) and roll them into a stiff cone-shaped cylinder. Tape this securely with masking tape and trim the bottom so that it can be set evenly on a flat surface.

Take dried milkweed-pod halves that have the fuzzy parts cleaned out and are shaped with one end cupped up and the other end coming to a narrow point approximately ½ to ¾ inch wide. Put glue on the back of the milkweed pod where it will come into contact with the cone and, starting at the bottom of the cone, glue the pods in place with the cup-shaped ends down. It helps to run a straight pin through the glued area so that the pod will stay in place until the glue has dried. (I leave mine in.) Work your way up to the tip of the cone.

When the cone is filled, spray the entire "tree" with an evergreen-colored spray paint, taking care not to miss the little spaces between the pods. When the paint is dry, paint the tips of the "boughs" with white poster paint to resemble snow. Spray the tree lightly with spray glue, then sprinkle some silver glitter over the tree (do not overdo it).

To make the burdock balls for decorations, take a sheet of waxed paper and cover it with the little pieces of burdock. Spray them with gold paint. When they are dry, dip the prickly little hair ends in glue and then in glitter. Place a dab of glue in each milkweed "bough" cup and stick the little glittered balls on the tree. Place another ball atop the tree. Voilà! A unique Christmas tree. These are nice little trees to give to elderly people who are living alone or confined to a nursing home.

Milkweed-Pod Hanging Decorations

Spray-paint cleaned pod halves with any color paint. Decorate with any color of glitter or glue gauzy pieces of cotton to the insides and nestle pretty earrings or bright buttons in them, glued in place. Line some with old pieces of satin, and create scenes in the larger ones. Punch a tiny hole in one end and thread with heavy gold or sil-

NATURAL MILKWEED-POD
TREE DECORATION

ver thread for a hanger. I use milkweed pods just as nature left them, preferably ones with the silk dangling out. Beautiful on the Christmas tree! No paint or glitter needed.

Egg Decorations

To prepare the egg for decorating, you must first empty it. We keep the equipment needed to empty our eggs in a handy place, and whenever we are using eggs for cooking or scrambling, we save the shells. Take a 30-cc plastic syringe with a large-bore needle attached. The type you buy at farm supply stores for veterinary use is the best. Place a small piece of masking tape or Scotch tape on the small end of the egg to prevent large cracks. With a sharp-pointed knife or large needle, carefully punch a hole about ⅛ inch in diameter through the taped eggshell. Take the syringe and pull out the plunger, filling it with air. Stick the needle through the shell in the large end of the egg and blow the egg out. It may take two or three times to get all of it. With a solution of ¼ cup Clorox to 1 quart of water, fill the eggshell and let it sit a little while to clean out the inside of the shell, then empty it and store the shells in egg cartons. Keep the balance of the Clorox solution for other shells.

These eggshells can now be decorated with paint, ribbon, glitter, beads, buttons, and so on, or they can be cut in half and made into jewelry boxes or filled with little scenes. To cut in half or make openings, draw a faint line with a pencil where you want to cut, and very, very carefully go over the line with a single-edge razor blade. This takes time and patience. You mustn't press too hard. Craft catalogs carry special tools

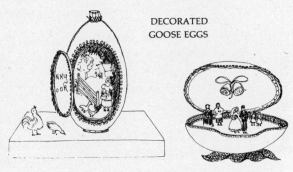

DECORATED GOOSE EGGS

for this as well as tiny hinges and materials for creating scenes. The two eggs shown here were created for me by my Aunt Lorraine with our own goose eggs. One is a twenty-fifth wedding anniversary celebration, jewelry-box style, and the other depicts our life-style here at Sunnybrook. The tiny door includes a photo of our home.

Odds and Ends

Spray pine cones, dried cattails, or ears of corn with gold or silver paint, then with spray glue and glitter. Cattails can be decorated with old beads. Twist small screw eyes into one end and hang them on the tree. As they turn and catch the lights, they sparkle beautifully. Several pieces of burdock just stuck together and sprayed with paint, then glittered, make a feathery-looking ball.

Milk-strainer pads can be cut into snowflake patterns and decorated. Fold a strainer pad in half, fold in half again, then in thirds. It will look like this:

Cut small pieces to form a design. Open it and press it flat with a heavy book until it lies flat. Spray your snowflake with spray glue, then glitter, first on one side and then on the other. If you can find some crushed isinglass, use this instead of glitter; it will sparkle brilliantly.

Acorns or other smooth-shelled nuts such as bitter walnuts make good faces for "little decorative figures." We especially like the acorns because the top resembles a little hat. Yarn hair is added and features painted on. Bodies can be made from corn husks, cardboard, cloth, or yarn, with pipe cleaners for arms. These figures are especially cute grouped in winter scenes.

Once you start working with these ideas, you'll come up with many more of your own.

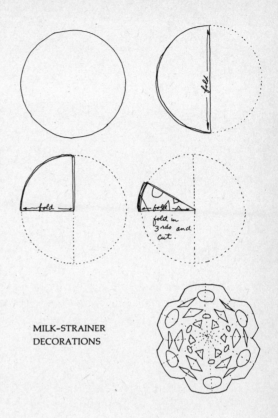

MILK-STRAINER
DECORATIONS

Handcrafted Gifts

Real Bone Candlesticks and Napkin Ring Holders

Finding a meat cutter who will cut the bones for you is the most difficult part of this project. Once you've located one, take him some beef shin bones, or better yet, get some from him. Ask him to cut rings ½ to 1 inch thick for napkin rings and other pieces 2 to 3 inches thick for candlestick holders. Use the parts of the shin bone that flare toward the knuckle for the candlesticks. This will give you a wider base, and

REAL BONE CANDLESTICKS
AND NAPKIN RINGS

they will stand better. Once the pieces are cut, soak them for 24 hours in a large kettle of baking soda and warm water. Use ½ cup of baking soda to 1 gallon of water. Remove the bones from the water and scrub them thoroughly inside and out. Rinse the kettle and refill with the bones. This time cover them with a solution of 1 cup Clorox, 1 capful of dishwashing detergent, and water to cover. Bring them to a boil and simmer for 30 minutes. Remove from the heat and allow the bones to cool in the water overnight. Drain and let dry thoroughly. Sand any edges that are very rough, but leave them as natural as possible.

To stain the bones, brush or spray on a light coat of glue, let dry, and then stain with regular wood stain. Let dry again; then cover with a coat of clear shellac or leave as is.

To make candlestick holders, half-fill the long pieces with plaster of paris or melted lead. Take a candle and set it in place, holding it straight, just to make sure that if the inside of the bone is lopsided, the plaster of paris will set up so that it holds the candle upright in a straight line. As soon as the plaster is set enough to hold its shape, remove the candle and allow the plaster to set until it's hard. The candlesticks can be initialed by using a fine-point artist's brush and gold or silver paint.

Homemade Candles

Good-quality candles are not hard to make and, colored or decorated and set in a pretty dish for a holder, they make a nice gift. To make, you will need:

Wicks
Turpentine
Molds (milk cartons, plastic containers, tin cans, etc.)
10 ounces rendered beef tallow (see instructions for rendering as for lard, page 207)
4 ounces beeswax, old candles, or paraffin wax (of course, beeswax is best)
2 ounces powdered alum

You should first prepare the wicks. We use heavy white butcher twine. Cut pieces twice as long as your mold. Soak these pieces in turpentine and allow to dry. Since the bottom of your mold is usually the top of your candle, run the wick either through the end of the mold or wind a small piece and tape it securely to the bottom of the dry mold with masking tape. Create enough tension to keep it centered by winding the other end around a pencil or small piece of wood and fitting it over the opposite end of the mold.

Now, over low heat, slowly melt together the beef tallow, wax, and alum and skim off any debris that rises until the mixture is clear. Make sure that the tension of the wick is tight enough to hold it in the center of the mold, and carefully pour the liquid into the molds. Allow to harden thoroughly before removing. If you spray the molds with Pam or grease them before filling, it will make the candles easier to remove from the molds. If you want colored candles, melt a wax crayon of the desired color along with the tallow.

You can make decorated candles too. Or candles can be made with dried flowers. Tape a flower or two to the inside of the mold with clear tape. Cool the tallow mixture slightly, stirring constantly, before filling molds, and then pour the mixture into the mold carefully so as not to disturb the dried flower arrangement.

Candles can also be made in pretty jars or dishes. Tape wicks in place as instructed above, creating the proper tension. Cool the tallow mixture slightly, stirring constantly, and fill the dish. If the dish has a wide top, an arrangement of dried pine cones or flowers on the top make a pretty decoration. *This makes 1 large or 3 to 4 small candles.*

Homemade Soap

I'm including the following two recipes for soap. Though the hard soaps can be carved, colored, scented, and given as gifts, this isn't really why I've included them. For a few pennies and a few minutes a year invested, these soaps save me several dollars. The hard soap is a good hand soap, and though not a high-sudsing type, it does a good job of cleansing your hands even of pitch from trees and tar. It's better than any soap or spray on the market for removing stains and the proverbial "ring around the collar." Simply wet the fabric where it is stained and rub it with the soap, then throw it in the washing machine along with everything else. It will take out most stains, and my girls swear by it for removing tough grass stains from their white slacks and shorts. This soap recipe makes about 8 pounds of soap, about a year's supply, for the price of a can of lye (about 50 cents).

The second soap is a liquid soap. For the cost of 2 pounds of washing soda (sal soda), about 30 cents, you can make 3 gallons of soap. We mix this liquid soap in the blender half and half with our favorite dishwashing detergent, such as Ivory, Joy, and so on. This alone saves several dollars a year. We also use it in the dishwasher. We sell milk, so all of our storage jars are done in a dishwasher for safety. Until I discovered this soap, detergent and electricity were cutting into our profits. Now I have cut my costs in half or more. This liquid soap is low sudsing and does a fantastic job of cleaning, but it did leave us with a mineral coating because of our hard water. We solved the problem by using ¼ cup of the liquid soap placed directly in the bottom of the dishwasher for the first wash, and using 2 tablespoons of commercial detergent in the cup that is used for the second wash. It does a great job of cleaning, and there isn't a single water spot on anything. It is also great for tough stains—rub it on them before starting the dishwasher.

HARD SOAP

Assemble the following items before you begin your soap-making project:

1 cardboard or wooden box, the size of a large shoe box
brown paper or a piece of muslin large enough to line the inside of the box
6 pounds lard or mixed clean fats
1 can lye (13 to 14 ounces)
1 large glass jar or bowl, at least a 2-gallon size
1 quart cold water
1 long-handled wooden spoon or clean stick to stir the lye solution
2 tablespoons household ammonia
2 tablespoons borax powder
1 large *enamel* pan (the lye in this mixture will pit any other type of pan)
1 old blanket
1 piece of fine wire about 18 inches long

Fit the brown paper or muslin into the box; make sure it fits smoothly and tape it into place. Melt the fat in the enamel pan over low heat until it reaches 95 degrees F. While the fat is melting, place the lye in the glass jar or bowl (another enamel pan can also be used) and carefully add the cold water, stirring all the time with the spoon or stick. It's best to do this outside, as the lye mixture foams and gets very hot. I make sure that there are no little children around when I do this, as lye burns are very dangerous. (If by accident you should splash some of this solution on yourself, wash it off immediately with cool water and then with cider vinegar.) Allow the lye mixture to cool to about 95 degrees F. With the fat at the same temperature, remove the pan of fat from the stove and slowly pour the lye mixture into it, stirring constantly. Add the ammonia and borax powder and continue to stir until the mixture saponifies (that is, thickens until it reaches the consistency of honey). This usually takes 20 to 30 minutes, though it can take a little longer. Do not stir beyond the point when it reaches the thickness of honey or it will begin to separate. Pour the mixture into the prepared box and cover the box with a piece of cardboard and then an old blanket to keep in the heat. Allow the box to stand without disturbing until hardened, about 48 hours. Remove the solid mass from the box and cut with a thin piece of wire into even-size chunks. Do not use a knife, or you will break the soap into uneven pieces. Stack the cut pieces to allow air to circulate, and leave them out in the open for 2 more weeks to season. If a fine layer of white ash coats the cut pieces, scrape it off before storing.

To color or scent these soaps, you will have to purchase oils and oil-based colorings from a craft shop. *Makes about 8 pounds*

SOFT SOAP

3⅓ pounds clean tallow, lard, or mixed greases
2 pounds sal soda (washing soda)

2 gallons plus 2½ quarts hot water
1 large-size bottle of favorite liquid dishwashing detergent
½ cup ammonia

Put everything except the liquid detergent and ammonia into a large covered crock or enamel, aluminum, or stainless steel pail that will hold 3 to 4 gallons of soap and stir daily until the fat is eaten up and the mixture is smooth. This takes about 2 weeks. Add the ammonia and the bottle of liquid detergent and stir well. Stir again before each use. *Makes about 3 gallons*

One book cannot begin to tell you all the ways you can have a better life for less. The ideas in this book are basics, just to get you started. You will want to learn more as you go along, and you will come up with some good ideas of your own once you start thinking along these lines. Good luck and have fun!

BIBLIOGRAPHY
AND INDEX

BIBLIOGRAPHY

Hertzberg, Ruth, Beatrice Vaughan, and Janet Greene. *Putting Food By.* Brattleboro, Vermont: Stephen Greene Press, 1973.

Hill, Lewis. *Fruits and Berries for the Home Garden.* New York: Alfred A. Knopf, 1977.

Owen, Millie. *A Cook's Guide to Growing Herbs, Greens, and Aromatics.* New York: Alfred A. Knopf, 1978.

Rombauer, Irma S., and Marion Rombauer Becker. *Joy of Cooking.* Indianapolis: Bobbs-Merrill, 1961.

The following booklets may be obtained through your local agricultural extension agent, or by writing to: Superintendent of Documents, United States Government Printing Office, Washington, D.C. 20402

Some may be obtained directly from the college extension offices that published them; addresses for these will be noted. There is usually a small fee for these booklets.

"Burning Wood," NE-191 (U.S.D.A. and Extension Service, 1977) or Northeast Regional Agricultural Engineering Service, Riley-Robb, Cornell University, Ithaca, New York, 14853

"Hobby Greenhouses and Other Gardening Structures," NE-77 (U.S.D.A. and Extension Service, 1977) or Northeast Regional Agricultural Engineering Service, Riley-Robb, Cornell University, Ithaca, New York 14853

"Home Processing of Poultry" (4-H Bulletin, U.S.D.A. and Extension Service) or Pennsylvania State University, College of Agriculture Extension Service, University Park, Pennsylvania 16802

"Insects and Diseases of Vegetables in the Home Garden," U.S.D.A. Bulletin No. 380

"Raspberry and Strawberry Pest Control for the Home Garden," U.S.D.A. Booklet No. 1183

"Slaughtering, Cutting and Processing of Lamb and Mutton on the Farm," U.S.D.A. Bulletin No. 2153

"Slaughtering, Cutting and Processing Pork on the Farm," U.S.D.A. Bulletin No. 2138

INDEX

A NOTE ABOUT THE AUTHOR

Janet Chadwick was born in St. Albans,
Vermont, in 1933 and was educated
there at Holy Angels' School and the
Bellows Free Academy. With her husband
and six children, she began a gradual tran-
sition to a sufficient life-style in 1969,
while living in Burlington, Vermont. In
1974 they moved to their property in
Monkton, Vermont, and began their effort
to reach full food sufficiency.

A NOTE ON THE TYPE

The text of this book was set, via computer-
driven cathode ray tube, in Palatino, a type
face designed by the noted German typog-
rapher Hermann Zapf. Named after Giovan-
battista Palatino, a writing master of
Renaissance Italy, Palatino was the first of
Zapf's type faces to be introduced to
America. The first designs for the face were
made in 1948, and the fonts for the complete face were issued between 1950 and
1952. Like all Zapf-designed type faces,
Palatino is beautifully balanced and exceed-
ingly readable.

The book was composed by American
Book–Stratford Press, Inc., Brattleboro, Ver-
mont; printed and bound by R. R. Donnelly,
Crawfordsville, Indiana.

Typography and binding design by Camilla
Filancia